MURDER, LIES, AND COVER-UPS

MURDER, LIES, AND COVER-UPS

WHO KILLED **MARILYN MONROE, JFK,**
MICHAEL JACKSON, ELVIS PRESLEY,
AND **PRINCESS DIANA?**

DAVID GARDNER

Skyhorse Publishing
A Herman Graf Book

Skyhorse Publishing books may be purchased in bulk at special discounts for sales promotion, corporate gifts, fund-raising, or educational purposes. Special editions can also be created to specifications. For details, contact the Special Sales Department, Skyhorse Publishing, 307 West 36th Street, 11th Floor, New York, NY 10018 or info@skyhorsepublishing.com.

Skyhorse® and Skyhorse Publishing® are registered trademarks of Skyhorse Publishing, Inc.®, a Delaware corporation.

Visit our website at www.skyhorsepublishing.com.

10 9 8 7 6 5 4 3 2 1

Library of Congress Cataloging-in-Publication Data is available on file.

Cover design by Rain Saukas
Cover photos are in the public domain.

Print ISBN: 978-1-5107-3140-0
Ebook ISBN: 978-1-5107-3141-7

Printed in the United States of America

CONTENTS

CONTENTS

MICHAEL JACKSON

INTRODUCTION

Few deaths have affected so many lives as the five examined in this book. The passing of Princess Diana and President John F. Kennedy changed the way entire nations perceived themselves. Losing Elvis Presley and Michael Jackson was, for millions, akin to a death in the family, so entrenched were they in the fabric of our lives. More than half a century after Marilyn Monroe died, alone and naked in her bedroom, her image lives on in every high street.

In each case the deaths were sudden, shocking . . . and way too young. Somewhat surprisingly, Jackson was the oldest at fifty, JFK was forty-six, Elvis, forty-two and both Princess Diana and Marilyn were thirty-six.

All five deaths were also, inevitably, the subject of an enormous amount of dissection, both by the authorities and the media. But because we were spoon-fed so much about them when they were alive—these strangers we discussed, critiqued and worshipped as though they were our closest friends—we were content to largely accept the versions we were presented of the way they died and the reasons they were no longer with us.

Of course, we heard about all the conspiracy theories surrounding President Kennedy's assassination but didn't we really just want to believe it was the work of one deranged 'Commie' with a magic bullet?

Despite his chequered past with young boys, Jackson was the innocent victim of a financially stretched playboy doctor. Conrad Murray was busy talking on the phone to his girlfriends close to the time he had administered a powerful anaesthetic to Jackson to help him sleep. Jackson never woke up.

Monroe, always walking the tightrope between fame and insecurity, fell into such a pit of despair that her final cry for attention was a fatal overdose of barbiturates.

Similarly, Presley, fried peanut-butter sandwiches, pills and paranoia transforming him into a bloated caricature of his 'Blue Suede Shoes' prime, was a victim of his own indulgence.

And Diana? Well, the Paris car crash was an accident, wasn't it?

As a journalist, I covered two of these tragedies at first hand and so I knew back then that there was much more to the stories surrounding Princess Diana and Michael Jackson than ever became public. In Diana's case, the establishment drove the narrative with a patriotic intensity that set out to destroy former Harrods owner Mohamed Fayed, the father of Dodi Fayed, who also died in the crash, with a ruthlessness that smacked of Johnny-foreigner racism. I dare anyone who reads this account of the events leading up to, during and after Diana's death to believe it was accidental.

Paul Burrell, who was Diana's butler at the time, claimed that the Queen told him that 'dark forces' were at work. The facts, examined through the lens of hindsight, clearly show that such sentiments were no exaggeration.

In Jackson's case, I sat through almost every day of Dr Conrad Murray's 2011 trial in Los Angeles and came to the conclusion that the vain physician was indeed being made the scapegoat—a necessity for any media-conscious law enforcement agency investigating a high-profile 'crime'. His behaviour was unethical and dishonest but he was far from alone. Others shared the blame but were allowed to get off scot-free.

As with Princess Diana's death, powerful forces had high stakes in how JFK's assassination was portrayed. Some may argue that, when national security is an issue, the line between right and wrong becomes more blurred but consider this: more than one hundred people with links to the Dallas murder died in the wake of the shooting, many of them in distinctly sinister circumstances. This was not the act of a lone gunman—not even close.

Some of those same forces at the apex of government and organised crime in the United States collided to determine Monroe's fate. It wasn't until later—much later—that FBI files kept on the blonde bombshell disclosed gossip about her affairs with both JFK and his younger brother, Robert F. Kennedy. There was no easy exit from such a tangled web.

As for Elvis, he was closeted in life and death by his 'Memphis Mafia' entourage of friends, leeches and hangers-on, so much so that they were willing to lie that he was found dead in his bed, rather than tell the truth that he was discovered with his pyjamas around his ankles after falling headlong from the toilet. No one would deny that Elvis was struggling with his demons later in life but he was turning things around and hoping to get back with ex-wife Priscilla. The more you get to know about his final days, the less likely it seems that his death was a mistake or a suicide . . . and the larger the likelihood of murder looms.

I'm not telling you what to believe here. Some of what you will read in the ensuing pages you will have read before, some explanations have already been dismissed as conspiracy theories. But you will find that a simple recounting of what is known to be true offers more credibility to these 'theories' and taints the established versions with a heavy whiff of corruption.

As I started examining these deaths, I was astounded at just how many of the facts had either been covered up or twisted. Lies run like honey through all of these cases, trying to smooth over the dark, jagged edges and make it seem like all is well; that there is no reason to worry or delve any further.

The very opposite is true. In each of these five cases, there are very disturbing causes for concern. Questions remain but I suggest we should be very suspicious of the answers we have been given up to now.

MARILYN MONROE

The candle in the wind flickered and died on a balmy California night in August 1962.

To the immense shock of Marilyn Monroe's millions of fans around the world, the movie goddess who, on the surface, seemed to have everything—stunning looks, powerful suitors and riches beyond her wildest dreams—had taken her own life.

Or had she . . .

Sure, there were empty bottles of Nembutal sleeping pills at her side and it was certainly no secret she'd been struggling under the weight of her fame and the bitter disappointments of her turbulent personal life.

Discovered naked and lying face down on her bed, still clutching a white telephone in one hand, it was the script-perfect tragic ending to a fairytale life gone sour. She had had too much too soon and flamed out like the candle Sir Elton

John would use many years later to sing farewell to her and, in a poignantly rewritten version, to Princess Diana.

But in the months and years since Marilyn's death, as more details emerged of her intimate, secret relationships with some of America's most powerful people, it slowly became clear that there was more to the tragedy than was first thought.

The unthinkable became more plausible with each new disclosure. Could it really be possible? Was Marilyn murdered?

Even more incredible was the possibility, supported by some biographers who spent years interviewing hundreds of Marilyn's friends and associates, that her death was orchestrated and carried out as part of a murky plot that reached all the way to the White House.

It now seems certain she had passionate affairs with President John F. Kennedy *and* his brother, Robert F. Kennedy, then America's Attorney General, both married men with a great deal to lose, and associates spoke of a 'smoking gun'—a secret diary in which Marilyn had supposedly recorded her illicit trysts.

There were even suggestions that she may have been pregnant with Bobby Kennedy's baby—a scandal that would have enormous ramifications to his political ambitions.

Some close to the star were convinced that shadowy CIA assassins—or even Mafia hit men—were dispatched to poison her, such have been the conspiracy theories that continue to surround her death to this day.

Others insist that all the smoke and mirrors were just that: facts lined up in such a way to make a more sensational story when the truth was that the actress fatally miscalculated a desperate cry for attention.

Even the official autopsy report didn't offer a definitive reason for the death. The Los Angeles Medical Examiner came back with a conclusion of 'probable suicide'.

Little is what it seems in this most mysterious of celebrity tragedies. It didn't even happen on the day entered on her death record but late the previous evening. The inconsistencies in the autopsy and the police investigation could never have happened today in such a high-profile case. Dangerous forces were at work behind the scenes. Of that there can be little doubt.

With the help of previously classified FBI records and years of research, this book aims to cut through the speculation and the many lies and cover-ups surrounding Marilyn's premature death, and explain what really happened at 12305 Fifth Helena Drive in Brentwood that fateful night.

We still have her films, of course, and the indelible images that mean her unmistakable blonde beauty is just as recognisable now as it was fifty years ago. But the unsettling suspicion remains that Marilyn's death was not at her own hand and that, if she hadn't made such powerful friends—*and* enemies—she could have lived to a ripe old age.

Within these pages, I will make a compelling case to explain why one powerful faction in America plotted the 'perfect murder' of the unwitting actress, only for an even more powerful group to go to extreme lengths to cover it up.

The only innocent here is Marilyn Monroe. She was the victim, much as she had been her entire life . . .

THE LEGEND

To know just a little about Marilyn Monroe's nightmare childhood is to understand why even the love of millions of fans in her Hollywood heyday was never quite enough to still the gnawing insecurity that would haunt her every relationship.

Born plain Norma Jeane Mortenson in the charity ward at the Los Angeles County Hospital on 1 June 1926, she had to quickly learn how to deal with rejection.

The father on her birth certificate—a baker named Edward Mortenson—separated from her mother, Gladys, before she was born and there was a suggestion that the real biological father was Charles Gifford, who was Gladys's boss at Consolidated Film Industries, where she worked as a film cutter. Whoever the father was, he didn't play any further role in Marilyn's life.

Just twelve days after she was born, Norma Jeane was abandoned a second time when her penniless mother was forced to hand her daughter over to foster parents, Albert and Ida Bolender. The stage was set for a dysfunctional childhood, with Norma Jeane bounced from one set of foster parents to another and in and out of an orphanage while her own mother battled poverty and mental illness.

Her childhood, described in the *New York Times* obituary as 'Oliver Twist in girl's clothing', was starved of any kind of love. One foster family gave her empty whisky bottles to play with instead of dolls.

The Bolenders, devout members of a branch of the United Pentecostal Church, 'were terribly strict', Marilyn said later.

'They didn't mean any harm—it was their religion. They brought me up harshly.'

For those first, formative years, Gladys was just 'the woman with the red hair' who rarely visited until she managed to buy a home near the Hollywood Bowl when her daughter was seven and moved in with her. It was not to be a good experience. A few months after they were reunited, Gladys suffered a nervous breakdown.

In her memoir, *My Story*, Marilyn recalled hearing 'a terrible noise on the stairway outside the kitchen'. The little girl ran to see what was causing the commotion, only to find her wild-eyed mother in the middle of a schizophrenic meltdown. 'She was screaming and laughing,' wrote Marilyn. 'They took her away to the Norwalk Mental Hospital.'

It was a traumatic episode that lived with her. 'I kept hearing the terrible noise on the stairs and my mother screaming and laughing as they led her out of the home she had tried to build for me,' she remembered.

Scared and lost, the youngster was declared a ward of state and placed in the care of Gladys's best friend, Grace McKee, who faced similar money problems as Marilyn's mother and periodically put the child back in the Los Angeles Orphans Home to help make ends meet.

As an adult, Marilyn's use of her body to get what she wanted would raise eyebrows but her ambivalence about sex no doubt stemmed from the abuse she suffered as a child. She described later how she was lured into the bedroom of a lodger called 'Mr Kimmel', who was staying at a foster home she'd been farmed out to when she was nine.

'I was passing his room when his door opened and he said quietly, "Please come in here, Norma,"' she wrote in her autobiography. He closed the door and locked it behind her. 'Now you can't get out,' he smiled.

'I was frightened but I didn't dare yell. I knew if I yelled I would be sent back to the orphanage in disgrace again,' she continued. 'Mr Kimmel knew this too. When he put his arms around me I kicked and fought as hard as I could, but I didn't make any sound. He was stronger than I was and wouldn't let me go. He kept whispering to me to be a good girl.'

Finally managing to break free, she told her 'Aunt Grace' what had happened but her stand-in mother refused to believe such a 'fine man' would do such a thing. She was equally disbelieving when her husband Ervin Goddard forced himself on Marilyn in a drunken frenzy in 1937.

'I can't trust anything or anyone,' Grace complained, according to Marilyn. However, her response was not to kick out her husband but to pack her young charge off to live with some other relatives.

In such a bleak upbringing, there were few constants to cling to. 'As I grew older, I knew I was different from other children,' Marilyn later confessed. 'Because there were no kisses or promises in my life.'

It was hardly surprising then that her first marriage at the age of sixteen was a means to an end that had little to do with children and picket fences and certainly nothing to do with love. It was a way to escape her unhappy childhood.

'I was placed in nine different families before I was able

to quit being a legal orphan,' she later said. 'I did this at 16 by becoming an adult.'

Jim Dougherty, a twenty-one-year-old neighbour's son who worked a blue-collar job at Lockheed Aircraft, was her convenient choice but, after tying the knot on 19 June 1942, the relationship soon became little more than a 'friendship with sexual privileges' and, as her nascent career in Hollywood gained some traction, she no longer had any need for a husband with whom she had nothing in common other than a second name.

Her wedding photos show a smiling Norma Jeane clutching a bouquet of flowers. Four years later, when her divorce was granted on 13 September 1946, her future as Marilyn Monroe was beginning to take shape and she never spoke to Dougherty again.

She landed her first modelling contract with the Blue Book modelling agency after being spotted working at a munitions factory during World War II. The transition from curly-haired brunette to blonde bombshell was still in its early stages the previous year, when she was photographed for *Yank* magazine. In April 1946 she was on the cover of *The Family Circle* dressed up like Dorothy from *The Wizard of Oz* and playing with a little lamb. But what she really wanted was to act and she was prepared to do anything required to make it happen, including sleeping with the studio executives with the power to make her dreams come true.

Her first—and perhaps most crucial—move was to dye her hair blonde and change her name. Monroe was her mother's maiden name and Marilyn just sounded 'sexier' than Norma Jeane.

Ben Lyon, a 20th Century Fox executive, was the first to see Marilyn's potential as the new Jean Harlow and he was instrumental in persuading her to come up with a new name. But the model-turned-actress had bigger fish to fry. She was working hard and taking acting and dancing lessons, but she was typecast as a ditzy blonde and all she could get were non-speaking parts. Her first contract came and passed without her making any kind of impact.

She was determined not to fall into the kind of financial abyss that had consumed her mother. Short of cash in 1949, she agreed to pose naked on a swathe of red silk for photographer Tom Kelley for a paltry $50.

It was time to put her looks to better use.

Her first target, 20th Century Fox founder Joe Schenck, persuaded his buddy Harry Cohn, head of Columbia Pictures, to offer his mistress a $65-a-month, six-month contract, which she signed in March 1948. The contract wasn't renewed but Marilyn needn't have worried. By then she'd hooked up with Johnny Hyde, a vice president at the William Morris talent agency. He was fifty-three and she was just twenty-two.

Although she did sleep with him, she made no secret of the fact that it was, at best, an affectionate business arrangement. Hyde was besotted nevertheless and made it his business to make Marilyn a star. First came a role in the 1950 film *The Asphalt Jungle*, as the young mistress of an ageing criminal, and then came her breakthrough in *All About Eve* (also 1950), opposite Bette Davis. She was on her way.

Hyde arranged for a cosmetic surgeon to remove a small bump of cartilage from her slightly bulbous nose to soften her appearance in 1950 and signed her up for a seven-year deal with 20th Century Fox.

In 1952 she was featured on the cover of *Life* magazine along with the headline: The Talk of Hollywood.

When *Playboy* bought up the nude shots from the Kelley shoot and featured Marilyn as the magazine's first Playmate in December 1953, the ensuing scandal only boosted the actress's sex-symbol image. Unashamed, she said she needed the money to pay her rent. When asked by a woman journalist, 'You mean you didn't have anything on?' she replied with her trademark breathlessness, 'Oh yes, I had the radio on.'

The film roles came thick and fast and, hits or misses, the Monroe myth grew inexorably through the 1950s. She shared top billing with Cary Grant in *Monkey Business* and with Richard Widmark in *Don't Bother to Knock* in 1952, and starred alongside heavy hitters Betty Grable and Lauren Bacall in *How to Marry a Millionaire* and with Jane Russell in *Gentlemen Prefer Blondes* the following year.

The famous scene in which her white dress billows around her legs as she stands over a subway grate in 1955's *The Seven Year Itch* became one of the most iconic, enduring images of the twentieth century.

In 1956, she won over the critics for her performance as saloon singer Chérie in *Bus Stop* and was said to be devastated when she wasn't nominated for an Oscar. *Some Like It Hot*—co-starring Tony Curtis and Jack Lemmon in drag—was a huge hit in 1959 and was later hailed 'the greatest American comedy film of all time' by the American Film Institute. It also proved that she could be funny.

Marilyn turned up the heat in 1960's *Let's Make Love* with Yves Montand and in her final film, *The Misfits*, with Clark Gable in 1961.

But her private life was making just as many headlines during this period.

In the early 1950s the rising star could do little wrong, especially after she started dating American baseball hero Joe DiMaggio. Their romance had begun with a blind date in Newport Beach, California on 8 March 1952. He was so dumbstruck by her blue suit and white, low-cut blouse that night that one news outlet reported, '. . . the great Joe DiMaggio struck out.'

But both felt the chemistry and soon the two most famous people in America were a couple. They wed in a flurry of publicity on 14 January 1954 and the retired athlete tried his best to transform the sex siren into a doting wife. Perhaps not surprisingly, he failed, but there were other issues too.

He was a neat freak, while she was a slob. He hated Hollywood; she was its biggest star. She was a flirt; he was possessive and 'insanely jealous'. Few doubted their love for each other; they just couldn't make it work. The final straw came just eight months into their marriage, when Marilyn filmed the skirt-billowing scene in *The Seven Year Itch*.

DiMaggio was visiting the set and reportedly fumed as the take was shot over and over again as both cast and crew looked on in awe. When they got home, his simmering anger blew up into a massive row and, shortly after that, they split.

Marilyn's divorce application was granted on 27 October 1954 on the grounds of mental cruelty. She had described DiMaggio to the court as cold, silent and indifferent towards her and it seemed that, after less than a year of marriage, their relationship was irretrievably broken.

Her third husband couldn't have been more unlikely to fans taken in by her 'dumb blonde' persona. But Marilyn was no fool and Arthur Miller—then America's most popular playwright—didn't just fall for her famous curves; he also believed in her as an actress.

They met on the set of *As Young as You Feel* in 1951 and quickly hit it off, even though Miller was married with two young children. She offered him an escape from the oppressive domesticity of his home life. He was her ticket to the respect in the industry she craved.

Although the Pulitzer Prize-winning author of plays like *All My Sons*, *Death of a Salesman* and *The Crucible* flew back to the East Coast early to assuage his conscience, the couple continued corresponding through Marilyn's ill-fated romance with DiMaggio and, one month after filing for divorce, she was on her way to New York to carry on where they'd left off three years earlier.

They kept their affair secret until Miller's marriage to wife Mary collapsed, and he and Marilyn were wed on 29 June 1956. But it wasn't long before reality set in on a trip to England, where Marilyn was starring in *The Prince and the Showgirl* (1957) opposite Sir Laurence Olivier.

The brooding, intense writer and the insecure, needy actress weren't such a good match as it turned out. Miller left England early, disturbed by his new wife's off-set antics and embarrassed by Olivier's obvious disdain for her. It was pretty much downhill from there.

During the marriage, Marilyn suffered two miscarriages and was left smarting by her husband's preoccupation with work and his apparent disregard for her. While he would spend countless hours working in his study, she guzzled champagne in her bedroom, waiting for their fleeting moments of togetherness.

The inevitable death knell for the relationship came after French actor Yves Montand was cast opposite Marilyn in *Let's Make Love*. Her dalliance with the married actor—who incidentally remained with his wife—poured salt on the wounds of the marriage, which limped into the filming of *The Misfits*, a movie Miller wrote for Marilyn.

But she hated the movie and became convinced Miller was undermining her on set, leading to a huge row, with Marilyn smashing her bedroom mirror and kicking over tables in a furious rage.

The film was finished—and so, too, was the marriage. They divorced shortly before *The Misfits* premiered in 1961.

Marilyn's lovers included Marlon Brando, Frank Sinatra and Tony Curtis, who famously said afterwards, 'When I was in bed with Marilyn, I was never sure—before, during or after—where her mind was. She was an actress. She could play a part. She could give the part what she thought a man wanted. I never asked for more.'

But it was her lust for powerful men—an appetite that served her well in her rise through Hollywood's shark-infested waters—that would ultimately lead to her downfall.

If Norma Jeane had been forced to contain her ambitions, Marilyn Monroe had no such obstacles in her way.

She was the most wanted woman in the world; it was only natural that the most powerful man on the planet would come calling.

MARILYN MONROE FACT FILE

1. The dress Marilyn was wearing to sing her famous 'Happy Birthday, Mr. President' on 19 May 1962 was so tight that it had to be sewn on her 37-23-36 curves. It was sold at auction in 1999 for $1,267,500.

2. She washed her face fifteen times a day because she was so worried about getting pimples.

3. In 1947 she was crowned Miss California Artichoke Queen.

4. She was *Playboy*'s first ever Playmate of the Month in 1953 after Hugh Hefner bought the rights to a 1947 nude photo shoot for the princely sum of $500. Hef also purchased the burial vault next to Marilyn at Westwood Memorial Park in Los Angeles so he can spend eternity at her side.

5. The first time she signed an autograph as Marilyn Monroe in 1946, she had to ask how to spell it (she didn't know where to put the 'i' in Marilyn). She didn't change her name legally until 1956.

6. She wore glasses.

7. Her first modelling job at the Radioplane Corporation factory paid only $5 for an article on 'Women in War Work'.

8. She was originally cast instead of Audrey Hepburn as Holly Golightly in 1961's *Breakfast at Tiffany's*. Writer Truman Capote wanted Marilyn for the part but her acting coach, Lee Strasberg, advised her it would be bad for her image to play a prostitute.

9. Her first roommate in Hollywood was actress Shelley Winters. Marilyn was twenty-one and Shelley was twenty-seven at the time.

10. Far from being the dumb blonde, Marilyn was an avid

reader and had a library of over four hundred books when she died, including Tolstoy, Freud and James Joyce.

DANGEROUS LIAISONS

Chomping on a cigar with his feet up on the rail in the presidential box, John F. Kennedy knew Marilyn Monroe was preparing something special for him. After all, he'd argued with wife Jackie over the actress's involvement in his birthday party at Madison Square Garden and she'd pointedly refused to attend as a result, preferring to go horse riding in Virginia.

When an aide called a couple of days before the 19 May 1962 celebration to check he was OK with Marilyn performing in the show, the President guffawed and insisted he had no problem with her singing a little song for him.

But he certainly wasn't expecting anything like this.

Even for Hollywood's sexiest star, Marilyn looked sensational. Her backless flesh-coloured Jean Louis dress—covered with 25,000 rhinestones—was so tight it had to literally be sewn onto her naked body, leaving almost nothing to the imagination. Yet it was her breathy, sensual rendition of 'Happy Birthday, Mr. President' that would go down in history as one of the most memorable performances ever.

When she'd finished singing, JFK went on stage to huge applause and joked, 'Thank you. I can now retire from politics after having had "Happy Birthday" sung to me in such a sweet, wholesome way.'

To the 15,000-strong crowd at the Garden for what was more a political fund-raiser than a real birthday celebration—Kennedy didn't actually turn forty-five for another ten days and still had a sizeable campaign debt to pay off from his triumphant 1960 election—it was certainly a memorable party piece.

But to JFK and his younger brother, Bobby, who was sitting just a few seats along in the same row in the vast auditorium with his wife, Ethel, it was a performance dangerously fraught with a much deeper resonance. For, if numerous friends and associates of the brothers are to be believed, both Kennedys had passionate illicit flings with Marilyn, tag teaming one another in a shocking crossroads of Camelot royalty and Hollywood glamour.

Marilyn first met JFK in the early 1950s at a party thrown by her agent, Charles Feldman, in Los Angeles, when both were building their careers. They didn't strike up a romantic relationship then but she was said to have had stars in her eyes from their very first meeting. By the time she was formally introduced to the soon-to-be-president in the spring of 1960, she'd been married three times and Kennedy had wed wife Jackie in 1953. But that didn't stop Marilyn from having a full-blown infatuation with the dashing politician.

'I wish he hadn't married Jackie,' she told a friend. 'I'd like to be his wife.'

The conduit for Marilyn's first meeting with Jack was his sister, Patricia, the sixth of Joe and Rose Kennedy's nine children, who was living with her heavy-drinking husband, dashing English actor Peter Lawford, in Los Angeles when she befriended the impressionable actress. To Patricia, Marilyn was a glamorous guest she could show off to her high-flying brother. With his famous wandering eye and her desperate need for validation, the outcome was inevitable.

In his book, *Marilyn's Last Words*, Matthew Smith claimed that their secret dalliances took place at the Beverly Hills Hotel on the West Coast and at the Carlyle in New York. On one occasion, he said Marilyn disguised herself as a secretary, wearing a wig and carrying a notepad, to get into his suite undetected.

On a weekend stay at Bing Crosby's Palm Springs home in March 1962, Jack was spotted at a poolside party with Marilyn. 'The president was wearing a turtleneck sweater and she was dressed in a robe. She had obviously had a lot to drink,' former Los Angeles County Assessor Philip Watson told biographer Anthony Summers.

'It was obvious they were intimate, that they were staying there together for the night.'

But Marilyn was dangerously talkative and was starting to boast out of turn to her friends about the relationship. For JFK, the Madison Square Garden birthday event was the final straw—and also for Jackie Kennedy, who could no longer turn a blind eye to such a public spectacle.

The affair was likely little more to the President than a thrilling conquest—apparently one of many. To Marilyn, though, it was much more. The great Marilyn Monroe certainly wasn't used to getting the silent treatment.

'She was calling him a lot. She wanted to see him. Everyone knew it,' said one Secret Service agent.

But the calls were not returned.

'I spent enough time with the man to know that no woman, not even his wife, was sacred to him,' Frank

Sinatra's friend and valet George Jacobs told biographer J. Randy Taraborrelli.

'His need was like that of Alexander the Great: to conquer the world. To him, Marilyn was one more conquest, a trophy—maybe the Great White Shark of Hollywood, but still a record, not a romance,' he added.

Worried about Marilyn's incessant attempts to reach him and her growing instability, JFK dispatched brother Bobby, who was eight years his junior, to California to calm her down.

Then the Attorney General, Bobby had followed in his brother's footsteps all the way up the greasy pole in Washington. Although by now it was eminently clear that an affair with Marilyn was like kryptonite to the Kennedys, Bobby was apparently smitten when they met up at the Lawfords' beachfront estate in Santa Monica.

Just like his brother, the married Kennedy apparently launched into his own affair with the sex bomb.

Chaos inevitably ensued, according to some of Marilyn's biographers, but being the early 1960s, it was all quietly swept under the carpet out of view of the public. Hardly a hint of the Kennedys' infidelities was revealed until after their deaths, even though many insiders later came forward to claim they knew all about them.

While even Marilyn had acknowledged there wasn't much chance of luring her relationship with the President out of the shadows, Bobby was another matter.

According to private detective Milo Speriglio, Marilyn was rumoured to have fallen pregnant while her fling with Bobby was in full swing. He wrote that she took her plight to father-of-seven Bobby, convinced she could persuade him to divorce Ethel and marry her. The dilemma reportedly struck fear into the family because JFK could easily have been drawn into the scandal amid gossip that the child may have been fathered by either brother. Speriglio even went so far as to claim that Marilyn had an abortion at Bobby's insistence before he, like his brother, dropped her like a stone.

Two days after the termination, claimed the private eye, Bobby had disconnected the number he gave Marilyn for his private line. She was on her own again.

In the weeks and days before her death, Marilyn was said to be desperately trying to reach Bobby, who wouldn't return her calls. Her biggest dream of being accepted and embraced by the most powerful men in the country had been exposed as a lie. They had used and discarded her and not even the name of Marilyn Monroe and all the stardom that came with it could protect her from that harsh reality.

Now she was a child again, fighting against all the odds to be heard. And just like Norma Jeane, she didn't know who to trust.

THE FBI FILES

Marilyn was involved in orgies. She made a sex tape and had a lesbian affair with Joan Crawford. She was a closet Communist and her murderer was a mystery married man who was a household name.

Marilyn's life was a parade of rumours: some true, many not. But these were not the musings of a Hollywood gossip columnist or a fan with an overheated imagination—they come direct from the files of the FBI!

The actress had no clue the agency's famously Machiavellian director, J. Edgar Hoover, was compiling a bulky file on her that was started in 1955 and wasn't closed until some years after her death in 1962. Nor did she ever get the opportunity to question its contents.

In the early days, America's obsession with rooting out Communism and the resulting Hollywood witch-hunt was the chief reason for compiling memos about Marilyn. But as whispers about her relationships with the Kennedys became louder in Washington, Hoover had his own very personal motives for keeping a closer eye on the actress.

According to political insiders, both President Kennedy and his brother, then the Attorney General, were keen to get rid of Hoover following the 1960 election. But their appeal for his resignation backfired, according to private investigator Milo Speriglio in his book, *Marilyn Monroe: The Final Word*.

'Hoover dropped a thick file on the president's desk, demanding that he and his brother read it immediately. The file contained a stack of photos, which included clandestine film of Marilyn Monroe with each of the Kennedys. Needless to say, the subject of resignation was dropped,' he wrote.

Under the Freedom of Information Act, the FBI has now released once-classified documents from its probe into Marilyn's life, with many names and other details still heavily redacted.

Here's a sample of some of the entries:

16 August 1955: A heavily redacted note to Hoover saying that Marilyn's manager had applied for a Soviet visa on her behalf.

27 April 1956: An anonymous source reports that Marilyn was taken on a tour of Brooklyn by 'a *Life* photographer who is a party member'.

6 March 1962: In a memo to Hoover from Legat, Mexico, an agent writes, 'While on vacation in Mexico, Marilyn was said to have "associated closely with certain members of the American Communist Group in Mexico (ACGM)." Source characterized the ACGM as a loose association of a predominantly social nature of present and/or past members of the Communist Party, USA, and their friends and associates who share a common sympathy for Communism and the Soviet Union.'

The agent writes about Marilyn's 'mutual infatuation' with a Mexican she met on the trip. His name is blacked out but it was thought to be screenwriter José Bolaños. 'This situation caused considerable dismay among Miss Monroe's entourage and also among the ACGM.'

The memo said Frank Sinatra organised the Mexico visit and that Marilyn was accompanied by an interior decorator called Eunice Churchill, a sixty-five-year-old widow from Los Angeles whose husband 'was a violent trade unionist'. The note adds, 'Subject reportedly spent some time with Robert Kennedy at the home of Peter Lawford in Hollywood.'

Clearly, the sunshine getaway was an emotional rollercoaster. The FBI source writes that Eunice Churchill said Marilyn 'is very vulnerable now because of her relationship by Arthur Miller and also by Joe DiMaggio and Frank Sinatra. She telephoned Sinatra to come and comfort her and he wouldn't do it.' The source said Marilyn was 'completely enamoured' with Bolaños, thinking he was 'rich, stable, intellectual and dependable'. Marilyn continued her relationship with the dashing filmmaker when she returned to the US and even told her maid, Lena Pepitone, that they had talked about marriage but it seems she quickly tired of him and dropped him soon after arriving back in Los Angeles.

Early 1962 (exact date unclear): An FBI Informant reports that Marilyn 'said she had luncheon at the Peter Lawfords with President Kennedy just a few days previously. She was very pleased as she had asked the president a lot of socially significant questions concerning the morality of atomic testing and the future of the youth of America. She has already been asked by Lawford to appear at the president's birthday party.'

Marilyn's 'views are very positively and concisely leftist; however, if she is being actively used by the Communist Party, it is not general knowledge among those working with the movement in Los Angeles.'

9 July 1963: Almost a year after Marilyn's death, a field agent refers to an article by gossip columnist Walter Winchell in the 8 July 1963 issue of the *New York Mirror*, which said 'the married man responsible for' Marilyn's death was getting considerable coverage in the foreign press, although he had not been named.

Winchell said there was no proof the man was 'the villain' and that 'many of Miss Monroe's friends now believe the overdose of sleeping pills was an accident.'

The memo said the 'clues' to the man's identity were that he was 'happily married and has children and that you can see him in a crowd and reach out and touch him; that he is a great man, famous, known the world over; that he can be seen on television and in movie theaters; that people look up to him and consider his wife and children lucky; that he is mentioned almost daily in newspapers and magazines; and that he is considered a "truly honourable man."'

It continues, 'The article alleges the affair between this man and Miss Monroe began during "the worst time of her life and the best time of his."' The article states that she telephoned the man on Sunday night, 5 August 1962, and that, when he said he would not leave his wife and could not see Miss Monroe 'any more', she swallowed a 'handful' of sleeping pills.

20 January 1965: Mrs Alta Melton, American chairman of Mothers of World War II, wrote to Hoover saying she was living in a trailer park in Winter Haven, Florida, and was handed a pamphlet titled 'Suicide or Murder?' about Marilyn's death and her relationship with RFK. 'Such reading can do much to undermine one's character and I would like to know if there is any truth to any of it,' she added. In a note attached to the log entry, an FBI agent has added, 'An alleged relationship between the Attorney General and Marilyn Monroe has come to the Bureau's attention previously.'

19 October 1964: The FBI received a letter from a former agent who was at the time working in the office of the California governor. He writes that he 'does not know the source and cannot evaluate the authenticity of this information'. The note goes on to claim, 'Robert Kennedy has been having a romance and sex affair over a period of time with Marilyn Monroe. Robert Kennedy was deeply involved emotionally with Marilyn Monroe, and had repeatedly promised to divorce his wife to marry Marilyn.'

It continues, 'Marilyn also had an intermittent lesbian affair.' Although the name was redacted, Marilyn herself admitted in tape recordings made for her psychiatrist Ralph Greenson to bedding actress Joan Crawford.

The note claimed RFK and Marilyn attended a sex party

at which 'a tape recording was secretly made and is in the possession of a Los Angeles private detective agency'. It adds, 'All the voices are identifiable.'

There is a series of entries regarding Marilyn's romance and marriage to playwright Arthur Miller because of his alleged Communist links.

One on 27 September 1956 noted the couple's marriage in a civil ceremony on 29 June 1956, followed by a Jewish wedding on 1 July. It goes on to detail his appearance before the House Committee on Un-American Activities and his 'alleged links to some 29 organizations cited as Communist fronts'.

The final entry from 15 February 1965 said an unknown person visited a New York address, where someone 'exhibited a motion picture which depicted deceased actress Marilyn Monroe committing a perverted act upon an unknown male'.

According to the person who screened the film, 'former baseball star Joseph DiMaggio in the past has offered him $25,000 for this film, it being the only one in existence'. The man apparently turned down the offer.

The memo concludes, 'Since the dissemination of above information at the present time may compromise source, this information should not be discussed outside the bureau.'

MURDER, LIES & COVER-UPS

Marilyn arrived for her last, lost weekend with Frank Sinatra looking every inch Hollywood's hottest screen siren.

Dressed from head to toe in green and wearing her signature black sunglasses, she didn't appear to have a worry in the world. But twenty-four hours later, the broken star fled home to Los Angeles after a scandalous stay in Lake Tahoe, Nevada, tainted with rumours of sex parties, Mafia blackmail threats and a drugged-out confrontation with Ol' Blue Eyes.

Six days later, she was dead.

Marilyn's last days in 1962 were awash in a haze of booze. She started out chasing down her favourite Piper-Heidsieck champagne with Bloody Marys during the day and taking handfuls of prescription pills to combat her chronic insomnia at night. But pretty soon she was drinking and downing pills all times of the day and night.

Her failure to turn up on time or remember lines on her latest movie, the ironically titled *Something's Got To Give* (1962), resulted in her being fired and sued by 20th Century Fox chief Peter G. Levathes when he finally lost patience with her antics. Only by dint of her sheer surefire star power—and the support of co-star Dean Martin, who rebuffed attempts to replace her with rivals Lee Remick or Shirley MacLaine—did Monroe manage to win the part back. She even negotiated a pay hike.

It was to celebrate Marilyn's successful showdown with her studio bosses that Sinatra invited his old lover to a star-studded bash at his newly opened casino hotel, the Cal-Neva on Lake Tahoe, on the weekend of 28 and 29 July 1962.

As she struggled to keep her life from unravelling, Marilyn had two people that friends said could have saved her.

One was on the inside at Cal-Neva. Frank Sinatra was the ringmaster, entertaining Rat Pack friends like Martin and Sammy Davis Jr, and singer Buddy Greco after flying

Marilyn in on his private jet to the resort he'd opened just two weeks earlier with his partner, the notorious Mob god-father Sam Giancana.

On the outside was former husband Joe DiMaggio, who flew to the casino to see Marilyn but wasn't allowed in because of a simmering feud with Sinatra.

There were stories afterwards that Sinatra orchestrated the weekend with his Mob cohorts to put the squeeze on Marilyn not to divulge any details of her dalliances with his friends, the Kennedys.

In his book, *The Last Days of Marilyn Monroe*, writer Donald H. Wolfe even went so far as to claim the addled actress was involved in an orgy and was photographed in an uncompromising position so she could be blackmailed in future if it became necessary.

'When she arrived that Saturday, you'd never believe that she had a care in the world,' remembered Buddy Greco, now in his eighties and living in England.

> I was sitting with Frank, Peter Lawford and a bunch of other people outside Frank's bungalow, when a limousine pulls up and this gorgeous woman in dark glasses steps out. She's dressed all in green—everything green; coat, skirt and scarf. Before I realised who it was, I thought, 'My God, what a beautiful woman. No taste in clothes but what a beautiful woman!'

But later that night, the crooner saw a very different Marilyn.

> Suddenly the room went silent and very still. It was

ROBERT F. KENNEDY
deceased

Robert Kennedy had been having a romance and sex affair over a
period of time with Marilyn Monroe. He had met her, the first date
being arranged by his sister and brother-in-law, Mr. and Mrs. Peter
Lawford. Robert Kennedy had been spending much time in Hollywood
during the last part of 1961 and early 1962, in connection with his
trying to have a film made of his book dealing with the crime investigations. He used to meet with producer Jerry Wald. He was reported to be intensely jealous of the fact that they had been making
a film of John F. Kennedy's book of the PT boat story.

Robert Kennedy was deeply involved emotionally with Marilyn
Monroe, and had repeatedly promised to divorce his wife to marry
Marilyn. Eventually Marilyn realized that Bobby had no intention of
marrying her and about this time, 20th Century Fox studio had decided
to cancel her contract. She had become very unreliable, being late
for set, etc. In addition, the studio was in financial difficulty
due to the large expenditures caused in the filming of "Cleopatra".

The studio notified Marilyn that they were cancelling her contract. This was right in the middle of a picture she was making.
They decided to replace her with actress Lee Remick. Marilyn telephoned Robert Kennedy from her home at Brentwood, California, person-
to-person, at the Department of Justice, Washington, D. C. to tell
him the bad news. Robert Kennedy told her not to worry about the contract — he would take care of everything. When nothing was done,
she again called him from her home to the Department of Justice, per-
son-to-person, and on this occasion they had unpleasant words. She
was reported to have threatened to make public their affair. On the
day that Marilyn died, Robert Kennedy was in town, and registered at
the Beverly Hills Hotel. By coincidence, this is across the street
from the house in which a number of years earlier his father, Joseph
Kennedy, had lived for a time, common-law, with Gloria Swanson.

Peter Lawford, ██████████████████████████████████ knew from Marilyn's friends
that she often made suicide threats and that she was inclined to fake
a suicide attempt in order to arouse sympathy. Lawford is reported
as having made "special arrangements" with Marilyn's psychiatrist,
Dr. Ralph Greenson, of Beverly Hills. The psychiatrist was treating
Marilyn for emotional problems and getting off the use of barbiturates. On her last visit to him, he prescribed seconal tablets, and
gave her a prescription for 40 of them, which was unusual in quantity
especially since she saw him frequently.

On the date of her death, March 4, 1962, her housekeeper put the
bottle of pills on the night table. It is reported the housekeeper
and Marilyn's personal secretary and press agent, Pat Newcombe, were
cooperating in the plan to induce suicide. Pat Newcombe was rewarded
for her cooperation by being put on the Federal payroll as top assistant to George Stevens, Jr., head of the Motion Picture Activities
Division of the U. S. Information Service. His father, George Steve-
ens, Sr., is a left-wing Hollywood director, who is well know for producing in the making of slanted and left-wing pictures. One of these
was the "Diary of Anne Frank". Pat Newcombe was flown within 48

(2)   ENCLOSURE 61-9454-28

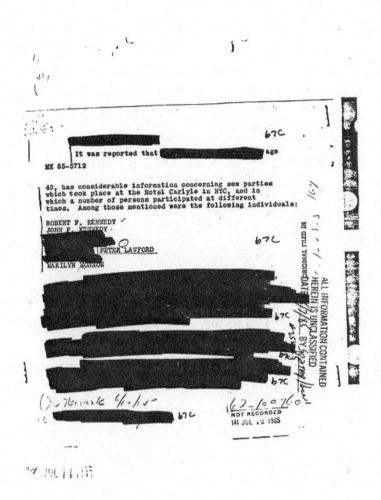

'Marilyn and the Kennedys: Two redacted FBI documents revealing details of RFK and JFK's liaisons with Monroe.'

surreal. As if somebody had turned the sound off. I looked at Frank. I could immediately tell he was furious.

His eyes were like blue ice cubes.

He was looking at the doorway where Marilyn was stood, swaying ever so slightly. She was still in the same green outfit she'd worn all day. But the woman I'd met that afternoon—smart, funny, intelligent, fragile—had gone. Now she looked drunk and, well, defiant. She was clearly angry and I think I heard her say: 'Who the f*** are they all staring at?'

'It was clear Sinatra was worried,' Greco told writer Peter Evans. 'She was in a state where she could have said anything. Sinatra motioned to his bodyguard, Coochie, to get her out of there.

'Coochie, a big guy, escorted her out. Actually, he picked her up and carried her out. It wasn't the star we were used to seeing,' he added.

A Cal-Neva doorman told Wolfe he saw Marilyn by the pool early on the Sunday morning, 'barefoot, swaying back and forth'. He said she was looking up the hill at DiMaggio, who was staring down at her, half-hidden in the mist from the lake.

It would have been the last time he saw her alive.

There had been talk of them getting back together and even remarrying after she dumped her Mexican screenwriter lover José Bolaños but she returned to her Brentwood home alone after Sinatra washed his hands of her.

That wasn't to say she didn't have plans. In fact, having taken on the mighty Fox and won, she was once more a hot commodity.

In the next few days, she had talks on a series of projects, including a plan to make a musical version of the novel *A Tree Grows in Brooklyn* with Sinatra. She was putting together a coffee-table book of pictures with photographer George Barris and moving forward with a pet project to make a movie about her Hollywood heroine, Jean Harlow. Before the weekend, she made a date to meet up with Gene Kelly the following Monday to discuss making a film with him.

Amid this throng of renewed activity, there was still an aura of loneliness.

'Do you know who I've always depended on?' Marilyn asked one Los Angeles reporter. 'No strangers, not friends. The telephone. That's my best friend. I love calling friends, especially late at night when I can't sleep.'

None of the people Marilyn spoke to that week said she sounded particularly depressed or upset.

On the morning of Saturday, 4 August 1962, handyman Norman Jeffries was busy working on the floor of Marilyn's home when he looked up to see his employer standing there, wrapped in a giant bath towel.

'I will never forget the sight of her,' he told biographer Anthony Summers. 'She looked sick, desperately sick—not only in the physical sense—and I thought there must be something terribly wrong. She must have taken a lot of dope or something, or maybe she was scared out of her mind. I had never seen her look that way before.'

Marilyn's press agent and majordomo, Pat Newcomb, had stayed the night and recalled the actress was in an irritable mood. She was particularly annoyed because

Newcomb had slept for fifteen hours straight while she herself had again had trouble getting any sleep at all.

In her last months, Marilyn suffered night terrors and would have to get up and sit in a chair until the dark cloud lifted. Psychiatrist Dr Ralph Greenson was called over to the house and immediately noticed Marilyn appeared to be heavily sedated. He had been trying to break his famous patient's reliance on Nembutal barbiturates in favour of chloral hydrate as a sleep aid and stayed until about 7pm before heading off for dinner.

At around 7.15pm, Marilyn appeared in good spirits when she talked on the phone to Joe DiMaggio Jr about his recent decision to end his engagement. Thirty minutes later, there was another of those 180-degree mood changes.

Actor friend Peter Lawford had been badgering her to go down to the beach for a party that night but this time, when he spoke to her on the phone, she sounded out of it. He had to shout her name into the handset several times before she responded.

'Say goodbye to Pat [Lawford's wife], say goodbye to the President and say goodbye to yourself because you're a nice guy,' she told him, according to biographer Donald Spoto.

There have been countless theories over what happened in the hours that followed in the small, simply furnished house—the first Marilyn had ever owned. But one fact is indisputable: the actress didn't make it through the night.

Sergeant Jack Clemmons was serving as acting watch commander in West Los Angeles when his desk telephone rang at 4.25am on 5 August 1962 and an unidentified caller reported a single sentence before hanging up.

'Marilyn Monroe is dead; she committed suicide.'

Because it was a slow night, he decided to investigate himself and arrived at Monroe's bedroom at 12305 Fifth Helena Drive in Brentwood about ten minutes later to find the star lying face down on her bed, her shoulders exposed but a sheet pulled over her lifeless body.

Whatever the real reason for her death, there was no doubt there was a cover-up and there were so many lies that even the perpetrators couldn't keep up with the stories they were spinning.

According to biographer Donald Spoto, Marilyn's housekeeper, Eunice Murray, told Sgt Clemmons she first discovered her employer's body 'at midnight', only to later change her story to about 3am. She was busy laundering clothes in the middle of the night when the police arrived, suggesting someone had something to hide, although, inexplicably, she was never asked who it was or why.

Murray was hired by Marilyn the previous year at the instigation of Greenson and the actress suspected her employee was told to spy on her for the shrink, who made a point of keeping in very close contact with his star patient. It was Murray who called Greenson to the house, saying she saw a light still on in Marilyn's bedroom late at night, which was apparently very unusual. Afraid to wake her, she called for help.

The doctor ordered the housekeeper to knock on the door. When she couldn't get a reply, Greenson told Murray to also call Marilyn's internist, Hyman Engelberg, and said he was heading right over from his home a mile and a half away.

Both of the doctors and Murray were at the house when Sgt Clemmons arrived. The officer wasn't happy with their explanation that they waited before calling for help because they needed permission from 20th Century Fox's publicity department. Even in those golden days of the powerful Hollywood studios, that was hard to swallow.

Reports of other strange goings-on that night began to emerge. Breaking glass and raised voices were heard coming from Marilyn's house by a neighbour; an ambulance was supposedly parked outside and a helicopter hovered overhead earlier on that fateful Saturday night.

A hysterical woman—who was never identified—was also heard screaming, 'Murderers! You murderers! Are you satisfied now that she's dead?'

On the weekend Marilyn died, Bobby Kennedy, then the Attorney General, was staying at the Northern California ranch owned by wealthy attorney John Bates, about sixty miles from San Francisco. He was due to give a speech to the California Bar Association and Bates was his host.

RFK's representatives always insisted that was where he remained the entire time. He was seen at church there on the morning after the tragedy, as the world woke up to the news that the screen siren was gone. But biographer Matthew Smith insists that RFK was told to 'get your ass down to LA because she's out of control' after Marilyn let slip to some confidantes that she was planning to hold a Monday-morning press conference where she would 'blow the lid off the whole damn thing'.

Exactly what she planned to say, if anything, was never revealed but there was long rumoured to be a 'red diary' in which Marilyn would jot down secrets JFK and Bobby whispered to her during their clandestine trysts. According to some biographers, it was this notebook Bobby was trying to reclaim when he allegedly made two trips to see Marilyn in the hours before her death.

A neighbour, Betty Pollard, said her mother was playing bridge with a friend when they noticed Kennedy going into Marilyn's house some time before 5pm. Smith claims RFK returned several hours later and lost his temper with Marilyn after demanding she hand over her diary.

Deborah Gould, the ex-wife of actor Peter Lawford, told writer Anthony Summers the real reason for the delay in reporting the death to police was 'to get Bobby out of town'.

She wasn't necessarily accusing the Attorney General of foul play. Summers puts a different spin on Kennedy's alleged visit to see Marilyn, suggesting he may well have been at the house because he was genuinely concerned for her health after she made the rambling call to Lawford—the Kennedys' brother-in-law through his first wife, Patricia—earlier that Saturday night. According to this more sympathetic theory, Bobby may have rushed over to Marilyn's house, only to find her dying or already dead, leaving him with a difficult dilemma.

'Even had he never had an affair with Marilyn—and all the evidence points to the contrary—for a Kennedy to be found with a dead Marilyn Monroe, even on a legitimate mission of mercy, would have meant certain political disaster,' wrote Summers in his 1985 biography, *Goddess: The Secret Lives of Marilyn Monroe*.'

If her death was not an accident—or by her own hand—who else wanted Marilyn dead? And who killed her?

Teamsters boss Jimmy Hoffa hated the Kennedys and reportedly thought he could either blackmail or shame the family by sending Mob enforcers to kill Marilyn and then implicate them in the murder.

Another possibility: certain government agencies such as the CIA or Secret Service may have been so concerned at what Marilyn had gleaned through her relationships with the Kennedy brothers that, when she threatened to expose them, she became too much of a risk to be left alive.

There were more questions following the autopsy by Dr Thomas Noguchi, then a new hire in the LA Medical Examiner's office. Police investigators had already questioned why there was no water glass near Marilyn if she'd swallowed as many as thirty or forty pills and now Dr Noguchi was wondering why her stomach was empty if she'd ingested that many capsules. And if she'd taken an overdose of Nembutal barbiturates, as the toxicology tests pointed to, there should have been a telltale yellow dye on the linings of her throat, oesophagus and stomach. There was no stain.

Experts claimed the only likely answer was that Marilyn had taken—or been forcibly given—the lethally large dose via an enema.

'I did not think she committed suicide,' said former LA Deputy District Attorney John Miner thirty years later. Miner, who was present at the autopsy, added that his inquiries showed that Marilyn was making plans for the future and that 'she felt that she had put everything bad behind her and could now go forward with her life.'

Many of her friends went one step further. Photographer George Barris, who took the famous pictures of Marilyn in the surf during her last summer and spoke to her on the phone the day before she died, said in his book, *Marilyn: Her*

Life In Her Own Words, 'It will always be my conviction that she was murdered.'

The lack of any definite conclusion from the coroner and the question marks, contradictions and suspicious behaviour of almost all of the main players makes it virtually impossible to believe there wasn't a cover-up on some level. From there, it isn't such a big leap to think that whoever was responsible for her death got away with murder.

Ten years before her passing, during the heady early days of her meteoric rise to fame, Marilyn had made a special request of her make-up artist friend Allan 'Whitey' Snyder.

'Promise me that if something happens to me you'll do my make-up, so I'll look my best when I leave,' she asked him.

On 7 August 1962, Joe DiMaggio called in the favour. 'Whitey, you promised—will you do it, please—for her?' asked the Yankee Clipper.

'I'll be there, Joe,' Whitey told him before driving to the Westwood Village Mortuary, off Wilshire Boulevard, to do Marilyn's make-up one more time.

It was DiMaggio who decided he wasn't going to turn his former wife's funeral into the kind of celebrity circus that had undoubtedly hastened her demise. Sinatra wasn't invited; neither was Dean Martin or Sammy Davis Jr. Peter Lawford, Marilyn's conduit to the Kennedys, was also left out in the cold.

According to one witness, Sinatra was so determined to be present that he brought his own security people to pretend they were working there and help slip him in but the ploy failed.

Only thirty relatives and close friends watched Marilyn's final chapter play out in the mortuary chapel while hundreds of photographers, reporters and fans waited outside. Marilyn's long-time acting teacher, Lee Strasberg, gave a eulogy and a pastor offered a brief address. 'Over the Rainbow', her favourite song, was piped in.

Before the casket was closed, a weeping DiMaggio kissed Marilyn with a final goodbye. 'I love you, my darling. I love you,' he said, putting a posy of roses in her dead hands.

Although their marriage had floundered, DiMaggio and Marilyn had been seeing each other again in the months before her death and on 1 August 1962 the retired slugger confided to pals that he had proposed to his ex-wife again and she had agreed. But there was one major thorn in his hard-won happiness over winning the actress back—the shadowy figure of RFK.

DiMaggio still had friends among Marilyn's closest confidantes and he would have been painfully aware of her clandestine affair with the Attorney General. He would also have understood all too well the truth that Marilyn had closed her eyes to the fact that RFK would never leave wife Ethel and their children.

To a proud, possessive Sicilian like DiMaggio, the way the Kennedys toyed with Marilyn's emotions would certainly have made his blood boil, particularly as he was pursuing her himself.

According to the FBI file, the last call Marilyn took on the night she died was from her ex-husband's son, Joe DiMaggio Jr, who was in the US Marines stationed at Camp Pendleton, near San Diego.

'They were very friendly,' the file reports. 'Marilyn told him she was getting sleepy.

'Joe DiMaggio Sr knows the whole story and is reported to have stated when Robert Kennedy gets out of office, he intends to kill him,' it continues. 'Joseph DiMaggio Jr knew of the affair between Robert Kennedy and Marilyn.'

With anyone else at any other time, this death threat alone would be enough to send major alarm bells ringing right to the very top but DiMaggio hadn't made much of a secret of his disdain for RFK and, hours later, he was grieving the loss of the great love of his life along with the rest of the world.

Of course, DiMaggio never made good on his death threat but he didn't let go of his memories of Marilyn so easily. He never married again and, three times a week for the next twenty years, he delivered fresh flowers to her grave. When he died in 1999, his last words were, 'I'll finally get to see Marilyn.'

Other than its colour, it's not an ostentatious last resting place. The pink marble wall crypt #24 at the Corridor of Memories in Los Angeles has a bronze plaque carrying the simple inscription:

MARILYN MONROE
1926–1962

There is no trace left of Norma Jeane now; no sign of the vulnerable, lost girl who was overtaken by stardom that rolled over her old life so fast she could never quite keep up. But more than fifty years after her death, there are simply too many questions that remain unanswered for Marilyn Monroe to rest in peace.

MARILYN'S DEATH—TIMELINE
4 AUGUST 1962

7.15pm: Marilyn sounds cheerful and upbeat on the phone with Joe DiMaggio Jr, who recalls the time because he was watching the seventh inning of a Baltimore Orioles baseball tie with the Los Angeles Dodgers and the time matches with the game record.

7.30pm: Peter Lawford calls Marilyn to invite her to his house but she declines. According to Lawford, her speech was slurred and hard to decipher. The call ends abruptly and the line remains busy when Lawford tries to reconnect.

8pm: Lawford calls Marilyn's housekeeper, Eunice Murray, and asks her to check on her employer. Murray says Marilyn is fine.

10.30pm: Marilyn's agent, Arthur P. Jacobs, hurriedly leaves a concert at the Hollywood Bowl after being told by the actress's lawyer, Mickey Rudin, that the actress has overdosed.

Midnight: Murray notices a light under Marilyn's door and, unable to get a response after knocking, telephones psychiatrist Dr Ralph Greenson.

5 AUGUST 1962

12.30am: Greenson arrives and looks through French windows to see Monroe lying lifeless on her bed clutching a telephone. After breaking the glass to open the locked door, he discovers she is dead. He calls her physician, Dr Hyman Engelberg.

1am: Lawford is told by Rudin that Marilyn is dead.

4.25am: Emergency call to police reporting Marilyn's death.

4.35am: Police arrive at Marilyn's house.

5.40am: Undertaker Guy Hockett arrives at the scene. He puts the time of death as being between 9.30pm and 11.30pm.

6am: Murray changes her story and says she called Greenson after waking around 3am and noticing Marilyn's light was still on. Greenson and Engelbert now claim the time of death to be around 3.50am.

MARILYN'S SECRET TAPES

It was *Marilyn Monroe Uncensored*—an audio recording—that revealed the most intimate secrets of Hollywood's fabled sex symbol. Dressed only in her underwear, Marilyn made the soul-searching tape in the privacy of her bedroom as an extraordinary experiment for her personal psychiatrist, Ralph Greenson. It was supposed to be for his ears only and did, indeed, remain under wraps for forty years.

When the tapes finally emerged, they threw fresh doubts on the official suicide theory of her death and fuelled conspiracy theorists still convinced the truth was more sinister.

Marilyn bared her innermost thoughts and emotions in a way few celebrities have ever done, especially at a time when the public images of the stars were so tightly controlled by the studios. She talked about Jack and Bobby Kennedy, about her marriages and why they failed, about her sexual problems and the other men—and women—in her life. As she herself put it, they were 'the most private, the most secret thoughts of Marilyn Monroe.' Even more intriguing, she spoke of her excitement about her plans for the future. She sounded bright and insightful and brimming with ideas about the next phase of her life. She complained about her nosy housekeeper and plotted to fire her, again hardly the mindset of a star at the end of her tether.

The implication is that either her death was accidental, or she was murdered.

The reason the tapes remained buried for so long was because Marilyn gave them in confidence to Dr Greenson, maybe on the actual morning of her death or at least a day or so before.

'I have absolute confidence and trust you will never reveal to a living soul what I say to you,' she told him.

In fact, the only person he played them to was Los Angeles Deputy District Attorney John Miner, who, in turn, promised to keep them private to preserve the doctor-patient privilege. The psychiatrist wouldn't allow Miner to take the tapes but he did permit him to take extensive and 'nearly verbatim' notes.

It wasn't until two decades after Dr Greenson's own death that Miner disclosed what was in the tapes in a belated effort to try to set the record straight on some key factors surrounding the mysterious death of the screen siren. He only revealed the contents then because he was concerned that Dr Greenson's reputation had been maligned over the years with suggestions that his treatment and over-prescription of drugs had somehow led to Monroe's suicide. Whatever her emotional state at the time, Marilyn made the tapes as a way of helping her deal with the insecurities that still plagued her despite her immense fame.

In his 2004 book, *Marilyn's Last Words: Her Secret Tapes and Mysterious Death*, writer Matthew Smith made the contents of the homemade recordings public for the first time. Here are some excerpts—they make for fascinating reading.

On her sex life, Marilyn had a surprising confession: 'What I told you is true when I first became your patient. I had never had an orgasm. I well remember you said an orgasm happens in the mind, not the genitals. You said there was an obstacle in my mind that prevented me from having an orgasm; that it was something that happened early in my life about which I felt so guilty that I did not deserve to have the greatest pleasure there is. I would win overwhelmingly if the Academy gave an Oscar for faking orgasms. I have done some of my best acting convincing my partners I was in the throes of ecstasy.'

On her looks: 'I stood naked in front of my full-length mirrors for a long time yesterday. I was all made up with my hair done. What did I see? My breasts are beginning to sag a bit. My waist isn't bad. My ass is what it should be, the bester there is. Legs, knees and ankles still shapely. And my feet are not too big. OK, Marilyn, you have it all there.'

On her father-fixation with Clark Gable, her co-star in 1961's The Misfits: 'In the kissing scenes, I kissed him with real affection. I didn't want to go to bed with him, but I wanted him to know how much I liked and appreciated him. When I came back from a day off the set, he patted my ass and told me if I didn't behave myself, he would give me a good spanking. I looked him in the eye and said, "Don't tempt me." It was different when I got to know him. Then I wanted him to be my father. I wouldn't care if he spanked me as long as he made up for it by hugging me and telling me I was Daddy's little girl and he loved me.'

On her dream role: 'I dreamt that I was sitting on Clark Gable's lap with his arms around me. He said, "They want me to do a *Gone With the Wind* sequel. Maybe I will, if you will be my Scarlett." I woke up crying.'

On her 1957 The Prince and the Showgirl **co-star Sir Laurence Olivier:** 'Olivier came into my dressing room to give me hell for screwing up. I soothed him by telling him I thought his *Hamlet* was one of the greatest films ever made. He was superficial—no, that's not the word—supercilious, arrogant, a snob, conceited. Maybe a little bit anti-Semitic in the sense of some of my best friends are Jews. But damn him, a great, great actor.'

On her rivalry with Liz Taylor: 'If I have to do any more pictures for those b*****s at Fox, I am going to be the highest paid actress in Hollywood, double what they pay Taylor, and a piece of the gross.'

On her plans to appear in a Shakespeare production: 'I have thrown all my pills in the toilet. You see how serious I am about this? I am going to do Juliet first. What with what makeup, costume and cameras can do, my acting will create a Juliet who is fourteen, an innocent virgin, but whose budding womanhood is fantastically sexy. I've some wonderful ideas for Lady Macbeth and Queen Gertrude. I feel certain I'll win an Oscar for one or more of my Shakespearian women.'

On Joan Crawford's treatment of her daughter, Christina, when the little girl had the flu: 'I could see that Crawford was getting so angry; she was going to hit the child. I felt she had a cruel streak towards the child.'

On her lesbian fling with Crawford: 'I told her straight out that I didn't much enjoy doing it with a woman. After I turned her down, she became spiteful. An English poet best described it, "Heaven hath no rage like love to hatred turned; and hell hath no fury like a woman scorned".'

On her habit of using enemas to take prescription drugs: 'I don't understand this big taboo about enemas. Mae West told me she is given an enema every day. Mae says her enemas will keep her young until she is a hundred.'

On Frank Sinatra: 'He has helped more people anonymously than anybody else. And the miserable press smears him with lies about his being involved with the Mafias and gangsters. What a wonderful friend he is to me. I love Frank and he loves me. It is not the marrying kind of love. It is better because marriage can't destroy it. How well I know. Marriage destroyed my relationships with two wonderful men.'

On Joe DiMaggio: 'Joe couldn't stay married to Marilyn Monroe, the famous movie star. Joe has an image in his stubborn Italian head of a traditional Italian wife. She would have to be faithful, do what he tells her, devote all of herself to him. Doctor, you know that's not me. But we didn't end our love for each other. Any time I need him, Joe is there. I couldn't have a better friend.'

On Arthur Miller: 'It's different with Arthur. Marrying him was my mistake, not his. He couldn't give me the attention, warmth and affection I need. It's not in his nature. Arthur never credited me with much intelligence. As bed partners, we were so-so. He was not that much interested: me faking with exceptional performance to get him more interested.'

On JFK: 'This man is going to change our country. No child will go hungry. No person will sleep in the street and get his meals from garbage cans ... I tell you, Doctor, when he has finished his achievements he will take his place with Washington, Jefferson, Lincoln and FDR as one of our greatest presidents. I'm glad he has Bobby. It's like the navy. The president is the captain and Bobby is his executive officer. Bobby would do absolutely anything for his brother. And so would I. I'll never embarrass him. As long as I have memory, I have John Fitzgerald Kennedy.'

On RFK: 'But Bobby, Doctor, what should I do about Bobby? I want someone else to tell him it's over. I tried to get the president to do it, but I couldn't reach him. Now I'm glad I couldn't. He's too important to ask. You know when I sang "Happy Birthday" for him, I sweated profusely; I was afraid it would show. Maybe I should stop being a coward and tell him myself. His Catholic morality has to find a way to justify cheating on his wife, so love becomes his excuse. And if you love enough, you can't help it and you can't be blamed. All right, Doctor, that's Marilyn Monroe's analysis of Bobby's love for me.'

WHAT REALLY HAPPENED?

For more than half a century, the idea that a depressed Marilyn Monroe died naked and alone in her bed after taking a massive overdose of drugs has become an iconic pop-culture touchstone. But let's clear up one thing right now—the

Los Angeles Medical Examiner's 1962 report was wrong; it wasn't suicide.

Put simply, nothing adds up to support the 'official' cause of death. In my opinion—one shared by many who have looked deeply into the case over the years—it's not a question of whether Marilyn was murdered but by whom. Friends said she was happy and looked forward to the future with an optimism and zest that had been missing in previous months. She was making plans for exciting new projects, new movies, rounds of golf and maybe even another go at marriage with Joe DiMaggio.

There was no suicide note, nor evidence in Marilyn's stomach that she'd swallowed forty to fifty missing Nembutal sleeping pills and as many as seventeen chloral-nitrate pills. There were huge gaps in the timetable of events and the scene had been swept as clean as a whistle.

What the actress could never have anticipated as she settled down for a quiet night in at her Brentwood, Los Angeles home on 4 August 1962 were the powerful forces marshalling against her. Her final moments were to be played out as a pawn in a high-stakes game of chicken that she had no clue she was caught up in.

Only at the very last minute would she have realised her life was in jeopardy.

So much is suspicious about the death of Marilyn Monroe but the investigation into what really happened to the doomed actress begins with a bruise.

The Medical Examiner who carried out the autopsy on Marilyn's body, Thomas Noguchi, offered at the time a cause of death as probable suicide. But as the years passed, even he admitted to doubt.

He wrote in his original report,

The unembalmed body is that of a thirty-six-year-old, well-developed, well-nourished Caucasian female weighing 117 pounds and measuring sixty-five and one-half inches in length. The scalp is covered with bleached blonde hair. The eyes are blue . . . a slight ecchymotic area [bleeding under the skin] is noted on the left hip and left side of lower back.

Later—much later—he said this same bruise 'might have indicated violence'.

He qualified his comment by adding that he would have expected to find fresh bruises around the throat or skull if there was foul play. But in his memoir, *Coroner (1983)*, he adds, 'Nevertheless, that fresh bruise on her hip still remains unexplained. And as a possible clue to violence, it is curious that most of the investigative reporters who later became interested in the case failed to pick it up.'

The reason the bruise didn't seem consistent with an overdose death was that investigators didn't initially consider the possibility that the drugs were pumped into the bloodstream via an enema. If that was, indeed, the case— and most experts agree now that is the most likely scenario— the mystery bruise would be consistent with Marilyn being forcefully held while the administration was made without her consent.

It's no surprise, considering all we know about this investigation, that Marilyn's stomach and its contents and her intestine were never tested and, when Dr Noguchi tried to correct the error, he was told the organs had disappeared.

So the obvious question is: who would do such a thing and why?

The clues lie in the people interested enough in Marilyn's thoughts and actions to bug her home. Two people planted listening devices in the house that were in operation on the night she died.

Private eye Fred Otash, the investigator who notoriously knew where all the bodies were buried in Hollywood of the 1950s and 1960s, had been asked by Marilyn herself to help her record her calls but, at the same time, he surreptitiously hid away bugs for Peter Lawford to keep tabs on her for the Kennedys.

Bernie Spindel, a freelance operator who counted Mob-linked Teamsters boss Jimmy Hoffa as one of his best customers, had installed another set of wiretaps. Hoffa and his Mafia cohorts hated the Kennedys, who had targeted organised crime as an urgent priority following JFK's election triumph in 1960 and were looking at ways to destroy them.

To the Kennedys, Marilyn was a potential embarrassment that needed to be handled carefully. To the Mafia, she was the Achilles' heel they could use to get to their arch-enemies in Washington.

There was a third element involved in the conspiracy— FBI Director J. Edgar Hoover. He, too, had reason to fear the Kennedys, who were trying to force him out of the self-aggrandising fiefdom he'd built the agency into through his years in charge.

Neither recording has ever been made public but accounts from both sides do appear to mesh.

Documents belonging to Otash, who died in 1992, were discovered by his daughter, Colleen, stashed away in a storage unit and one note written by the investigator says he listened to Marilyn die after he taped an argument she had with Bobby Kennedy and Peter Lawford.

'I listened to Marilyn die. She said she was passed around like a piece of meat. It was a violent argument about their relationship and the commitment and promises he made to her,' Otash wrote. 'She was really screaming and they were trying to quiet her down. She's in the bedroom and Bobby gets the pillow, and he muffles her on the bed to keep the neighbours from hearing. She finally quieted down and then he was looking to get out of there.'

Otash would confess to *Vanity Fair* just before his death that he listened in on JFK having sex with Marilyn. 'Yes, we did have [Lawford's house] wired. Yes, I did hear a tape of Jack Kennedy fucking Monroe. But I don't want to get into the moans and groans of their relationship. They were having a sexual relationship—period.'

Even with their immense sense of entitlement, the suggestion by some conspiracy theorists that Bobby was directly responsible for killing Marilyn to silence her seems way too implausible. For all their cheating and skulduggery, JFK and RFK weren't going to the lengths of having their girlfriends bumped off, especially when it involved someone as high profile as Marilyn. The Mafia had no such qualms.

Otash's story that Bobby left Marilyn's house in a hurry on the evening of 4 August correlates with the version told by the brother of Mob boss and Sinatra confidante Sam Giancana, who claims to name the killers in his 1992 book with his brother, Chuck Giancana, *Double Cross: The Explosive, Inside Story of the Mobster Who Controlled America*.

Chuck Giancana says his brother was tipped off that Bobby was in California that fateful weekend and likely to pay Marilyn a visit. He said a 'trusted assassin', Leonard 'Needles' Gianola, was flown in to carry out the hit, along with his sidekick, Mugsy Tortorella, and two other professional killers, one from Kansas City and the other from Detroit.

Using the eavesdropping equipment planted by Bernie Spindel, they waited close to Marilyn's home for the Attorney General to arrive. Listening in on the conversation, they heard an angry altercation between RFK and Marilyn. 'She became agitated—hysterical, in fact—and in response, they heard Kennedy instruct the man with him, evidently a doctor, to give her a shot to "calm her down",' wrote Giancana. 'Shortly thereafter,' he adds, 'the Attorney General and the doctor left.'

Waiting until darkness, the assassins broke into the home sometime before midnight and overwhelmed Marilyn. 'Calmly, and with all the efficiency of a team of surgeons, they taped her mouth shut and proceeded to insert a specially "doctored" Nembutal suppository into her anus. Then they waited,' he continues.

The enema, prepared by a Chicago chemist, was apparently a favoured method used by the Mob to 'whack' their enemies. It was, says Giancana, fast and effective and the men placed a naked Marilyn back on her bed before sneaking off into the night.

The idea was that then 'Act Two' of the drama would unfold with Marilyn's dead body bringing hordes of police and press to the house and the finger of suspicion would swiftly point at RFK after it emerged that he had visited Marilyn just hours earlier.

The scandal of the married Kennedy having an affair with the world's most famous actress would be sufficient to wreck his political ambitions. He could even be suspected of playing a part in the murder. But the plot ended up playing out very differently.

The first people to learn of Marilyn's death were not the police but Kennedy and Lawford, according to the Mafia wiretaps. And the English actor was sent to Marilyn's home with Otash to sweep the house before the authorities were alerted.

Leaving nothing to chance, Hoover was also notified and provided a team of FBI agents to protect the Attorney General. According to some reports, they commandeered all of the incoming phone records to the house, which were never heard of again.

With such powerful people pulling the strings, it was hardly surprising that the likes of Murray and Greenson were so willing to switch their stories.

The suicide tale fitted the public perception of the tragic movie star and rumours of her romantic entanglements with the Kennedys would not emerge until many years later, after their own lives had been cut short by violence.

Spindel's home would be raided by agents working for the New York District Attorney—a friend of RFK—and all his tapes were seized. Despite launching a lawsuit to recover 'tapes and evidence concerning the causes of death of Marilyn Monroe which strongly suggest that the officially reported circumstances of her demise were erroneous', the recordings were never returned.

As for Marilyn's little red book—the diary she was said to have kept, detailing her relationships—Lionel Grandison, the Los Angeles Deputy Coroner in 1962 who signed Marilyn's death certificate, said he saw the diary in the Medical Examiner's office in the hours after the death.

By the next day it had disappeared.

The candle that once shone so brightly wasn't simply blown out by the cruel winds of life—it was snuffed out in a firestorm Marilyn unwittingly sparked with her fame and beauty, never realising just how much danger it left her in.

JOHN F. KENNEDY

People who lived through the Kennedy assassination will forever remember exactly where they were and what they were doing when the clock was frozen at 12.30pm on Friday, 22 November 1963.

One moment President John F. Kennedy was waving to the adoring crowds in Dealey Plaza in downtown Dallas, his wife Jackie all in strawberry pink at his side in the back of an open-topped Lincoln Continental. Then a shot rang out and the open-mouthed President, his wave frozen in a helpless fist, turned to the First Lady, trying to comprehend the enormity of what had just happened.

Her Chanel suit splattered by her husband's blood, Jackie cried out, 'They have killed my husband! I have his brains in my hand.'

Bang, bang, bang! Three assassins' bullets did their job. The country had lost its leader, and brave Jackie, whose dignity in the face of tragedy would win the admiration of the world, had lost her husband.

For decades historians and conspiracy theorists would argue about hitman Lee Harvey Oswald's motives for history's most infamous murder but that would never change the fact that one woman was left a widow and her children fatherless in a brief moment of madness.

Alas, Kennedy's brother, Bobby, who strongly suspected the Mafia was involved in the hit, died before he could get to the truth, assassinated less than five years later at forty two as he campaigned for the presidency in Los Angeles.

Tragically, JFK's wife and son would also die—Jackie through terminal non-Hodgkin's lymphoma, a rare form of cancer, in 1994 at the age of sixty four and JFK Jr in a 1999 plane crash, aged thirty eight—without knowing the full facts about the death. Even now, the FBI and Central Intelligence Agency prefer to allow the fog of conspiracy theories to shroud the real motive for the assassination to cover up some long-ago skulduggery.

The answers are out there; the case is closed. Here, I will endeavour to explain what really happened on that fateful day and why.

Questions remain, of course. The assassination, as vivid as it remains in the minds of many, still happened a long time ago and concerted efforts have been made to cover up the truth by both the authorities and the protagonists. The number of potential witnesses to the truth who have died in mysterious circumstances over the past half century is quite staggering.

The Kennedys represent, in many ways, a bright light in America's past, spearheading the battle for human rights and, on the surface at least, representing all that was good and optimistic about their nation's newfound stature in the world in the early 1960s. By contrast, the Mob was the dark underbelly of American culture, with a power and influence in the latter part of the twentieth century more pervasive than even fans of *The Godfather* movies might imagine. This underworld was much more about greed and bloody murder than it was about honour and brotherhood. If you crossed them, there was a very real chance you'd pay with your life.

In the following pages, I will present compelling evidence that will show how America's most feared Mafia bosses felt very deeply that they had been double-crossed by JFK, Bobby and their father, Joe.

And in this confluence of the good and bad in America in the 1960s, it was the bad that won out.

THE LEGEND

For a man who lived so much of his life on the public stage, John Fitzgerald Kennedy was comfortable with secrets and lies. Harangued by his critics as all style and precious little substance, he is still worshipped by the American public, who consistently rank him alongside Thomas Jefferson and Abraham Lincoln as among the nation's most beloved leaders.

His life remains a mass of contradictions. A devout Catholic who showed little respect for the sanctity of marriage; the creator of the Peace Corps, who took the world to the brink of nuclear war in the Cuban Missile Crisis of October 1962; an action man living life to the fullest, who spent half of his life in bed battling illness. The great tragedy was that his millions of admirers—and even his detractors—were robbed of the chance to see all that JFK could achieve.

Born on 29 May 1917 in Brookline, Massachusetts, he was the second oldest of seven children. His father, Joe, was a wealthy banker, who made a fortune on the stock market after World War II and went on to become US Ambassador to Great Britain. His mother, Rose, was a Boston debutante.

Both had high hopes for their children but John—known as 'Jack'—was a poor student and, at Harvard University, showed little interest in anything other than sports and women. At the start of his second year, he wrote to his friend Lem Billings, 'I can now get tail as often and as free as I want, which is a step in the right direction.'

He signed up for the US navy and was assigned to command a patrol torpedo boat in the South Pacific during World War II. It proved to be a tumultuous posting. A Japanese warship sank the boat on 2 August 1943, killing two sailors. Despite badly injuring his back, Kennedy saved the life of one man by carrying him to safety and led the survivors to a nearby island, where they were rescued six days later.

He won a navy bravery medal and the Purple Heart for his gallantry but his older brother, Joe Jr, was still the sibling their parents had singled out as a future President of the United States.

When Joe was killed when his fighter plane exploded over England in August 1944, the aspirations of the Kennedy clan moved to the second son, who soon began his heady ascent to the White House by winning a seat in Congress at the age of twenty nine. When he beat Richard Nixon by a razor-thin margin on 8 November 1960, forty-three-year-old Kennedy became the second youngest American president in history after Theodore Roosevelt, who was forty-two.

'Ask not what your country can do for you. Ask what you can do for your country,' he said at his legendary inaugural address on 20 January 1961.

His tenure was to last just 1,000 days.

JACK & JACKIE

As they lived life on the grandest of scales on the biggest of stages, they were America's couple, their every move closely observed by legions of admirers, both at home and abroad. But what about when the cameras were turned off; when the most famous Kennedys of all were simply Jack and Jackie?

No amount of fame and fortune could save them from the heartache of three miscarriages or Jackie's inner turmoil over her husband's compulsive philandering and their perfunctory sex life. But it was those intimate, private moments between them—often seized in between campaign speeches, political meetings and matters of State of critical importance—that meant the most to Jackie and offered a real glimpse into what made history's most fabled marriage tick.

The marriage wasn't perfect—even Jackie would never have dared to suggest that—but neither was it always teetering on the brink of disaster the way some revisionist biographers would have you believe. Behind closed doors, Jackie relished the simple pleasures of raising a young family, even if those doors happened to be the entrance to the White House.

They had met in May 1951 at a small dinner party organised by a mutual friend, *Chattanooga Times Washington* correspondent Charles Bartlett, at his home in Georgetown. Their marriage was a little more than two years later, when Jackie was twenty-four and Jack thirty-six, in Newport, Rhode Island, on 12 September 1953. It came with all the Kennedy trimmings, with more than eight hundred guests and a blessing from Pope Pius XII.

Jackie's contradictory feelings over her wedding dress were a harbinger of the kind of interference the young bride would face in the years to come. The gown by Ann Lowe, couturier to America's 1950s elite, made with enough ivory silk taffeta to cover half a football field, was widely admired but Jackie didn't much care for it because it was designed on the orders of other members of the Kennedy clan. She later admitted she thought it accentuated her flat chest and left her looking like a lampshade.

The couple's early married years were a flurry of elections and duties and rented homes, with barely a second to breathe on JFK's rocket trip to the presidency.

There was pain; Jack's bad back left him in agony for days at a time, often leaving his young wife at a loss to know what to do to help ease his misery.

There was heartache too.

In 1955 Jackie was overjoyed to discover she was pregnant, only to miscarry the baby. The next year, on 23 August 1956, a second pregnancy also ended in tragedy when the child, Arabella, was delivered stillborn.

Friends said the miscarriages represented a turning point in the marriage. After the stillbirth, it was Bobby, not Jack, who was waiting for Jackie to regain consciousness after the emergency Caesarean. Her brother-in-law also arranged for the burial of the child. It wasn't until 26 August—three days after the tragedy—when Jack finally spoke directly to his traumatised wife.

According to biographer C. David Heymann in *A Woman Named Jackie*, his first reaction was 'mild annoyance'.

'As often happens in times of turmoil, Jack and Jackie's differences in outlook, interests, and manner became more obtrusive,' said their friend Len Billings. 'They were both bitter, disillusioned, withdrawn, silent, as if afraid that conversation would deepen the wound.'

Jack characterised his wife's mercurial temperament by drawing a wavy line across a sheet of paper and a straight, bold line through the middle, to resemble his even temper. The breach led to talk of a possible divorce, so obvious was the antagonism to their friends.

Finally, a third pregnancy in 1957 was successful and a daughter, Caroline Bouvier Kennedy, was born on 27 November 1957. A boy, John Fitzgerald Kennedy Jr, followed on 25 November 1960.

The children gave fresh meaning to the marriage for both Jack and Jackie and some of the damage, at least, was glossed over, only to reawaken in 1963 when Jackie gave birth prematurely to a boy, Patrick, who passed away after just two days from infant respiratory distress syndrome. But strangely, it wasn't just the children Jackie credited with saving her marriage—it was her husband's ascendance to the White House.

As Jackie's favourite fashion designer, Oleg Cassini, said, 'When they got to the White House, they fell in love all over again.'

But while Jackie admitted sleeping in a separate bed to her husband on their first night at 1600 Pennsylvania Avenue, she said later that she cherished those years the most.

'It really was the happiest time of my life. It was when we were the closest—I didn't realize the physical closeness of having his office in the same building and seeing him so many times a day,' she recalled in private tapes recorded in 1964.

Happiness, she wrote to her friend William Walton in 1962, was 'the last thing I expected to find in the W. House'.

The typical White House day would begin at 7.45am, with Jack being woken by his long-time valet George Thomas, who lived on the third floor. He'd get up and eat breakfast in his own bedroom while reading the morning briefings and schedules for the day ahead. Then he'd take a bath.

'And I always thought it was so funny for people who used his bedroom—guests. Because all along his tub were all these little floating animals, ducks, and pink pigs and things,' recalled Jackie.

About this time, the children, Caroline and John, would come into the bedroom and watch cartoons on TV.

Later in the afternoon, whatever they were doing, the couple would meet again in the bedroom, where the President would slip off all his clothes for a forty-five-minute power nap.

'He'd get completely undressed and into his pyjamas and into bed,' said Jackie on the tapes that were kept secret for nearly half a century.

'Who could be bothered to get in your pyjamas for forty-five minutes? He'd hit that pillow and go to sleep and wake up again. I mean, I couldn't sleep—it would take me forty-five minutes to doze off, but it was good for him,' she said, adding that sometimes she'd just sit with her husband in the room, eating lunch and watching him doze.

'At night, we'd have supper always in the little Lincoln Sitting Room on trays. You know, I loved those days,' she recalled.

Jackie had a well-worn beauty regimen she'd stuck to since her teens—fifty to a hundred strokes a night of her hairbrush, assiduously sprinkled with cologne, using a pinch of skin cream to glisten her eyelashes and applying powder before and after putting on her lipstick.

One thing she quickly learned not to do was to ply her husband for details of the great events of the day. He would get irritable, saying he was desperate to relax.

During the day, Jackie might be smoking her L&M filtered cigarettes on the second floor, scribbling letters, painting, reading or watching over the children. According to biographer Sally Bedell Smith in *Grace and Power: The Private World of the Kennedy White House*, Jackie boasted to her oldest friend, Nancy Tuckerman, that she'd been advised there were 'ninety-nine things that I had to do as First Lady and I have not done one of them'.

The couple hardly went out together to socialise, preferring instead to host dinners for groups of four or eight, most of them part of a close inner circle but often with an additional guest artist or writer for added entertainment.

Most sought after of all were invites to their private dinner dances—they held six of the boozy soirées in less than three years. TV correspondent Nancy Dickerson wrote that 'blended with the spirit of Harvard and the patina of Jackie's finishing schools, the mixture was intoxicating.'

Jackie disclosed other, very personal details of their life together away from the public eye. Every night, Jack would say his prayers just as he had as a child.

'He'd come in and kneel on the edge of the bed and say them, you know. Take about three seconds—cross himself. It was just like a little childish mannerism, I suppose, like brushing your teeth or something. It used to amuse me so, standing there.'

But it was still far from plain sailing.

Jackie also revealed that, on the biggest night of her husband's life—after his January 1961 inauguration—she took an amphetamine party pill to get through it and then spent her first night in the White House in a separate bedroom from her husband.

On the tapes, she describes how she went back to the White House to rest after the rigours of the day. 'At about nine o'clock or something, when it was time to start getting dressed again, I couldn't get out of bed.'

She called her doctor in desperation. 'And she had two pills, a green one and an orange one, and she told me to take the orange one. So I did and I said, "What is it?" And then she told me it was Dexedrine, which I'd never taken in my life—and that I never have again.'

Later that night, the effects of the drug wore off and Jack sent her home while he carried on partying, returning to the White House at three or four in the morning.

'And I slept in the Queen's Room. He slept in the Lincoln Room then, so that was his first night in Lincoln's bed. And—well, he was just so happy,' she said, putting a brave face on what must have been a disappointment.

The orange pill was by no means the only pick-me-up medication Jackie used to stay energised. Both she and Jack regularly turned to the controversial services of Dr Max Jacobson, a German-born New York physician also known as 'Dr Feelgood' and 'Miracle Max'.

He was known for shooting amphetamines—better known as 'speed'—into the veins of a long list of celebrities, artists, politicians and jet setters. According to biographer C. David Heymann, his other clients included Winston Churchill, Judy Garland, Marlene Dietrich, Tennessee Williams and Edward G. Robinson.

In Christopher Andersen's 1996 book, *Jack and Jackie: Portrait of an American Marriage*, Jackie's friend, Corinne Claiborne 'Lindy' Boggs, offered her perspective on the re-lationship.

'Jackie was a woman full of love and full of hurt,' she explained. 'They were two private people, two cocoons married to each other, trying to reach into each other. I think she felt that since he was so much older than she was, that it was up to him to reach more than he did . . . but he couldn't.'

Unable to talk to other members of the Kennedy family and prevented by her position from seeking professional counselling, Jackie looked to a handsome young cardiologist, Dr Frank Finnerty, a professor at Georgetown University and a neighbour of Bobby's, to provide informal marriage therapy. Sally Bedell Smith wrote that Jackie struck up a close relationship with the physician after he treated her when she hurt her ankle in one of the family's infamous touch-football games.

She initially confided in him that she was aware of her husband's infidelities, reeling off a list of women the doctor didn't recognise –apart from Marilyn Monroe, who 'seemed to bother her the most'.

'She did know what was going on. This conversation shocked me,' Finnerty told Bedell Smith. She went on to reveal that sex with JFK was a washout because 'he just goes too fast and falls asleep'.

Finnerty said he offered Jackie advice on foreplay to improve sex with her husband and they even drew up a crib guide on how best to approach Jack to improve his performance in bed without offending him. None of this was mentioned, of course, in Jackie's tapes, recorded by historian Arthur M. Schlesinger Jr, but she did offer an insight into how she kept the marriage with such a charismatic—and difficult—man alive.

She explained,

I think it's good to be able to forgive quickly. That's a quality that Jack liked in me, being married—that if ever there'd be a slight little cloud, I'd always be there—I'd rush and say, 'Oh, dear, did I upset you? Did I say something wrong?' Or, 'I'm so sorry.' And he loved that, because I think it's hard for a man to make up first in a family, in a rather intimate way.

In other words, Jack never said he was sorry and Jackie, beautiful and adored as she was by the public, never called him out on it.

JFK FACT FILE

1. John F. 'Jack' Kennedy travelled with a set of bathroom scales because he was so obsessed with his waistline.
2. The day before he ordered a US ban on Cuban imports in 1962, he bought 1,200 top-grade Cuban cigars.
3. All four of his grandparents were the children of Irish immigrants to the United States. He was the only US president whose grandmother lived longer than he did.
4. He could speak as fast as 350 words a minute and, for one of his speeches in 1957, he was recorded as speaking at 327 words per minute—the fastest rate of public speaking ever.
5. His favourite novel was *Ulysses* by James Joyce.
6. He gave his entire $100,000-a-year presidential salary to more than two-dozen charities, including the Boy Scouts and Girl Scouts of America, the United Negro College Fund, and the Federation of Jewish Philanthropies.
7. He received the sacramental Last Rites four times—on a trip to England in 1947 when he was diagnosed with a rare disease of the adrenal glands and fell so sick on the *Queen Mary* on his way home that a priest was summoned; in Japan in 1951 after being stricken with a high fever; when he slipped into a coma after contracting an infection following back surgery in 1954; and on the day of his assassination, 22 November 1963, in Dallas.
8. He won a Pulitzer Prize for a book he wrote aged twenty-two, titled *Why England Slept*.

9. Prior to Dallas, he was the target of at least four murder attempts. One came shortly after his election, when a postal worker tailed him in a car full of explosives, and two more plots were foiled, in Tampa, Florida and Chicago.
10. JFK was the first president to dance with a black woman at an inaugural ball.

THE ASSASSINATION

It is an indelible image the world will never forget.

Three bullets were all it took to shatter America's innocence on the day a celebratory presidential cavalcade through downtown Dallas turned into a funeral for a nation's hopes and aspirations.

Time and again, the world would come back to that moment in the ensuing years. But remarkably, while the graphic film footage of the assassination beamed around the world within hours to show exactly what happened on 22 November 1963, confusion still reigns today as to why it happened and who was responsible.

The visit to Dallas was supposed to have been a curtain raiser for Kennedy's 1964 re-election campaign. The idea was to raise some money and mend some Texas Democrat fences in a state the party barely won in 1960.

The presidential motorcade should have arrived in Dealey Plaza at 12.10pm but was running late after twice stopping so the President could shake hands with some Catholic nuns and then some schoolchildren.

At 12.29pm, Kennedy's limousine—codenamed 'SS-100-X'—pulled into the plaza after a 360-degree right turn from Main

Street into Houston Street. In the car with the First Couple were Texas Governor John Connally and his wife, Nellie.

According to witnesses, the shooting began just after the limo made the turn onto Elm Street, past a grassy knoll near the Texas School Book Repository. After he was hit by the first shot, Kennedy raised his arms dramatically in front of his face and throat as he turned, shocked, towards his wife, who, still confused and disbelieving, tried to comfort him with her arm around his shoulder.

The bullet had entered the President's upper back, penetrated his neck, slightly damaged a spinal vertebra and the top of his right lung, and then exited his throat just below his larynx, nicking the left side of his suit-tie knot.

The second and third shots came clumped closer together. If anyone in the crowd thought perhaps they'd heard a firecracker or a car backfiring, the horrific scenes inside the limo quickly dispelled those thoughts.

Secret Service agent Clint Hill reacted first to the gunfire, jumping from the running board of the back-up security car and dashing to try to protect the President. But he was too late. The second shot had opened up the side of Kennedy's head as he leaned into his wife's embrace.

Turning around to check on the President, the Texas Governor was also hit in the upper-right back.

'Oh, no, no, no! My God, they're going to kill us all!' he cried out, clutching at his wound.

The second shot had gone through Kennedy's head and exploded out of a roughly oval-shaped hole, ending any hopes of survival. Horrifically, JFK's head matter, brain, blood and skull fragments covered the interior of the car and even splattered on the follow-up Secret Service car and its driver's left arm, as well as motorcycle officers riding on both sides behind the motorcade.

Afterwards, Mrs Kennedy had no memory of crawling out and reaching to the rear trunk lid. But it appears she was instinctively trying to collect up parts of her husband's head that was torn apart right in front of her eyes.

Accelerating away with Secret Service agent Hill clinging on, the limousine sped to Dallas's Parkland Memorial Hospital, where the President's condition was declared 'moribund', meaning he had no chance of survival. A Catholic priest was summoned to administer the Last Rites and JFK was officially declared dead at 1pm.

In the ensuing chaos, the authorities initially believed that the shooter may have been on the grassy knoll but witnesses quickly came forward to say they heard three gunshots coming from a window at the Texas School Book Depository.

Two employees watching from the fifth floor said they heard a gun going off directly above their heads.

It was only seventy-four to ninety seconds after the last shot that armed policeman Marrion L. Baker confronted a man in the second-floor lunchroom of the depository. The building's superintendent identified him as Lee Harvey Oswald—an employee—and he was immediately released. He left the building, through the front entrance, at approximately 12.33pm.

In those couple of minutes before fleeing the scene, Oswald hid his 8-pound Italian-made 1938 Mannlicher-Carcano 6.5-mm rifle equipped with a four-power scope behind a pile of boxes and rushed down from his vantage point on the sixth floor. He took a bus and a taxi ride back to his lodgings at 1026 North Beckley Avenue, arriving at about 1pm, and his housekeeper saw him waiting at a bus stop a few minutes later.

By this time, his boss at the book depository had reported the former Marine missing and he was being hunted as a possible suspect.

Dallas police officer J.D. Tippit spotted Oswald walking in a residential neighbourhood in Oak Cliff, three miles from Dealey Plaza, and called him over to his car. But when the officer got out, he was shot four times and left dying on the pavement by Oswald, who fled to the nearby Texas Theatre.

Police were called and forcibly arrested Oswald when he tried to pull a gun and punched an officer, shouting, 'Well, it's all over now!' The arrest came approximately seventy minutes after the President was gunned down.

Across the city, Kennedy's body was taken to Love Field and placed on *Air Force One*. Before the plane took off, a grim-faced Lyndon B. Johnson stood in the tight, crowded compartment and took the Oath of Office, administered by US District Court Judge Sarah Hughes. The brief ceremony took place at 2.38p.m. Also on the plane was Jackie Kennedy, still in her pink suit stained with her husband's blood.

Governor Connally was critically injured but survived. Doctors later stated that, after he was shot, his wife pulled him onto her lap and the resulting posture helped close his front chest wound, which was causing air to be sucked directly into his chest around his collapsed right lung.

James Tague, a spectator and witness to the assassination, also received a minor injury to his right cheek when one of the bullets ricocheted off the sidewalk.

Three previous presidents had been assassinated while in office—Abraham Lincoln in 1865, James Garfield in 1881 and William McKinley in 1901—but all came long before the age of TV.

Within minutes of the Kennedy assassination, the news was flashing around the world. Several photos and films captured every grisly detail of the killing, including the infamous Zapruder footage, thus ensuring the aftershocks from the tragedy would leave the nation reeling for decades to come.

INFIDELITY IN THE WHITE HOUSE

To the world, they were the perfect loving couple but JFK led a double life, as the charismatic leader of the free world and a reckless, unfaithful husband whose aides sneaked women into the White House to appease his insatiable sexual appetite.

The truth about the dark side of the Camelot fairytale only emerged after Jack's death, leaving his loyal wife humiliated and heartbroken. But while Jack may have been a prolific philanderer, he wasn't the only one to stray: Jackie also found comfort in the arms of other powerful men after realising she could never tame her husband's wild ways. In what might be seen as the ultimate betrayal, she even launched into a passionate four-year affair with Jack's married brother, Bobby, shortly after the 1963 assassination, according to some biographers. For a public besotted with Jackie's beauty and her stoic elegance, it was hard to believe.

So beguiling was their gilded image and so successfully did they keep the scandals under wraps that the Kennedys are still celebrated as America's First Couple today, more than half a century after Jack's presidency ended in a hail of gunfire. Both Roman Catholics, they would never divorce. But the pair left nothing to chance to cover up Jack's dalliances amid his rise to power. Patriarch Joe reportedly paid Jackie $1 million not to leave Jack before the 1960 election, knowing she was vital to his presidential hopes. The election won and her tears run dry by failed early attempts to rein in her sex-obsessed husband, Jackie subsequently turned a blind eye to the steady stream of stories about the President's infidelity with an array of beauties—among them Marilyn Monroe and smouldering gangster's moll, Judith Campbell.

His short term in office, romantically dubbed 'the thousand days', is almost as noteworthy for its 'thousand nights'. By all accounts, no young woman working at 1600 Pennsylvania Avenue was safe from Jack's amorous advances.

But it was Marilyn, who famously sang a sultry 'Happy Birthday, Mr President' to Jack in 1962, who came closest to breaking up the marriage. Jack even went so far as to suggest he'd make an honest woman of the blonde bombshell when she arrived for one of their mile-high trysts on *Air Force One*, clad in a black wig and dark glasses to copy Jackie's style. The actress donned the same disguise entering 1600 Pennsylvania Avenue for romps in the Lincoln Bedroom when Jackie was out of town.

As long as the notches on her husband's bedpost remained under wraps and she wasn't publicly embarrassed, Jackie was willing to forget—if not forgive—her mate's cheating.

According to Edward Klein, author of *All Too Human: The Love Story of Jack and Jackie Kennedy* (1997), the President's womanising was no secret to his wife. 'Jackie was completely aware her husband was a hopeless philanderer, and when he did it privately and without her knowledge, it bothered her far less than when he would fail to hide it in public,' he declared.

It was precisely this reason why Jack's affair with Monroe hurt Jackie so deeply. She wasn't there to witness the sex siren's steamy Madison Square Garden tribute to her husband for his forty-fifth birthday (when Monroe's sensuous, breathy version of 'Happy Birthday, Mr President' fuelled gossip about the relationship) and she certainly wasn't fooled by his attempts to dismiss the hurtful gossip it provoked. Biographer Christopher Andersen wrote that Marilyn, her career fading, thought Jack would leave Jackie and marry her. The author even claimed the actress called the White House and confessed to the affair.

Cold as ice, reported Andersen, Jackie warned her rival off her man. She told her sarcastically, 'Marilyn, you'll marry Jack, that's great . . . and you'll move into the White House and you'll assume the responsibilities of First Lady, and I'll move out and you'll have all the problems.'

In another potentially explosive relationship, Frank Sinatra introduced Jack to party girl Judith Campbell (later Exner). For two years she became one of his mistresses, regularly visiting him in Washington. It later emerged Judith was also a girlfriend of Chicago Mob boss Sam Giancana, raising fears that she could have leaked national-security secrets to the gangster. Exner, who died from breast cancer aged sixty five, in 1999, claimed she terminated a pregnancy by Jack a year before he died in Dallas.

Decades before Bill Clinton got into hot water for his fling with Monica Lewinsky, Jack carried on an eighteen-month affair with White House intern Mimi Alford, beginning when she was just nineteen, and appeared none too concerned about his conquests being close to home.

In his 1997 book, *The Dark Side of Camelot*, investigative reporter Seymour Hersh also writes that Jack had a number of sexual encounters with two young twenty-something secretaries, Priscilla Wear and Jill Cowen, known among the President's staff as 'Fiddle' and 'Faddle'. According to Hersh, one poolside tryst was cut short when a Secret Service man alerted the President to the fact that Jackie was preparing to take a swim.

'You could see one big pair of footprints and two smaller pairs of wet footprints leading to the Oval Office,' the agent recalled.

Another conquest was reputed to be actress and stripper Blaze Starr. During the Cuban Missile Crisis of October 1962, Jack reportedly said to her, 'Boy, if Fidel Castro had something like you, he would think more about making love and less about making war!'

While the public knew nothing of Jack's other women at the time, Jackie's friend Ralph Martin told biographer Andersen that the First Lady wasn't fooled. 'You know, in the end Jackie knew everything. Every girl. She knew her rating, her accomplishments.'

Driven to her wits' end by her husband's betrayals at a low point in their marriage, Jackie escaped the pressure-cooker life in DC on an Italian cruise in 1962 with Fiat's millionaire kingpin Gianni Agnelli and then sailed the Aegean Sea with Greek shipping tycoon Aristotle Onassis, on his yacht, the *Christina* O. There were also rumours of a fling with actor William Holden.

'Jackie regarded the pretty young things in the White House as superficial flings for Jack. She did retaliate by having her own affairs,' said Kennedy biographer Ed Klein. 'There was a period during which she was delighted to be able to annoy her husband with her own illicit romances.'

If Jackie's motive was to get her husband jealous, it worked. 'MORE CAROLINE, LESS AGNELLI,' read Jack's telegram to his wife after one overnight cruise when their daughter Caroline was left behind on the shore. Decades later, a report in *Vanity Fair* said the trip was 'notable for a fair amount of kissing, caught on film by the paparazzi'.

In malevolent circles, it was also whispered later that John Jr looked a lot more like Gianni than Jack. Concerned that, by flaunting her relationship with the married Agnelli, Jackie was making him look bad, the President demanded she spend more time with daughter Caroline and return home. Her response: she went scuba diving the next day with Agnelli.

When Jack was similarly suspicious about Jackie's 1963 Greek Islands cruise with Onassis, she defied him to add a second leg to Morocco instead of cutting the trip short. According to Peter Evans in his book *Nemesis* (2004), Jackie and Onassis became lovers on the trip, even though the Greek was already romancing her younger sister, Lee.

Evans claims Bobby Kennedy was so angry that he instructed Jackie to 'tell your Greek boyfriend he won't be coming back here until Jack's re-elected . . . a f****** long time after, like maybe never.'

Whatever happened on board the *Christina O*, the seeds were sown for Jackie's tumultuous relationship with the

Greek shipping magnate, whom she married in 1968 after JFK was murdered.

Evans also claims that Jackie was only recently married when she slept with heartthrob Hollywood actor William Holden in the same bed where her husband had made love to Marilyn Monroe.

Ironically, while the presidency certainly didn't stop Jack from cheating, his ascendance to the White House brought more stability to the marriage. A turning point came when, without his father, on whom he had always depended for advice but who had been felled by a stroke in December 1961, JFK summoned Jackie back from their country retreat to be at his side to help him weather the Cuban Missile Crisis. He may have turned to a stripper for sex but he needed Jackie's support. 'They both grew,' wrote Klein, 'and after considerable torment, they fell in love again.'

Soon after the Crisis, Klein writes, 'Jack was relaxing in the bathtub, chatting with close aide David Powers, when Jackie burst in, riding whip in hand . . . wearing a long white riding shirt—and nothing else.' Halting Powers in mid-sentence, Jackie ordered, 'Just cancel the rest of his appointments!'

For all their ups and down—the pain and passion of a flesh-and-blood relationship lived out in the public eye—the Kennedys were more in love than ever towards the end, said those closest to them. His cheating came with the territory. Klein reports that Jack confessed to his wandering eye even as he asked for Jackie's hand in marriage—and the ties bonding them were strong enough to fool an adoring public and overcome all but an assassin's bullet.

The tragedy was that Jack and Jackie had finally found a path back to one another just when his death meant the previously suppressed stories about his sexual shenanigans would be played out in front of the world, just as she'd always feared they would.

JFK'S ASSASSINATION—TIMELINE 22 NOVEMBER 1963

7.23am: Lee Harvey Oswald arrives for work at the Texas Book Depository in Dallas carrying a long package wrapped in paper. Asked by a colleague what it is, he replies, 'Just some curtains.'

11.38am: *Air Force One*, carrying President Kennedy and First Lady Jacqueline Kennedy, lands at Love Field in Dallas.

11.45am: The Kennedys join Texas Governor John Connally and his wife, Nellie, in open-topped limo for a motorcade tour through downtown Dallas, where an expectant crowd is numbered at more than 150,000 people.

12.29pm: Nellie Connally turns to JFK as the limo steers into a packed Dealey Plaza and tells him, 'Mr President, you can't say Dallas doesn't love you.'

12.30pm: A shot rings out and hits the President in the back. Almost immediately afterwards, two more shots are fired, one of them also hitting Governor Connelly, who cries out, 'My God, they are going to kill us all!'

12.33pm: Oswald is confronted by police officer Marrion Baker in the depository cafeteria but is not detained and catches a bus home.

12.55pm: A Catholic priest administers the Last Rites to the 'moribund' President at Parkland Hospital.

1pm: President John F. Kennedy is declared dead. At the

same time, Oswald arrives at his rooming house, 1026 North Beckley Avenue, switches his jacket and leaves again.

1.15pm: Oswald flees after shooting patrolman J.D. Tippit three times and leaving him for dead after the officer spots that he fits the murder suspect's description and starts to get out of his car.

1.30pm: Oswald hides in the Texas Theatre, watching a film called *War is Hell*. At the same time, White House Acting Press Secretary Malcolm Kilduff makes a public announcement of the President's death: 'President John F. Kennedy died at approximately 1:00 CST today, here in Dallas. He died of a gunshot wound to the brain. I have no other details regarding the assassination of the President.'

1.50pm: Oswald is arrested. He tries and fails to shoot a patrolman and yells, 'Well, it's all over now!'

2.38pm: Vice President Lyndon B. Johnson is sworn in as president on *Air Force One*.

2.47pm: *Air Force One* leaves Dallas with JFK on board in a bronze coffin.

11.26pm: Oswald is formally charged with the President's assassination 'in the furtherance of a Communist conspiracy' (this reference to a Communist plot was later removed from the charge).

LIES & COVER-UPS

Within hours of the assassination, the lies and cover-ups were already beginning to obfuscate the truth.

In the frenzied aftermath, Dr Earl Rose was determined to do his duty as Dallas Medical Examiner and carry out an exhaustive autopsy on the slain President. It was, after all, enshrined in law that the autopsy of anyone murdered in Texas had to be carried out in the state. But the pathologist had reckoned without Jackie Kennedy. The shocked widow wanted the medical examination carried out back at the Bethesda Naval Hospital in Maryland and no one—not even the redoubtable Dr Rose—was going to stop her.

In a bid to uphold the law, Dr Rose tried to block the door to Dallas's Parkland Memorial Hospital to prevent the President's aides from getting to the blood-spattered body. But he was brushed aside after a brief struggle with Secret Service agents and JFK's body was flown back to Washington, DC.

Jackie argued that she had the right to move her husband because he was a former naval officer but Dr Rose went to his grave in 2012 at the age of eighty-five believing he should have been allowed to do his job. Had he done so, the travesty of an illegal autopsy would have been avoided and the facts of JFK's death would have been made public right from the outset.

As it turned out, that's not what happened at all. Many senior people linked to the investigations into the assassination believe the autopsy photos were doctored to fit the 'Magic Bullet' lone gunman theory.

In 1992 hospital laboratory technician Paul K. Connor, who assisted during the JFK autopsy at Bethesda Naval Hospital, insisted in a signed statement that the official US government photo of Kennedy's body on the examining table was faked.

'No, that doesn't look like what I saw,' he wrote. 'A lot worse wound extended to the back of his head.'

Connor claimed that he and fellow lab technician Curtis Jenkins 'always used a rubber block' during procedures and not 'a metal head rest', as in the photo. He later claimed, 'there was no possible way' for photographs to show the President's head intact because it was 'kind of blown apart towards the rear'. If that were, indeed, the case, it would suggest Kennedy was shot from the front— leaving an ugly rear exit wound—and not from behind, as the Warren Commission would later conclude.

The Commission finding was also contradicted by Dr Paul Peters, who attempted to save Kennedy at Parkland Memorial Hospital, and recalled, 'I was trying to think how he had a hole in his neck and a hole in the occiput [rear skull], and the only answer we could think of was the bullet had gone through the front' and out the back 'since a wound of exit is always bigger than a wound of entry.' Unsurprisingly, Dr Peters's comments were left out of the final report on the murder.

The inquest wasn't any better, according to researcher Harold Weisberger. The investigator, who spent years probing the assassination and fighting bitter court battles to obtain key documents, insisted he had 'a long list of people' who committed perjury in an effort to make people believe that Lee Harvey Oswald was acting alone when he gunned down the President.

With public opinion increasingly antagonistic over the unsettling aftermath of the assassination, the White House decided that an independent inquiry was required to silence the doubters. But it ended up creating many more questions than answers.

Even before the Warren Commission was established to investigate JFK's death, senior government officials feared it would be hugely controversial and vilified by critics. And they couldn't have been more right.

Officially known as The President's Commission on the Assassination of President Kennedy—but named informally after its chairman, Chief Justice Earl Warren—it was established by President Lyndon B. Johnson on 29 November 1963, just one week after the shooting.

The 889-page report was delivered to the White House on 24 September 1964 and made public three days later, provoking a storm of dissenting opinion that continues to this day.

It concluded that Lee Harvey Oswald acted alone in killing JFK and critically wounding Texas Governor John Connally. The Commission also decided that Jack Ruby, a nightclub owner who fatally shot Oswald while he was in police custody on 24 November 1963, acted independently.

There was no conspiracy, domestic or international, involved, according to the inquiry. On the panel with Warren were two senators—Georgia Democrat Richard Russell Jr and John Sherman Cooper, a Republican from Kentucky— two Congressmen—House Majority Leader Hale Boggs, a Louisiana Democrat, and House Minority Leader and future Republican US President Gerald Ford, from Michigan—as well as former CIA Director Allen Welsh Dulles and John J. McCloy, former President of the World Bank.

The Commission largely succeeded—or failed, depending on what people thought about the sole-assassin theory. To support its conclusion, the panel agreed that a 'Magic Bullet' somehow passed through both the President and the

Dallas Governor and was discovered in near-pristine condition on Connally's hospital gurney—a theory especially maligned by sceptics, who argued it was an anatomical impossibility.

Critics claim the Commission was a fraud designed to cover up the real conspirators. They point to a memo written three days after the assassination by Assistant Attorney General Nicholas Katzenbach, which read, 'The public must be satisfied that Oswald was the assassin; that he did not have confederates who are still at large; and that the evidence was such that he would have been convicted at trial.'

Katzenbach later insisted that, like most of official Washington, he was convinced Oswald had acted alone but also believed theorising about a conspiracy harmed the national interest.

Historians have claimed that the 26 volumes of supporting documents provided by the Commission, which include the testimony of 552 witnesses and more than 3,100 exhibits, are often contradictory and have some serious omissions. Gerald Ford later wrote in the foreword to an updated edition of the commission's report, *A Presidential Legacy and The Warren Commission*, released after his 2006 death, that the CIA destroyed or kept from the Commission key evidence 'which can easily be misinterpreted as collusion in JFK's assassination'.

In a 2013 interview, Robert Kennedy Jr said his father, Attorney General Robert F. Kennedy, who publicly supported the Commission, privately felt it was a 'shoddy piece of craftsmanship'.

SILENCED!

More than a hundred people linked to the JFK assassination, including police officers, lawyers, witnesses, federal agents and journalists, have died in mysterious circumstances in the months and years since the tragedy. Did they know too much about what really happened before, after and during 22 November 1963? Here are some of the most sinister examples:

DOROTHY KILGALLEN

She was one of Hollywood's most read celebrity-gossip journalists and a regular panellist on the popular CBS show *What's My Line?* but Dorothy Kilgallen's biggest scoop—an exclusive jailhouse interview with Lee Harvey Oswald's killer, Jack Ruby—may have been a death sentence.

She reportedly told friends after her Ruby interview that she was 'about to blow the JFK case sky high.'

On 8 November 1965 she was found dead in her bed of an apparent overdose of drugs twelve hours after she had appeared on the regular Sunday-night broadcast of *What's My Line?* The mystery deepened because she was found in her sprawling apartment propped up in a bed she never slept in, with a book she'd finished months before. She died without ever revealing the contents of her conversation with Ruby. The notes on her JFK investigation were also missing after her death.

Throughout her career, Kilgallen consistently refused to identify any of her sources whenever a government agency questioned her and that might have posed a threat to the alleged JFK conspirators. Knowing what had happened to other investigative reporters, she left her notes to best friend Margaret Smith for safekeeping. Smith was found dead from unknown causes just two days after Kilgallen's overdose death.

MARY PINCHOT MEYER

JFK's White House lover, Mary Pinchot Meyer, was shot execution-style while walking along a towpath in Georgetown, just eleven months after the assassination.

The blonde socialite, a divorced mother of three, was secretly seeing Kennedy for two years while he was in the Oval Office and was a committed pacifist, who was said to be a strong influence on the President.

After the Dallas shooting, Meyer became convinced that the Mafia and the CIA were in cahoots over the conspiracy. Both were opposed to Kennedy's growing reluctance to pump up military measures against Cuba; the CIA was demanding a coup against Castro to consolidate the Agency's control over US foreign policy and the Mob was desperate to win back its lucrative casino and gambling rights on the Communist-controlled island.

A construction worker named Ray Crump was arrested soon after Meyer's 12 October 1964 murder but he was acquitted after an eyewitness insisted the accused didn't look anything like the killer. Years later, a trained CIA assassin, using the alias William L. Mitchell, allegedly confessed to the murder but he has never been located.

KARYN KUPCINET

Just a few days before the assassination, the actress daughter of Chicago journalist Irv Kupcinet was strangled to death as she tried to place a long-distance call from Los Angeles. The operator maintained Karyn screamed into the mouthpiece that Kennedy was going to be murdered. The slaying was seen as a chilling warning to her father, who knew Jack Ruby, to keep his mouth shut about what he knew about the JFK hit.

JACK ZANGRETTI

The manager of an Oklahoma motel told a friend a day after JFK's death that 'a man named Jack Ruby will kill Oswald tomorrow and in a few days a member of Frank Sinatra's family will be kidnapped to take some of the attention away from the assassination.' As Zangretti predicted, Frank Sinatra Jr was abducted from his hotel room at Harrah's Casino in Lake Tahoe, Northern California, on 8 December 1963, and later released unhurt. Two weeks after making the indiscreet remark, Zangretti was murdered in what appeared to be a gangland hit.

ROSE CHERAMI

A stripper in a nightclub run by Jack Ruby, Cherami claimed she'd seen Oswald in the club and, two days before the assassination, she told police the President was going to be murdered. She was killed in a hit-and-run 'accident' on 4 September 1965.

BILL HUNTER AND JIM KOETHE

The two reporters were allowed into Jack Ruby's apartment following the Kennedy shooting and both died in mysterious circumstances before revealing what they discovered. Hunter, of the *Long Beach Independent Press Telegram*, was shot dead when a police officer dropped his gun on 23 April

1964. Koethe, a writer with the *Dallas Times Herald*, was writing a book on the assassination when a man broke into his home and killed him with a karate chop to the neck on 21 September 1964.

WILLIAM SULLIVAN
The ex-number three in the FBI was shot dead in a 'hunting accident' on 9 November 1977, just days before he was due to testify in front of the US House Select Committee on Assassinations.

DAVID FERRIE
Ferrie is suspected of being the contract pilot who flew the real killers out of Dallas after the assassination and Jim Garrison, the New Orleans District Attorney who probed the killing, quizzed him about the claim in early 1967. The pilot was said to work for Mafia don Carlos Marcello as well as the CIA and was an 'acquaintance' of Oswald. In other words, he knew a lot about what happened. Perhaps that's why he was found dead on 21 February 1967 from a head injury. The death was ruled an accident.

GARY UNDERHILL
'Oswald is a patsy. They set him up. It's too much. The bastards have done something outrageous. They've killed the President! I've been listening and hearing things. I couldn't believe they'd get away with it, but they did!' The CIA contractor revealed his suspicions about his own agency to friends Robert and Charlene Fitzsimmons.

They're so stupid . . . They can't even get the right man.

They tried it in Cuba and they couldn't get away with it. Right after the Bay of Pigs. But Kennedy wouldn't let them do it. And now he'd gotten wind of this and he was really going to blow the whistle on them. And they killed him! But I know who they are. That's the problem. They know I know.

Underhill was found dead with a bullet in his brain on 8 May 1964.

ROGER D. CRAIG
The Dallas cop testified to the Warren Commission that the weapon found in the book depository was a 7.65 Mauser and not the Mannlicher-Carcano rifle documented in the official version. The evidence was dismissed because it contradicted the lone gunman theory and suggested two people were involved.

Craig was fired from the police force in 1967 and survived four murder attempts, telling friends that the Mafia had put a contract on him. He was shot at in 1967, a bullet grazing his head; his car was forced off a mountain road in 1973; shot at again in 1974; and wounded when his car engine exploded in 1975. On 15 May 1975 he was found dead from 'self-inflicted' gunshot wounds.

Yeah, right!

JACK RUBY
Ruby silenced Oswald but was then convinced the JFK conspirators were out to silence him in turn by injecting him with cancer cells. His death sentence had been overturned and he was facing a new trial and also battling lung cancer

when he died from a pulmonary embolism on 3 January 1967. Although he argued at his first trial in 1964 that his motive in killing Oswald was to prevent Jackie Kennedy from having to go on the witness stand, he told Warren Commission members in 1964 that he knew much more about a conspiracy and was afraid for his life.

JFK'S MISSING BRAIN

A macabre mystery may hold the key to the half-century controversy over the JFK assassination—whatever happened to the slain US President's missing brain?

Astonishingly, Kennedy's bullet-shattered brain vanished from America's National Archives in Washington in the aftermath of the shooting. All these years later, historians are still pressing for the release of millions of classified FBI documents on the slaying probe because they believe they may reveal the location of the gory presidential remains—and once and for all settle the controversy over the President's death.

In another gruesome twist to the tale, a US congressional inquiry into the murdered President's autopsy found that official photos purporting to be of Kennedy's brain were, in fact, those of someone else.

Conspiracy theorists insist the brain was stolen as part of a massive cover-up reaching the very top of the US government. Preserved in formalin, the brain would show unequivocally whether the gunfire on that fateful day in Dallas came from the rear, from the direction of the Texas School Book Depository, as in the official version of events. That would support the Warren Commission's long-defended conclusion that lone shooter Lee Harvey Oswald killed JFK.

Or it could prove the opposite; that the President was shot from the front—perhaps from the grassy knoll—as many experts have claimed for decades, and that the conclusions of the commission set up to investigate the tragedy were hopelessly wrong.

Seeking to find out the truth—and unable to find the brain itself—America's government-appointed Assassinations Records Review Board checked the brain photographs, which had been snapped shortly after Kennedy was taken to Dallas's Parkland Hospital following the assassination.

According to Douglas Horne, the board's chief analyst, the brain had been switched with another person's and showed much less damage than Kennedy sustained when his shocked wife Jackie scrambled onto the boot of their limo to collect parts of his brain matter in her hand. Doctors who tried to save the President told reporters immediately afterwards that they believed JFK was shot from the front and not from behind as the Warren Commission later concluded.

Horne claimed in his report that the brain was later swapped with another to make it look as though the President was shot from behind. 'I am 90 to 95 percent certain that the photographs in the Archives are not of President Kennedy's brain,' Horne revealed in a 1998 *Washington Post* interview. 'If they aren't, that can mean only one thing—that there has been a cover-up of the medical evidence.'

Intriguingly, it was the Kennedy family who deeded the allegedly bogus brain photos to the US National

Archives—and JFK's brother, Bobby, is the number-one suspect in the possible theft of the missing brain.

JFK's body should never have been moved from Dallas, where a local pathologist should legally have carried out the autopsy examination. But the Secret Service defied the local Texas medical authorities and strong-armed the dead President's body onto a plane with Jackie, still splattered with her husband's blood, and the medical examination was held at Bethesda Naval Hospital in Maryland, a thirty-minute drive from the White House. During the autopsy, the brain was put in a stainless-steel container with a screw-top lid and stored for a while in a cabinet in the Secret Service office.

It wasn't until 22 April 1965 that the brain was sent to the National Archives for safekeeping, according to official records from the US House Select Committee on Assassinations. But when archivists went to check on the contents six months later, the brain was gone from a secure room housing Kennedy's private papers. Also missing were eighty four slides of the brain and plastic boxes full of the President's body tissue.

Investigators contacted then-senator Bobby Kennedy, asking if he had any idea what had happened to his brother's remains. He had instructed staff at the Archives that no one was allowed to see the brain without his written permission. 'Senator Kennedy indicated that he did not know what happened to the materials, or who last had custody of them,' said the report. It concluded,

Despite these efforts, the committee was not able to determine precisely what happened to the missing materials.

The evidence indicates that the materials were not buried with the body at re-interment.

Although the committee has not been able to uncover any direct evidence of the fate of the missing materials, circumstantial evidence tends to show that Robert Kennedy either destroyed these materials or otherwise rendered them inaccessible.

The classified documents detailing still secret elements of the JFK investigation are held under lock and key in the 'special file' room at the FBI headquarters in Washington, classified 'too hot to handle'. Historians demanding to see the files are also hoping for an explanation of the Kennedy doppelgänger-brain photos.

'The brain photographs in the National Archives that are purported to be photographs of President Kennedy's brain are not what they are represented to be; they are not pictures of his brain, but rather are photographs of someone else's brain,' claims Horne, who worked on the Assassination Records Review Board in Washington for three years from 1995 to 1998. 'Following President Kennedy's autopsy, there were two subsequent brain examinations, not one: the first examination was of the President's brain, and those photographs were never introduced into the official record; the second examination was of a fraudulent specimen, whose photographs were subsequently introduced into the official record,' he added.

THE KENNEDY CURSE

The Kennedys might be one of the most famous of the American dynasties but they are also the most cursed. For all their triumphs and achievements, there have been almost as many tragedies.

As terrible as it was, JFK's assassination is just the darkest chapter in the horror story that has haunted generations of Kennedys, leading historians to speculate the family is jinxed.

The bad luck can be traced back to World War II, when dashing fighter pilot Joe Kennedy Jr, Jack's older brother who was tipped as a possible future president, was killed in action on 12 August 1944 when his bomber aircraft exploded over England.

On 13 May 1948 JFK's sister, Kathleen Cavendish, died in a plane crash in France.

Jack and Jackie suffered double heartbreak when their daughter Arabella was stillborn on 23 August 1956, followed by their son, Patrick, dying at just two days old on 9 August 1963 from infant respiratory distress syndrome.

After Jack's death in Dallas, it was hard to believe one family could stand much more heartbreak. But Bobby, Jack's younger brother and US Attorney General, was gunned down at the California presidential primary at the Ambassador Hotel in Los Angeles just after midnight on 5 June 1968 by shooter Sirhan Sirhan, a twenty-four-year-old Palestinian-born Jordanian.

After surviving a small plane crash on 19 June 1964 that killed the pilot and one of his aides, Jack's youngest brother Ted's political aspirations were crushed on 18 July 1969, when he drove off a bridge in Martha's Vineyard, Massachusetts, with twenty-eight-year-old Mary Jo Kopechne in the car. Kennedy escaped and fled the scene of the accident but his pretty young passenger drowned.

The next generation was also beset by the curse.

On 25 April 1984 David Kennedy, the fourth of RFK's eleven children, died in a Florida hotel room after overdosing on cocaine, painkillers and anti-psychotic medicine.

Thirteen years later, on 31 December 1997, Michael Kennedy, the sixth of RFK's children, was killed in a skiing accident in Colorado at thirty nine.

On 16 July 1999 John F. Kennedy Jr, JFK's son, died along with his wife, Carolyn, and her sister, Lauren Bessette, while flying his light aircraft to Martha's Vineyard. He reportedly became disorientated during the night flight and crashed into the ocean.

On 16 May 2012 Mary Kennedy, the estranged wife of Robert Kennedy Jr, was found dead after reportedly hanging herself at her New York home.

WHAT REALLY HAPPENED?

'Yeah, I had the son of a bitch killed. I'm glad I did. I'm sorry I couldn't have done it myself!'

With these words, a Mafia godfather confessed to orchestrating one of the most notorious murders in history—the November 1963 assassination of beloved US President John F. Kennedy.

The 'official' version is that lone gunman Lee Harvey Oswald fired three bullets to kill the President as he rode with wife Jackie on a motorcade through the packed Dallas streets. But after decades of debate and doubt, the full story can finally be told of how World War II army veteran Jack Van Laningham risked his life in an FBI plot in the mid-1980s to trap one of America's most feared Mafia bosses into revealing how the assassination was really carried out. Incredibly, the FBI has kept its file on the Mob conspiracy secret, fearing even now that, if the full details emerge, they could still harm relations with former Cold War foe Russia.

Now in his eighties, Van Laningham lives in Los Angeles. A stone's throw from the Pacific Ocean, his home is a far cry from the claustrophobic prison cell where he was incarcerated with New Orleans Mob boss Marcello in the 1980s. But the grandfather still looks over his shoulder, burdened by the secret he's carried with him since being forced to become an FBI informant.

Van Laningham had already been in the US military since 1946 and had bravely served in Japan and Vietnam when he met the beautiful eighteen-year-old Beryl Stimson in Norfolk, England, while stationed at the nearby Sculthorpe Air Base.

He was in England in November 1963 when he heard the news about the assassination. 'Who would have thought that twenty five years later I would be sharing a ten-by-five cell with the mother****** who killed the President?' he told me.

The car salesman's life began to unravel after he returned to the US and his marriage collapsed. Broke and living down and out in Bradenton, Florida, in 1984 Van Laningham made a choice that would change his life forever. Drunk and desperate, he grabbed a laundry bag and a hotel TV remote and robbed a bank, pretending he had a bomb. Wracked with guilt, two weeks later, he turned himself in and was sentenced to eight years behind bars at tough Texarkana Prison in Arkansas.

Carlos Marcello found himself at the same lock-up by a much more brutal route. Made as a mobster by infamous

Lucky Luciano, a ruthless violent streak fuelled his rise to the top of an organised-crime network spanning America's South, through Florida, Louisiana and Texas, and reaching as far as Cuba, where he ran the lucrative casinos.

A sign on his office door read ominously, 'Three can keep a secret if two are dead'.

Marcello was particularly bitter about the Kennedys because Bobby, then Attorney General, had singled him out in his battle with the Mob and had him deported to Guatemala because he didn't have US citizenship.

By a twist of fate, Marcello and Van Laningham, two men from very different backgrounds, developed an unlikely friendship in prison that soon came to the attention of FBI bosses, who had long suspected the gangster's involvement in JFK's death.

The FBI then made Van Laningham an offer he couldn't refuse—they bugged his cell and told him to get the crime boss to open up about his past. 'I was in the cell with him for one and a half years and everything was recorded,' he told me in a phone interview.

The radio had a bug in it and transmitted to another building next door and then through a high-powered connection to Dallas, where the tape deck was running twenty four hours a day.

I agreed basically because I thought that the President was the best America has ever had. I loved the guy. The FBI heard everything I got from Marcello—and I got everything! Who planned it, who was involved and who did the murder.

Marcello made his explosive confession on 15 December 1987, after going on an angry tirade about John and Bobby Kennedy, who had launched an unprecedented crackdown on organised crime in the US. Naturally cautious, he felt comfortable around Van Laningham and didn't hold back, admitting to having the 'son of a bitch' killed, and said he was only sorry he couldn't have pulled the trigger himself.

It was the first time Marcello had spoken openly about his role in the assassination but it wasn't the first time his name had been linked to the conspiracy. The House Select Committee on Assassinations—one of the half a dozen probes into the killing—concluded in 1979 that JFK was 'probably assassinated as a result of a conspiracy' and that Marcello and another godfather, Florida-based Santo Trafficante, 'had the motive, means and opportunity' to carry it out.

Van Laningham was first tracked down by author Lamar Waldron, who details the Mob conspiracy for the first time in his book, *The Hidden History of the JFK Assassination* (2013). Chronicling the long-secret FBI undercover operation—codenamed 'CAMTEX (CArlos Marcello—TEXas)'—Waldron also uncovered previously unreleased FBI documents supporting the ex-convict's claims.

Lulled into a false sense of security in the prison—which he effectively controlled, getting gourmet food, the best cell and sharp, pressed clothes—Marcello explained how he met up with Lee Harvey Oswald, the left-leaning dupe he'd selected to take the fall for the shooting. He also told how he'd flown in two unnamed shooters from Italy to carry out the 'hit'. Waldron writes that Marcello had a history of picking Sicilian war orphans and flying them out to do his executions before killing them, safe in the knowledge that they wouldn't be missed and severing any link he had to the murders.

Waldron, who has been investigating the assassination for twenty five years, also reveals Marcello's close ties to Jack Ruby, the Dallas bar owner who shot Oswald in apparent retribution for JFK's death. In fact, Ruby was a gangster working for Marcello, who had been caught dipping into the till of the club he managed to pay off his tax debts. Taken for a showdown with Marcello at the godfather's swampy Louisiana mansion, Ruby was told to shoot Oswald dead following the assassination or risk the lives of himself and his family, writes Waldron.

Despite all his efforts to incriminate Marcello, including passing a lie-detector test, Van Laningham complained the FBI never did anything with this wealth of information. Before his release in 1989, Van Laningham also learned that the godfather discovered he'd been double-crossed. 'Marcello knows all about what we did to him,' he told the US Justice Department. 'He will never rest until he pays me back.'

Although beaten up after he left prison by two mystery men, who were interrupted by a passer-by, Van Laningham outlived Marcello, who died at his home in Metairie, Louisiana on March 2 1993, at the age of eighty three. But he remains frustrated by the authorities' refusal to act.

'The FBI didn't want to know. They didn't really want me to get this kind of material from him. It is very difficult to get this information out into the world,' said Van

Laningham. 'Whenever the FBI finds out we are talking to anybody, they come down on them like a ton of bricks.'

The reason, says Waldron, is that the US government and the Mafia were locked in an unholy alliance in the early 1960s to overturn the Communist regime in Cuba and murder Fidel Castro.

By revealing the Mob's role in the presidential assassination, the FBI risked the US involvement in a possible Cuban coup being exposed and, if JFK's involvement in the plan to overthrow Castro had become public, 'it could have triggered World War III in those tense Cold War times,' writes Waldron. Rather than risk opening a can of worms, the FBI was told to quash the operation.

Waldron also claims Marcello had ties with active-duty CIA agents that could have embarrassed the authorities.

'This new information,' he adds, 'finally connects all the dots, tying Marcello to the shooters, to Lee Oswald and to Jack Ruby. What had formerly been a mass of compelling evidence—with a few key parts missing and some connections murky—now becomes a clear, coherent and concise story of JFK's murder.'

THE FBI FILES

Mafia don Carlos Marcello's dramatic confession to JFK's murder is revealed in an official memo sent by a Dallas Special Agent called Raymond A. Hult on 7 March 1986. Although the note names Jack Van Laningham, it says he should not be identified publicly and was 'a confidential source who has provided reliable information in the past.'

It continues,

On December 15, 1985, he was in the company of CARLOS MARCELLO and another inmate at the FEDERAL CORRECTIONAL INSTITUTE (FCI), Texarkana, Texas, in a court yard engaged in conversation. CARLOS MARCELLO discussed his intense dislike of former President JOHN KENNEDY as he often did. Unlike other such tirades against KENNEDY, however, on this occasion CARLOS MARCELLO said, referring to President KENNEDY, 'Yeah, I had the son of a bitch killed. I'm glad I did. I'm sorry I couldn't have done it myself.'

In a letter of 15 July 1988 to FBI Agent Carl Podsiadly, sent to the Dallas FBI office, Van Laningham provided more details and detailed his concerns for the safety of himself and his family.

I know that Marcello never lied to me but I no [sic] that the FBI did,' he wrote. 'The last month we spent together[,] December[,] we talked a lot. Marcello seemed to be very upset about the Kennedys. This is all he would talk about. . .
One night Marcello was talking about the Kennedys. He told me and my friend about a meeting with Oswald. He had been introduced to Oswald by a man called Ferris, who was Marcello's pilot. He said that the meeting had taken place in his brother[']s restaurant. He said that he thought that Oswald was crazy. He also told us about Jack Ruby. Marcello had met him in Texas. He set him up in the bar business there. He said that Ruby was a homo son of a bitch but good to have around to report to him

what was happening in town. Marcello told us that all the police were on the take, and as long as he kept the money flowing, they let him operate any thing in dalas [sic] that he wanted to.

Van Laningham was about to be transferred to another prison when the two men were talking on the prison patio on 15 December 1985.

Marcello was talking about his favorite subject[,] the Kennedys[,] and being deported. He flew into a rage[,] cussing the Kennedys[,] calling them every name he could think of. I thought he was going to have a stroke. He stopped talking for a minute and then continued. He said [']yeaw[,] [sic] I had the little son of a bitch killed, and I would do it again, he was a thorn in my side. I wish I could have done it myself.['] He stopped realizing what he had said and turned and walked over to some other inmates. My friend looked at me and said[,] [']I do not know about you[,] but I did not hear anything.['] My friend left and I could see that he was upset. I was in shock. I never believed that the little man would admit that he conspired to kill the President.

We went back to our room and nothing else was said. When I reported this conversation to the FBI[,] all that was said was that lie[-]detector tests would have to be taken. I told them that I did not have a problem with that. On the 17 December I was packing to leave the next day. Marcello was out[,] making his calls. He came back into the room and told me to sit down[,] that he had something to talk to me about. He said we have become good friends and we will remain friends as long as I kept my

mouth shut and told no one any thing [sic]. He said[,] [']I
want to tell you a story.['] he was dead serious and I was
scared. He said a Priest came to visit him from Italy years
before. The priest was old Mafia, [']my son[,'] he said[,]
[']if your enemies get in your way[,] you must berry [sic]
them in the ground, the grass grows over them, and you
go on about your business.['] He was telling me that[,] if
I crossed him[,] the grass would grow over me, as I would
be dead. My God[,] if he had murdered the President[,] he
would have no trouble with me. . .

Two years passed and they were not indicted. I asked
why but never got a strait [sic] answer. None of the promises that were made to me were kept. I am still in prison
and will remain until my time is up. I am pretty bitter
about the whole thing. I know that I did a good job, so the
feds have the gilty [sic] conscious [sic][,] not me. Never
trust a stranger[,] it does not pay.

In a postscript, Van Laningham adds, 'I learned in April 1988
that Marcello knows about my part in the investigation. He
does not know everything but enough. What will he do[,] I
can't say. He was returned to Texarkana so perhaps he will
die there. That would be fitting.'

The FBI agents involved in the case suggest that, by the
time Marcello was holed up with Van Laningham, he was so
old and senile that he'd lost a grip on reality—a claim dis-
puted by the frustrated informant, who insists the old Mafia
boss was still pin-smart when they shared a cell.

The fate of the other prisoner who supposedly witnessed
Marcello's confession—named by Van Laningham as 'Don
Wardell'—is also a mystery. According to investigative

reporters Anthony Summers and Robbyn Swan, the US Bureau of Prisons said no one of that name ever served time in Texas.

Van Laningham insists Wardell vanished without trace soon after the FBI learned what had happened.

THE MAFIA GODFATHERS WHO WANTED JFK DEAD

The rest of the world was in shock on the night of 22 November 1963 as two smiling men raised a toast in the corner of a Tampa restaurant.

With his trademark black-rimmed glasses, the balding Santo Trafficante Jr made little attempt to hide his joy, exulting, 'The son of a bitch is dead!'

The Florida Mafia boss—one of the most feared organised-crime figures in the country—beckoned his lawyer, Frank Ragano, to join him in the celebration.

'I think that was the night,' Ragano would say later, 'that I made my pact with the devil.'

But it wasn't until 13 March 1987 that Ragano claims his worst fears were realised. He says that, while driving around Tampa, the terminally ill Mob boss confessed to having JFK murdered.

'*Carlos e futtutu. Non duvevamu ammazzar a Giovanni. Duvevamu ammazzari a Bobby,*' he said in Sicilian (Carlos messed up. We shouldn't have killed Giovanni [John]. We should have killed Bobby), referring to fellow Mafia kingpin Carlos Marcello, who ruled over organised crime in the south-western United States from his New Orleans base.

If Ragano's claim was genuine, he was effectively confirming the tentative conclusion that the House Assassination Committee on Capitol Hill came to eight years earlier, in 1979.

Contradicting the earlier, questionable conclusions of the Warren Commission, the Committee decided that Kennedy was 'probably assassinated as the result of a conspiracy'. The Committee named both Marcello and Trafficante as having 'the motive, means and opportunity' to orchestrate the murder but the panel said it had no direct evidence against them.

G. Robert Blakey, Chief Counsel to the Committee, told the *Washington Post* it was 'a historical truth' that the Mafia killed Kennedy to get the administration off its back.

There is a strong narrative that suggests both men—and crooked Teamsters boss Jimmy Hoffa—were in it right up to their necks. The motives? Power and money—what else?

The roots of the conspiracy have strands leading back to JFK's wafer-thin 1960 election victory and the gambling mecca turned Communist stronghold of Cuba.

Allegedly shepherded in by the domineering Kennedy patriarch, Joseph, the Mob is suspected of stuffing ballot boxes and providing funds to boost JFK's faltering election campaign in Illinois, a key battleground state the Democrat upstart took by a mere 9,000 votes out of more than 4.6 million cast. The win was crucial and the Mafia—and Chicago crime boss Sam Giancana, in particular—believed the grateful new President and his clan would pay back the debt by discreetly giving them a pass to continue their crooked activities. Instead, JFK quickly appointed brother Bobby as Attorney General and he declared all-out war on organised crime, infuriating the wise guys who, as they saw it, got JFK elected in the first place.

Giancana was further incensed after hearing RFK call him 'that dago Giancana' on an FBI tape.

The flamboyant Chicago Mobster—a friend of Frank Sinatra and the successor to Al Capone—had another connection to Kennedy: at one point they had shared the same lover, Judith Campbell Exner. He also shared a desire with the Kennedy administration to overthrow Fidel Castro, who had removed every casino and gambling den in Havana—most of them owned by the American Mafia—when he came to power.

According to the 'Family Jewels', the informal name given to a set of declassified CIA reports documenting inappropriate or downright illegal activities by the US government's spy agency from the 1950s to the mid-1970s, the CIA partnered with the Mob in plots to assassinate Castro.

The documents show that the CIA recruited Robert Maheu, an ex-FBI agent and aide to reclusive billionaire Howard Hughes in Las Vegas, to approach Giancana's number two, 'Handsome' Johnny Roselli, under the pretence of representing multi-national companies with gambling interests that wanted Castro dead.

Roselli introduced Maheu to Giancana and Trafficante in 1960 and a secret deal was struck for the gangsters to use their contacts still in Cuba to poison Castro. The CIA files show that Giancana and Trafficante were supplied with six poison pills but their efforts to get them sprinkled into the Cuban dictator's food were unsuccessful.

The assassination attempt was abandoned after the failed CIA-backed Bay of Pigs invasion of Cuba in April 1961.

These two factors—the Mafia's hatred of the Kennedys for the ballot-box betrayal and its belief that the administration would go to extreme lengths *not* to allow its complicity in the Castro death plot to become public—explain both why the gangsters wanted to do away with the President and how they thought they could get away with it. However, for New Orleans crime lord Carlos Marcello, it was also very personal.

In 1959 JFK and Bobby Kennedy were both part of a commission investigating the relationship between trade unions and the Mafia, and Marcello was forced to go to Washington to answer questions. He invoked the Fifth Amendment, refusing to talk to the investigators, but it emerged during the hearing that he was not a US citizen. Two years later, RFK, by then the Attorney General, ordered federal agents to seize Marcello and deport him to Guatemala, his faked birthplace on forged papers, leaving the then-fifty-year-old in the middle of the jungle without any money or spare clothes.

He managed to sneak back into the US just two weeks later—no one ever found out how—and the vendetta was on.

Jimmy Hoffa, the pugnacious Teamsters leader, had also been targeted by Bobby Kennedy, who helped send him to prison on fraud and jury-tampering charges and, if Trafficante's lawyer, Frank Ragano, is to be believed, the union boss initiated the chain of events that culminated in JFK's shooting. He claims that, in July 1963, Hoffa—who was also a client—told him, 'Something has to be done. The time has come for your friend and Carlos to get rid of him, to kill that son of a bitch, John Kennedy.'

Ragano says in his book, *Mob Lawyer* (1994), that he delivered the message in a meeting at the Royal Orleans Hotel in New Orleans, not believing anything would ever come of it. But here's where the money comes in again. The Teamsters controlled a pension fund worth in excess of $1 billion and, in those days at least, that meant Hoffa controlled the cash.

Just a few minutes after the Dallas shooting, Hoffa called Ragano and said, 'Have you heard the good news? They killed the SOB.'

Ragano told the *Washington Post*,

I don't think he could order those two guys to do anything, but if they could lead Jimmy to think they did it because he ordered it, it would make the [Teamsters] pension fund more accessible. These are devious people, these are cunning people, they don't think the way we do, everything has double meanings. The whole motive revolves around one thing—forget everything else. The Teamsters pension fund. It all goes back to that—a billion dollars.

So by killing Kennedy, Jimmy would be beholden to Carlos and Santo and they would have [guaranteed] access to that pension fund. They had the motive and obviously had the capability. When [the CIA] wanted to get rid of Castro, who did they turn to? Santo—not one of their own agents. I don't pretend to know how it happened, but after I talked to Santo, four days before he died, all these pieces fell together. I could see the jigsaw puzzle.

Indeed, two weeks after JFK was killed, Marcello was furious because Hoffa hadn't arranged a $3 million loan from the Teamsters pension fund. 'Jimmy owes me and he owes me big,' the New Orleans hoodlum told Ragano.

Later that year, Hoffa confided, 'I'll never forget what Carlos did for me.'

The obvious question is why the conspirators murdered the President and not RFK, who was leading the Mob crackdown. Hoffa told a federal informant that JFK was a better bet because, 'when you cut down a tree, the branches fall with it.'

Marcello tried a different metaphor. 'If you cut off a dog's tail, the dog will only keep biting. But if you cut off its head, the dog will die,' he reputedly told Las Vegas promoter Edward Becker.

Along with just about everyone else who knew anything about what happened to JFK, there weren't many gangsters left to tell tales when all the dust had settled. Giancana was shot in the back of the head at his kitchen stove on 19 June 1975, just days before he was due to testify in front of the Church Committee investigating CIA and Cosa Nostra collusion in the Kennedy assassination. Hoffa famously disappeared in 1975 and is believed to be wearing concrete boots somewhere, courtesy of his old friends in the Mob. Roselli, Giancana's lieutenant, was dismembered, stuffed into a fifty-five-gallon oil drum and dumped off the Florida coast in August 1976.

Marcello and Trafficante were the only two mobsters left standing . . . and they took the full story of how they plotted the most famous assassination in history with them to the grave.

ELVIS PRESLEY

He was the rock'n'roll rebel who sent teenage hearts swooning and struck fear into Middle America with his provocatively swivelling hips and devil-may-care good looks. But at heart, Elvis Presley was still a God-fearing Southern country boy with a prudish streak and patriotic conservative values. As his pioneering days at the forefront of the musical revolution gradually petered out into an orgy of overindulgence, the contradictions in Elvis's public persona and his private life became ever wider.

The blue-eyed singer with the curling lip, who shocked parents with his outrageous, unapologetically sexual antics on stage in the 1950s, despised the hippies and anti-war demonstrators in the Swinging Sixties, blamed The Beatles for corrupting the young and was a staunch supporter of disgraced Watergate President Richard Nixon.

He didn't drink alcohol and abhorred street drugs but had a posse of doctors on call to feed him mind-numbing prescription pills around the clock. And he was fastidious about his appearance but allowed his weight to balloon out of control so badly he could no longer squeeze into his sequined jumpsuits. But there remained some constants about Elvis that friends agree were set in stone: his immense generosity, his undying loyalty, his abiding faith, and his deep love for his daughter, Lisa Marie.

His death on 16 August 1977 at the tragically young age of forty-two left a huge hole in the hearts of those closest to him and millions of fans around the world.

Despite all that has been written about Elvis through the years, the final, heroic chapter in the King's incredible story has been overlooked. He played all kinds of cheesy characters in his much-maligned Hollywood movies but his last real-life role was as an undercover agent for the FBI. This was the kind of part Elvis dreamed about playing in his movie career—a *Mission Impossible*-style hero risking his life in an elaborate sting to trap a dangerous crew of Mafia gangsters. But this time there was no happy ending. Law-enforcement sources believe the King paid the ultimate price for his brave decision to help the FBI crack a $2.5 billion organised ring of crime.

The singer's full, never-before-revealed role in Operation Fountain Pen—one of the agency's biggest investigations of the 1970s—is detailed in a heavily redacted 633-page FBI report that explains how the Mob-connected crooks were baited into trying to steal Elvis's private plane. Because of the sensitive nature of the investigation, many key details have remained classified until now. According to Presley insiders, the blacked-out FBI pages reveal Elvis's true-life heroics as President Richard Nixon's special federal 'Agent-at-Large'.

The hustlers, according to the file, were part of a much larger Mafia-backed organisation known as 'The Fraternity' and described by the Feds as 'a loosely-knit group comprised of approximately 30 to 40 of the world's top con-men'.

Although Elvis died before he was able to give evidence to put the scammers away, his behind-the-scenes co-operation with Operation Fountain Pen wasn't in vain. The probe helped the FBI open leads in seventeen different offices and crack fifty cases across the globe, according to the agency's website.

Those closest to Elvis—including his father, Vernon—believed Mafia gangsters who wanted to silence him from talking about the scam were behind the killing. Elvis and Vernon were due to testify in front of a federal grand jury on 16 August 1977—the day he died.

Friends pointed out that Elvis's meds must have been switched because he knew he was allergic to the opiate painkiller codeine and yet that was the drug that he accidentally overdosed on.

The star had everything to live for at the time. He was making a special effort to spend more time with Lisa Marie and he was secretly plotting to get back together with ex-wife Priscilla, the great love of his life. No one who knew Elvis believes he would ever have taken his own life and many no longer believe it was an accident.

For decades, the King's death has been held up as the ultimate morality lesson on the excesses of fame, when the truth is quite different. With the help of his FBI file, I will make the case that Elvis died a hero.

THE LEGEND

Elvis Presley was determined to prove people wrong about him right from the start.

His school music teacher told him he had 'no aptitude for singing' and, a few years later, he was advised to keep his job as a truck driver because he was 'never going to make it in show business'.

He had to battle the odds from the day he was born on 8 January 1935. His twin brother, Jesse, died at birth, wrote Elaine Dundy in her 1985 book, *Elvis and Gladys*, a tragedy that haunted the star throughout his life.

The two-room shack in Tupelo, Mississippi, where he grew up with his parents, Vernon and Gladys, couldn't have been more different to Graceland, the opulent mansion he would buy with his rock'n'roll fortune in Memphis, Tennessee. There was no electricity or running water and, when Elvis was a year old, his family was lucky to survive a tornado that swept through Tupelo, killing 235 people and destroying the church right across the street from where the Presleys lived.

Gladys doted on Elvis, despite having to work long hours in the cotton fields. Vernon's troubles getting share-cropping work, however, were compounded when he was caught altering a $4 cheque to a larger amount in 1938 and sentenced to a three-year term in the Mississippi State Penitentiary.

Little Elvis looked to music for escape and quickly found an outlet by singing gospel in church. In 1944 he made his musical debut on a Tupelo radio station and the following year won second prize—$5—in a local singing contest. But it wasn't until Elvis walked into the Memphis offices of Sun

Records in 1953 that the stars finally aligned. Founder Sam Phillips teamed his young protégé up with guitarist Scotty Moore and bass player Bill Black and they hit gold with their first single as a trio, 'That's All Right'.

Elvis's first RCA single, 'Heartbreak Hotel', was released in January 1956 and shot to the top of the charts in the United States. Soon everyone was talking about the cocksure newcomer—and they weren't just talking about his music.

Nervous about singing in front of bigger crowds and unsure what to do with himself during the instrumental breaks, Elvis started shaking his legs, the movements emphasised by his wide-cut trousers. What began as an unintentional stage tic quickly became Elvis's trademark as he slowed down the movements to a hip-swivelling grind and windmilled one arm in an overtly sexual gesture. The movements drove his swelling number of female followers wild— and infuriated his outraged critics. They also brought the newcomer now known variously as 'The King of Western Bop', 'The Hillbilly Cat' and 'The Memphis Flash' to the attention of the FBI.

After a 1956 show in La Crosse, Wisconsin, an urgent message on the letterhead of the local Catholic diocese's newspaper was sent to FBI director J. Edgar Hoover, warning that:

Presley is a definite danger to the security of the United States. [His] actions and motions were such as to rouse the sexual passions of teenaged youth.

After the show, more than 1,000 teenagers tried to gang into Presley's room at the auditorium. Indications of the harm Presley did just in La Crosse were the two high school girls whose abdomen and thigh had Presley's autograph.

The critics still weren't impressed either. 'Mr Presley has no discernible singing ability,' complained Jack Gould of The *New York Times*. 'His phrasing, if it can be called that, consists of the stereotyped variations that go with a beginner's aria in a bathtub. His one specialty is an accented movement of the body primarily identified with the repertoire of the blond bombshells of the burlesque runway.'

Ben Gross of the *New York Daily News* insisted popular music had 'reached its lowest depths in the "grunt and groin" antics of one Elvis Presley. Elvis, who rotates his pelvis, gave an exhibition that was suggestive and vulgar, tinged with the kind of animalism that should be confined to dives and bordellos.'

Ed Sullivan, host of America's most popular variety show, declared Elvis 'unfit for family viewing' and demanded the cameras only shoot him from the waist up.

But the controversy was anathema to Elvis, who was asked on a local TV show whether he'd learned anything from the furore he'd caused. 'No, I haven't. I don't feel like I'm doing anything wrong,' he explained. 'I don't see how any type of music would have any bad influence on people when it's only music. I mean, how would rock'n'roll music make anyone rebel against their parents?'

When he released his next single—'Hound Dog' paired with 'Don't Be Cruel'—it became apparent the public didn't care what the establishment thought of their handsome new hero. The record topped the charts for thirty six weeks—a mark that wouldn't be beaten for thirty six years.

The pattern followed with Elvis's movies. His first, *Love Me Tender*, was released in November 1956 amid groans from reviewers. It was a box-office smash. His second album, *Elvis,* was a similar success story and, by the end of his first full year at record giant RCA, he'd accounted for over half of the label's singles sales.

Three more singles shot to Number One in the first half of 1957—'Too Much', 'All Shook Up' and '(Let Me Be Your) Teddy Bear'—and Elvis's second hit movie, *Jailhouse Rock,* was released before everything screeched to a grinding halt with a 20 December draft notice.

The date of Elvis's army service was delayed until 24 March 1958 to allow him to finish filming *King Creole* but then Private Presley had no alternative but to report to Fort Chaffee, Arkansas, believing his career was effectively over. There was more bad news that summer when his mother, Gladys, to whom Elvis was extremely close, died of heart failure at just forty-six.

But the army would play an instrumental role in much of what was to follow, both good and bad. For one, he discovered amphetamines, becoming almost evangelical about their benefits after being introduced to 'speed' by a sergeant on manoeuvres. He also began practising karate, a hobby he kept up for the rest of his life. And, of course, he met fourteen-year-old Priscilla Beaulieu—the love of his life and future wife—while serving with the 3rd Armored Division in Friedberg, Germany.

Any fears that his fame would fade while he was in the army quickly proved groundless. Elvis recorded enough un-released material to give him ten Top 40 hits between his induction and his discharge two years later.

As for his rock'n'roll rebel image, it was enhanced by his lack of ego in the forces and his determination to be treated just like everyone else. If he still had any doubts as he returned to the United States in March 1960, they were soon dispelled by the adoring mobs that followed his train all the way back to Tennessee from New Jersey.

New songs—'It's Now or Never' and 'Are You Lonesome Tonight?' from his *Elvis is Back* album—signalled a new maturity in his sound that won over an even wider audience. His musical successes spanned from the rock'n'roll soundtrack to *G.I. Blues* (1960), his new film, through the country style of 'Something For Everything' to the gospel-infused 'His Hand in Mine'.

But Elvis's head had been turned by Hollywood and he had high hopes for his nascent acting career. However, his manager, Colonel Tom Parker, was seeing zeroes more than stars and, of the twenty seven movies Elvis made in the 1960s, almost all were universally panned. One critic dismissed them as a 'pantheon of bad taste'. But once again, the public wasn't listening and Hal Wallis, who produced nine of the movies, insisted at the time, 'A Presley picture is the only sure thing in Hollywood.'

As the Swinging Sixties and artists such as The Beatles and The Rolling Stones threatened to make the safe housewives' choice Elvis obsolete, those who had previously written him off began sharpening their pencils again. It was hard to see a way back for him this time. But Elvis had already conquered the worlds of music and movies and had targeted a new medium tailor-made for a triumphant return: television.

His 1968 comeback TV special was Elvis's first live concert since 1961. In his black leather jumpsuit, the revitalised star was a ratings phenomenon and right back where he belonged at the top. He had set the stage for the next stop on his rock'n'roll journey as the King of Las Vegas and cemented his legacy as the bestselling solo artist of all time, with record sales in excess of 600 million.

Much of Elvis's rise and fall has been thoroughly documented in scores of biographies but his final days have always been shrouded in mystery and confusion. In these pages, I'll lift the lid on what really happened and reveal how the Memphis Mafia covered up the truth about what took place right to the very end.

ELVIS FACT FILE

1. Elvis Presley recorded more than 600 songs in his music career but he didn't write a single one of them.
2. On his eleventh birthday, Elvis received a guitar but he was disappointed—he wanted a bicycle!
3. He only performed five concerts outside the United States—all in Canada in 1957.
4. In 1954, when Elvis was recording at Sun Studios, he auditioned for an amateur gospel quartet called the Songfellows. They turned him away.
5. Elvis bought Graceland for $102,500 when he was just twenty-two. It was named after the original owner's daughter, Grace.
6. Elvis's favourite toothpaste was Colgate, his favourite aftershave was Brut and his favourite soft drink was Pepsi.
7. The book Elvis was reading on the toilet when he died was called *Sex and Psychic Energy*.
8. His famous, sleek black hair was dyed—his natural colour was brown and he was blond as a boy.
9. Elvis owned a forty-pound chimpanzee named Scatter, who had a habit of terrifying female guests by peeking under their skirts.

10. Not long after Elvis's body was interred at Memphis's Forest Hill Cemetery, near his mother's grave, there was a failed attempt to steal his remains. His father, Vernon, later moved them to the more secure Meditation Garden at Graceland.

BAD COMPANY

With their black suits and dark sunglasses, the Memphis Mafia may have been employed as bodyguards, drivers and roadies but they really only had one job—'Taking Care of Business' for Elvis Presley.

They were the King's oldest and closest friends and—in the early days, at least—they acted as a buffer to keep his feet on the ground and the craziness of his massive fame at bay. The 'Mafia' regarded themselves as Elvis's own presidential Secret Service and even threw themselves in front of their boss to prevent him from getting hurt in a Las Vegas shooting in the early 1970s. All of them, their boss included, wore matching rings with a thunderbolt and the initials 'TCB' (Taking Care of Business).

But as Elvis became increasingly detached from the real world, it was some of those same friends who helped push him down the path to self-destruction with their wild partying, gambling and drug taking.

Although he wasn't a member of the all-male gang, Elvis's manager, Colonel Tom Parker, played an even more insidious role in his only client's downfall, locking him into an ironclad lifelong contract and encouraging his use of 'uppers' drugs to keep him performing and raking in more money. Unable to

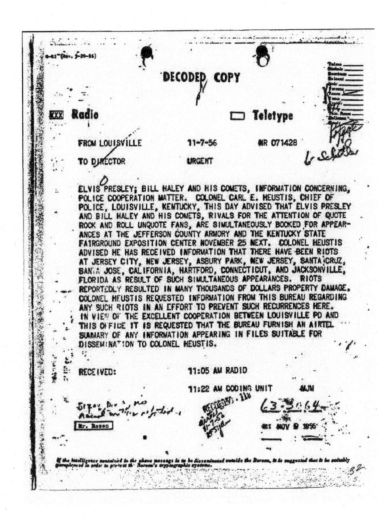

'An FBI memo indicating concerns over 'riots' that had been induced by Elvis and rock 'n' roll rivals Bill Haley & His Comets at the height of their popularity. '

escape from bloodsucker Parker's clutches, Elvis's behaviour became more and more outrageous as his career stagnated and he sought other ways to get his kicks.

Soon it was only other celebrities who could keep up with the round-the-clock madness and penetrate the close-knit Southern brotherhood that Elvis ruled over like a benign despot dictator. After Elvis based himself in Hollywood and Las Vegas, he would party with the likes of Rat Packer Sammy Davis Jr, notorious hell-raisers Robert Mitchum and Billy Murphy, Academy Award-nominated actor Nick Adams and Welsh heartthrob Tom Jones. Other pals would include Dennis Hopper, who starred in Elvis's favourite movie, *Rebel Without a Cause* (1955), and was known for his drug use, and Johnny Cash, who came up playing the same kind of gigs but wasn't afraid of the harder drugs that Elvis shied away from.

Then there was, of course, the ever-changing conveyor belt of beautiful women eager to meet the legendary entertainer.

The more Elvis revelled in the excesses of stardom, the further he cut himself off from his audience and the simple, God-fearing life he'd been raised to. Day and night soon blended into twenty four hours of non-stop partying, with Elvis and his buddies increasingly turning to speed and other prescription pills to keep up.

It was inevitable that Elvis would eventually crash and burn—almost to the end, there were hangers-on; not true friends but those who were there to serve up their master's drugs and women, with virgins apparently lining hotel hallways at some stops for an 'audience' with their no-longer-so-svelte hero.

Among the best known of those who lived and slept at Graceland were Sonny and Red West, Billy Smith, Marty Lacker and Lamar Fike. They would play savage games like 'War', invented by Elvis, which involved the guys splitting into two teams and knocking each other over by any means possible. And they would spend thousands of dollars on fireworks and then throw them at one another. One close shave left Elvis with a scar on his neck and a friend nearly lost an eye.

For Elvis and his pals, wrote biographer Peter Guralnick, 'Hollywood was just an open invitation to party all night long. Sometimes they would hang out with Sammy Davis, Jr., or check out Bobby Darin at the Cloister. Nick Adams and his gang came by the suite all the time, not to mention the eccentric actor Billy Murphy.'

Asked later how Elvis kept going, Fike answered, 'A little somethin' to get down and a little somethin' to get up.'

One of Elvis's closest showbiz friends was Nick Adams, so much so that there was speculation they had had an affair. 'He and Elvis would go motorcycle riding late at night and stay up until all hours talking about the pain of celebrity,' wrote another Presley biographer, Kathleen Tracy.

In Vegas, the partying really got out of control.

Said Elvis's tour manager and long-time Memphis Mafioso Joe Esposito,

It was a party like you wouldn't believe. Go to a different show every night, then pick up a bunch of women afterwards, go party the next night. Go to the lounges, see Fats Domino, Della Reese, Jackie Wilson, The Four Aces, the Dominoes—all the old acts.

We'd stay there and never sleep, we were all taking
pills just so we could keep up with each other.

The one person who should have protected Elvis, if only
to keep his gravy train on the tracks, was Colonel Parker
but he made it abundantly clear right from the start that he
would push his cash cow as hard as humanly possible to
maximise his profits in the shortest possible time. Parker's
contracts with Elvis gave him 50 per cent of most of the
singer's earnings and even the Memphis Mafia blamed the
Colonel for feeding Elvis's drug habit so he could honour his
gruelling schedules.

Sacrificing quality for quantity, he signed Elvis up for an astonishing twenty seven mostly mediocre movies in the 1960s.
When he made deals for the star's transformative Vegas concerts, it was for two shows a day, seven days a week, unlike
the much more manageable two or three performances a week
by other top stars such as Frank Sinatra or Dean Martin.

Elvis's hairdresser, Larry Geller, wrote how he saw the
Colonel and the singer's doctor on the night of 21 May 1977,
trying desperately to revive the comatose star by dunking
his head in a bucket of iced water. 'Eyes closed, jaw slack,
Elvis looked helpless, as if he were in a coma. I could hear
him moaning faintly,' Geller wrote in his 1989 biography.

> Less than two minutes later the Colonel emerged, quick-
> ly closing the door behind him. He stalked over to me,
> pointed his cane heavenward, looked coldly into my eyes
> and declared, 'The only thing that's important is that that
> man is on that stage tonight. You hear me? Nothing else
> matters! Nothing!' With that, he was gone.

It was not as though the TCB crew were going to save him either. By the time Elvis finally listened to his father Vernon and ex-wife Priscilla, both suspicious of the greedy motives of the Colonel and worried about some of the antics of the 'Mafia', he was a swollen caricature of his once vibrant self. And his prescription-drug addiction, fuelled by years of abuse enabled by his hangers-on, left him vulnerable and unable to save himself.

ELVIS IN VEGAS

Elvis arrived in Las Vegas in 1956 as a wide-eyed, hip-gyrating twenty-one-year-old who was virtually ignored by the casino crowd, which favoured older, more polished crooners and big-band jazz. By the time he played Sin City for the last time in the winter of 1976, he was the unchallenged King of the Strip after selling out 837 consecutive shows over the previous 7 years. But behind the bright lights, Vegas brought out the violent, dark side of the restless entertainer.

Barely eight months after Elvis left the Hilton building for good, he was found dead at his Graceland mansion—another victim of the Boulevard of Broken Dreams.

Feeling increasingly caged and bored by his massive fame, which meant he was mobbed whenever he left his penthouse suite, Elvis turned to guns, martial arts and drugs for his entertainment. It was in Vegas—a town where any diversion, legal or otherwise, is just a phone call away, particularly for the biggest star on the planet—where the reckless superstar planted the seeds of his own demise.

Few who witnessed that first visit opening for comedian Shecky Greene in the New Frontier's Venus Room expected Elvis to return at all, let alone in glory.

'For the teenagers, the long, tall Memphis lad is a whiz; for the average Vegas spender or showgoer, a bore,' *Las Vegas Sun* reviewer Bill Willard wrote at the time. 'His musical sound with a combo of three is uncouth, matching to a great extent the lyric content of his nonsensical songs.'

His 1964 movie, *Viva Las Vegas*, helped the singer win the city's heart and he was back in May 1967 to get hitched to Priscilla Ann Beaulieu in the owner's suite in the Aladdin. But Elvis's historic seven-year residency beginning in 1969 at the International, which later became the Hilton, revived his career as a live performer after years in B-movie exile— and marked the beginning of his decline into over-eating, over-medicating and angry, out-of-control behaviour that his manager, Colonel Tom Parker, desperately tried to hide from his adoring fans.

For all the drudgery and mediocrity of his Hollywood period, Elvis's studio bosses had insisted he stay in shape— just a few extra pounds would quickly be magnified on screen—and on time. His Vegas backers were much less ex- acting. As long as he turned up twice a night for two months every year, they didn't much care what condition he was in. The shows were a sell-out either way.

It was a licence for Elvis to do whatever he pleased. At the outset, he would stay out all night, carousing with his entourage and an ever-present posse of showgirls. Vegas became an oasis of indulgence. But Elvis wasn't interested in gambling—he got $10,000 free chips a day but never used them—and he obtained his prescription drugs from a cabal of five doctors he kept on tap day and night, none of them knowing about the others. He didn't have much need for the Mob, which was still a dominant presence in Vegas when his residencies began.

Colonel Parker had his own, discreet organised-crime connections to smooth over any problems the performer may have had with wise guys, and the manager went to great lengths to ensure his one and only client wasn't used as a Mafia photo opportunity.

It was very different to the days of the Rat Pack, when Sinatra and company would mix freely with the gangsters who ran the casinos. Added to that was Elvis's law-and-order obsession. He would boast to friends that he was helping to clean up Vegas and would pass on information to his FBI contacts.

All in all, it didn't make him popular with the Mafia—and the simmering feud would come back to bite, as would his growing dependence on narcotics.

The King's love affair with the city faded as his waistline grew and came to a head when Priscilla finally told him she'd had enough. Elvis apparently threatened her karate-world-champion lover Mike Stone, saying that he would go after him with an M16 rifle. The star's girlfriend at the time, former Miss Tennessee Linda Thompson, recalled him storming around their Vegas suite clutching the gun, refusing her pleas to put it down.

On several occasions, he famously shot at his TV when actors Robert Goulet or Mel Tormé came on because he was angry over past slights.

Shock rocker Alice Cooper, no stranger to the bizarre, once visited Elvis in Vegas and was handed a gun and told to shoot his hero. 'Elvis took me into the kitchen, opened a drawer and pulled out a loaded pistol, telling me to put it to his head. I recognised it straight away, a snub .32,' remembered Cooper. 'I didn't know what to do. I had this gun in my hand and was expecting one of his security to come in any second, see me holding a weapon and shoot me dead,' he said in an interview years later. 'A little voice in my left ear was telling me, "Go on, this is history, kill him, you'll always be the guy who killed Elvis." In my other ear was another voice saying, "You can't kill him, it's Elvis Presley—wound him instead, you'll only get a few years!"

'A fraction of a second later Elvis did a flying kick on the gun, and sent it flying, before tripping me and pinning me to the ground by my neck, announcing, "That's how you stop a man with a gun!"'

At the time of his death, Elvis owned thirty seven handguns and rifles and one machine gun. He'd come to Vegas as a naïve outsider with unlikely dreams of conquering the world's entertainment capital.

Mission accomplished but at what price?

ELVIS & THE FBI

Elvis may have done more than any other single entertainer to usher in the Swinging Sixties but he blamed The Beatles and Jane Fonda for corrupting young people and even volunteered to be a secret informant for the FBI.

What Elvis didn't know was that the Feds were already keeping a close eye on him.

Although he never committed a crime, it was no surprise the FBI kept tabs on the King of Rock'n'Roll. Right from his earliest days, it was Elvis who faced complaints that he was leading the nation's youth down the rocky road to ruin.

The star's bulky 683-page FBI file reflects that concern from some establishment types, as well as the kind of unwanted attention his celebrity drew.

Elvis was an ardent patriot who wrote a six-page letter begging then-President Richard Nixon for a meeting and suggesting he be made a 'Federal Agent-at-Large' in the Bureau of Narcotics and Dangerous Drugs. Among the gifts the King gave the President when they met at the White House on 21 December 1970 was a Colt 45 pistol. Intriguingly, the official photograph of Nixon and Elvis shaking hands has been requested for reproduction more than anything else in the National Archives, including the Bill of Rights and the Constitution of the United States.

A read through the bureaucratic memos in the FBI file offers an intriguing snapshot into some of the behind-the-scenes dramas Elvis faced in his everyday life and a hint of the contradictions that confused his fans and even those closest to him.

In one note, a worried community leader bemoans the threat to America posed by Elvis's swinging hips. In another, the singer himself is pontificating about the danger The Beatles represented with their 'filthy unkempt appearances and suggestive music'.

Starting in 1956 and ending in 1971, here are some of the more intriguing excerpts from the Elvis files:

16 May 1956: Letter from the Catholic diocese of La Crosse, Wisconsin, demanding action over Elvis's 'degenerate' performances to local teenagers: 'As a newspaper man, parent, and former member of Army Intelligence Service, I feel an obligation to pass on to you my conviction that Presley is a definite danger to the security of the United States,' the unnamed citizen wrote.

He went on to call Elvis's two shows 'the filthiest and most harmful production that ever came to La Crosse for exhibition to teenagers'. He said eyewitnesses described the performance as 'sexual self-gratification on stage' and 'striptease with clothes on'.

'There is also gossip of the Presley Fan Clubs that degenerate into sex orgies,' the letter continued. 'From eyewitness reports about Presley, I would judge he may possibly be both a drug addict and a sexual pervert. Only a moron could not see the connection between the Presley exhibit and the incidence of teenage disorders in La Crosse.'

The FBI wrote back saying it had no jurisdiction in the matter.

4 November 1956: Letter sent to FBI Director J. Edgar Hoover from an anonymous writer in Memphis, Tennessee, complaining about Elvis's immoral behaviour:

> It is essential that some agency with sufficient organization and influence do something toward better censorship in our country. There are minds who will scarcely stop short of complete indecency to explicit their wares upon the public, and youth is not able to discriminate between the right and wrong of it.

The Feds wrote back saying it was a 'fact-gathering agency' and not the nation's moral watchdog.

7 November 1956: Radio Teletype from Louisville FBI Bureau over local police fears that riots could break out at the Kentucky State Fair as both Elvis and Bill Haley & The Comets were on the bill. The stars, said the note, were 'rivals for the attention of quote rock and roll unquote fans'.

The FBI response was to suggest that the local police chief contact officials in other towns in New Jersey, California and Florida, where the duelling singers reportedly triggered riots.

11 March 1959: Letter sent to RCA Victor Records at 155 East 24th Street, New York from an anonymous person claiming plans had been hatched for a 'Red Army' soldier in East Germany to kill Elvis while he was stationed with the US Army in West Germany.

Colonel Parker, the star's manager, was shown the letters and said they were identical to earlier correspondence the FBI had already looked into from a woman in Ohio. Parker said the woman was 'nuts'.

30 December 1959: Memo from Major Warren E. Metzner of the US Military Police investigations branch from Bonn, West Germany, regarding a bogus skin doctor's attempt to blackmail Elvis. The major didn't want to put Elvis to any trouble because he'd been 'a first-rate soldier' but as the star had reported the extortion bid, the FBI needed to be informed.

Elvis apparently claimed South African dermatologist Laurens Johannes Griessel-Landau was a homosexual who made advances to several of his enlisted friends after carrying out treatments on his face and shoulders. But when Presley fired him, Griessel-Landau 'went into a fit of rage, tore up a photo album of Presley's and threatened to ruin his singing career and to involve Presley's American girlfriend [a sixteen-year-old daughter of an air-force captain].'

The girlfriend was, of course, Elvis's future wife, Priscilla, but the doctor's temper tantrum then took a sinister turn, reported the major.

He 'threatened to expose Presley by photographs and tape recordings which are alleged to present Presley in compromising situations. Presley assures me that this is impossible since he never was in any compromising situations,' he added.

To get rid of Griessel-Landau, Elvis paid him $200 for the treatments and bought him a $315 plane fare to London. Before flying out, he demanded another $250 from Elvis and then an additional $2,000.

Elvis was later cleared of any wrongdoing and Griessel-Landau was allowed to depart from Germany.

10 January 1964: A postcard was mailed from Huntsville, Alabama to 'President Elvis Presley' saying, 'You will be next on my list.'

Also named on the hit list was country singer Johnny Cash and President Lyndon Baines Johnson. The Secret Service was informed of the threat to the Commander-in-Chief.

29 July 1970: An anonymous caller contacted Colonel Tom Parker demanding $50,000 for the identity of a hood supposedly planning to kidnap or kill Elvis while he was performing in Las Vegas. Elvis's lawyer believed there may have been a link to a paternity case the star was fighting at the time. As a result, security was stepped up at Elvis's shows at the International Hotel in Vegas.

30 December 1970: Elvis asked if he could tour the FBI HQ and meet with J. Edgar Hoover. According to a briefing memo, the King wanted to tell Hoover—whom he apparently considered 'the greatest living American'—that 'The Beatles laid the groundwork for many of the problems we are having with young people by their filthy unkempt appearances and suggestive music while entertaining in this country during the early and middle 1960s.' In Elvis's opinion, the source for the disaffected youth of the day was owed to the existence of 'the Smothers Brothers, Jane Fonda and other persons in the entertainment industry of their ilk,' because they had 'poisoned young minds by disparaging the United States in their public statements and unsavory activities'.

The note said Elvis 'was interested in becoming active in the drive against the use of narcotics, particularly by young people'.

The note was less than enthusiastic about Elvis's request. It said his 'gyrations' in the late 1950s and early 1960s were controversial and he was 'certainly not the type of individual whom the Director would wish to meet. It is noted that at the present time he is wearing his hair down to his shoulders and indulges in the wearing of all sorts of exotic dress.' Elvis was meeting President Richard Nixon that same day at the White House.

Hoover agreed to the tour but dismissed the request to meet him with a curt reply.

4 January 1971: Undeterred by Hoover's snub, Elvis offered his services as an informant. An internal memo said Elvis had privately offered his services to President Nixon at their meeting a few days earlier and had been given a badge of the Bureau of Narcotics and Dangerous Drugs. 'Presley was carrying this badge in his pocket and displayed it,' it added. The writer continued, saying Elvis had been approached by people 'whose motives and goals he is convinced are not in the best interests of this country and who seek to have him lend his name to their questionable activities. In this regard he volunteered to make such information available to the bureau on a confidential basis whenever it came to his attention.'

Hoover gave Elvis the brush-off, writing back, 'You may be sure we will keep in mind your offer to be of assistance.'

DRUGS, BOOZE & WOMEN

To his frantic twenty-year-old lover, it appeared Elvis was dying.

He was unconscious, with blood pouring from his mouth, and Alicia Kerwin was terrified. The young bank teller knew practically nothing about the music legend, other than the fact he was twice her age, he had a daughter and, the first time they met at Graceland, all they did was talk for two hours.

He'd persuaded her to join him on a drug run to one of his tame Las Vegas doctors in April 1977 and the three-day trip had ended up with Elvis so zonked out on Placidyls and muscle relaxers that Alicia couldn't wake him. Now she was panicked, believing he was haemorrhaging—only to eventually discover he'd fallen asleep with red Jell-O in his mouth.

That June she cut it off, wrote Alanna Nash in her 2010 book, *Baby, Let's Play House*. 'It was just too much for a young kid,' Alicia said later. 'Just the idea of Elvis Presley. Too much, too fast. Way too much to handle.'

This was Elvis towards the end of his life—heavily dependent on drugs to both get him through the day and to get him to sleep and so desperate for love that he picked increasingly unsuitable partners.

No longer able to summon the beautiful young actresses that littered his earlier love life, he was reduced to begging local Memphis girls to keep him company. As a footnote, Nash said that Alicia died fourteen years later after moving to Vegas and overdosing on the same kind of drugs that made her recoil from Elvis.

While Alicia had little interest in Elvis's fame, Ginger Alden first met him at the age of five with her mother, who was a huge fan. She would cement her name in the King's story fifteen years later as the last woman he was romantically linked to—and the last person to see him alive. But it was hardly a great love story. Even when he was telling Ginger how much he loved and needed her, keeping up the credo he'd lived by for much of his life, Elvis continued to see other women.

Elvis, the superstar who still sent pulses of women around the globe racing; the heartthrob who romanced Hollywood beauties like Natalie Wood and Ann-Margret in the late 1950s and early 60s.

The truth was that Elvis had left Las Vegas months earlier a ruined man. He'd been humiliated by the end of his marriage to Priscilla and stunned at the collapse of his subsequent four-and-a-half year relationship with Linda Thompson.

Tall, blonde and curvaceous, Thompson was twenty-two and—she told Larry King in a 2002 interview—still a virgin when she met Elvis but, after telling her he wanted to spend the rest of his life with her, the singer sunk deeper and deeper into drugs and made little attempt to cover up either his pill addiction or his orgy of meaningless sex with random Vegas hangers-on. At least his God-fearing roots kept him away from booze. He rarely ever touched alcohol, preferring Pepsi Cola.

Just as Priscilla had first caught his eye in Germany when she was fourteen, his tastes veered dangerously towards younger teenage girls. In most cases, all he wanted them to do was hold his hand and soothe him to sleep.

Unable to find happiness with women, he spent so outrageously that his bank account became seriously depleted. He bought a handful of private jets and splashed $140,000 on a fleet of Cadillacs. Needless to add, the enjoyment they brought him was fleeting.

If anyone could have helped Elvis that final, fateful day, it would have been Ginger Alden but she was sound asleep in his bed until it was too late.

Elvis had cried wolf one too many times. There was no one left to save him.

ELVIS'S LITTLE BLACK BOOK

Elvis Presley's little black book read like a who's who of America's most beautiful women. But there was one phone number the heartthrob prized above all others—Marilyn Monroe.

Intriguingly, many of the beauties scribbled into the book's well-thumbed lined pages were *not* bedded by the world's sexiest icon. The truth was that he was intimidated by famous women and became shy and ill at ease when he met many of them. He would call them ma'am and become

Above: Marilyn in happier times with her third husband, playwright Arthur Miller. Rumours that the two were affiliated to the Communist Party as well as Marilyn's flings with John F. Kennedy and his brother Bobby brought the close surveillance of the FBI.

Below: Marilyn Monroe with John F. Kennedy and his brother Robert (left) on the night of her infamous performance of 'Happy Birthday Mister President' at a Democratic fundraiser on 19 May, 1962.

Above left: JFK and Jackie arriving at Love Field Airport, Dallas on 22 November, 1963. He was shot dead on Dealey Plaza just hours later.

Above right: Princess Diana arriving at the Serpentine Gallery in London in June 1994. Freed from Palace constraints, her increasingly daring outfits delighted the media and irritated the Royal Family.

Below: Elvis performing in Las Vegas in December 1975. Vegas revived his career as a live performer in the seventies but 'Sin City' indulged the entertainer's recklessness and ultimately contributed to his demise.

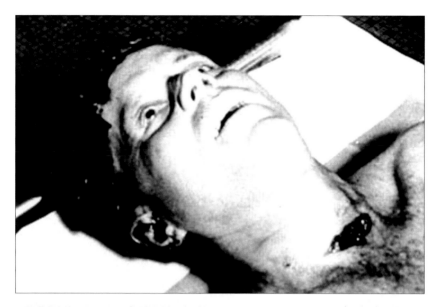

Above: An official autopsy photo of JFK at Bethesda Naval Hospital, Maryland on the day of his assassination. In 1992, hospital laboratory technician Paul K. Connor, who had assisted during the autopsy, declared that it had been faked. 'There was no possible way' for photographs to show the President's head intact because it was 'kind of blown apart towards the rear,' he claimed.

Below: One of the photographs that has led to decades of speculation that Diana was pregnant at the time of her death. It was taken during her holiday in St Tropez with Dodi and Princes William and Harry in the summer of 1997.

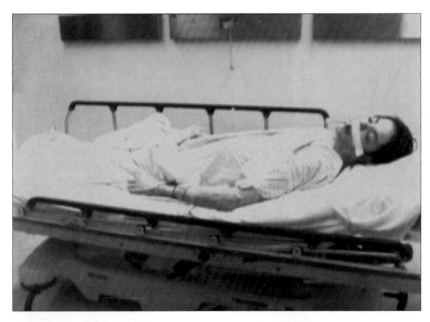

Above: Michael Jackson lying dead on a hospital stretcher in a photograph that was shown during the trial of Dr. Conrad Murray in 2011.

Below: Dr. Conrad Murray blowing a kiss to a member of the courtroom audience after being convicted by a jury in Los Angeles of causing the involuntary manslaughter of Michael Jackson.   *All photos © Getty Images*

too tongue-tied to tempt actresses, like his 1969 *Change of Habit* co-star Mary Tyler Moore, into his bedroom.

There was no such problem when Elvis and Marilyn were set up for an explosive one-night stand that both stars kept secret from their fans and the media alike.

According to Elvis's former agent, Byron Raphael, his bosses at the William Morris talent agency tried to fix up the couple as a publicity stunt in 1956 but Marilyn turned it down because it was 'too public'.

Elvis didn't give up, however, and two weeks later, he called Raphael and asked him to pick up Marilyn and take her to his room at the Beverly Wilshire hotel in Los Angeles. 'When he saw her, they came together and, without a word, started kissing,' said the agent in an interview:

> I was in shock and didn't know what to do.
>
> Then Marilyn, who was ten years older, said, 'You're pretty good for a guitar player.'
>
> After two minutes they went into the bedroom and I didn't know if I was supposed to leave, or stay and wait for them, so I sort of just dozed off. The next thing I knew I was startled awake by the door opening and I dove behind the bar. And they both walked out stark naked. I didn't say a word, I just stayed quietly.

Following the private tryst, Elvis sent Marilyn home in a taxi.

A few days later when I mentioned Marilyn to Elvis, he said, 'She's a nice gal, but a little tall for me.'

I knew that this was the sort of thing that could ruin their careers. They were two of the most famous people in the world and Marilyn was still married to Arthur Miller at the time—so I never said a word.

Elvis used his black book to call up another bombshell, actress Mamie Van Doren, who also happened to be married at the time the King asked to attend her Las Vegas show. He romanced her after the performance—and even crooned 'Love Me Tender' in the back of a pink Cadillac—but Mamie managed to resist his 'magnetic sexuality'.

Other sirens in the contact book that Elvis never plucked up the courage to call included Jayne Mansfield, Liz Taylor and Brigitte Bardot. He met a young Sophia Loren when she plopped in his lap in the Paramount Studio cafeteria while he was filming *King Creole* in 1958 but was too nervous to ask her out. And he snagged Jane Russell's number when they met at a 1957 benefit but, again, never followed through.

Mary Tyler Moore later revealed that Elvis 'had a big crush on me. He was in wonderful condition,' she said of him. 'He was fit and working out.' Mary was flattered but added that Elvis was 'so shy and beside himself—he was ma'aming me!'

But one thing was for sure—there were always plenty more numbers of gorgeous women for Elvis to call in his little black book.

DARK DAYS

In his final days, Elvis was haunted by a recurring dream of his beloved mother, Gladys, reaching out from beyond the grave—beckoning him to join her. He became obsessed by the belief that his life would end on almost the exact anniversary of his mother's death and at the very same age.

Friends even said Elvis was determined to cram a lot of living into those last few months. He spent more time with Lisa Marie and even sought out old friends he'd fallen out with to mend fences.

Close friend, singer Pat Boone, said, 'I felt Elvis had a premonition of his death.'

'It seemed to me that in his last few weeks Elvis was trying to fill his life with memories,' added Bill Burk, a columnist for the *Memphis Press-Scimitar*, who was also close to the King. 'It was out of character, suddenly, from the way he had been for the last couple of years.'

Those final years had been the darkest for Elvis. His devoted private nurse, Letitia Henley Kirk, who had worked for the singer since the late 1960s, fought a losing battle to keep him in shape and admitted his mood increasingly soured as his waistline grew.

In their 1997 biography, *Down at the End of Lonely Street: The Life and Death of Elvis Presley*, writers Peter Harry Brown and Pat H. Broeske claimed Elvis regularly wolfed down banana puddings that fed twelve people and became obsessed with a childhood favourite, fried peanut-butter-and-banana sandwiches. The more fat-laden, the better he liked them.

Even when taunted in some quarters of the media for being 'fat and forty', Elvis did little to change his unhealthy habits. When he wasn't touring to line his greedy manager's pockets, Elvis would lock himself away in his black-ceilinged bedroom, watching three TV sets simultaneously, with two radio stations playing in the background: one gospel, the other country.

While in the past he had somehow managed to hide his excesses from his fans, the façade was beginning to drop.

Elvis's personal hairdresser and friend for fourteen years, Larry Geller, got a scary insight into the singer's later plight when he saw him collapse in a drug-induced stupor about three months before he died. Cutting the star's hair, he said Elvis was a 'bloated, blotched caricature of the magnificent man he'd been only a few short years before.' If he didn't dye his famous client's hair, he said, it would have been a pure white.

'By that point in his life, Elvis was a heavy user of a variety of drugs, most of them prescribed for him by his personal physician "Dr Nick." The King was a mess, not only physically but emotionally, and he was going down fast,' Geller wrote in his biography, *If I Can Dream: Elvis's Own Story* (1989).

Nevertheless, Elvis finished what was to be his final tour in June 1977 determined to turn his life around. He wanted to be a better dad to Lisa Marie and settle down with fiancée Ginger Alden. According to pals, Elvis thought he'd finally found the right girl to replace Priscilla, even if she was less than half his age and was treated as an outsider by some of his Memphis Mafia sidekicks.

Ginger was just twenty and living with her parents in their modest Memphis home when her life was suddenly turned upside down. Her sister, Terry—then the reigning Miss Tennessee—got a call from Elvis, asking if she'd like to go over to Graceland, and the beauty queen asked to bring along her two sisters.

When Elvis appeared to greet the three siblings, it was Ginger who immediately caught his eye and he later spent hours that night reading to her from one of his many spiritual books. Strangely, the tour around his home that first night was one of the few times she spent downstairs at Graceland. The rest of their romance was carried out almost exclusively in his upstairs bedroom suite, where he would spend days wandering around in his pyjamas. They never ate at a table—their meals were always delivered to them in bed.

Elvis swept Ginger off on tour to Vegas, where he first placed a gold diamond cluster on one finger and then a ring of sapphires and diamonds on her other hand, insisting, 'You have to have backups.' A couple of days later, he gave her a new Lincoln Mark V car. When they first made love, Elvis refused to take off her robe and lingerie, telling her, 'I don't believe people should be completely undressed until they're married.'

The next day, he gave her another diamond necklace and a diamond watch.

But in the 2014 memoir *Elvis and Ginger: Elvis Presley's Fiancée and Last Love Finally Tells Her Story*, Ginger describes a darker side to the relationship. She claims she was woken up one night when Elvis fired a pistol at the wall over their headboard because he'd asked her to get him some yoghurt and she hadn't moved. 'It was an attention-getter,' he told her. He also hurled a bottle of Gatorade sports drink against the wall after becoming enraged when Ginger refused to break off her relationship with her hometown sweetheart.

Ginger remembers Elvis running out into the yard with a machine gun after spotting Lisa Marie being chased by someone with a gun. It was only when she persuaded him it was a child with a toy pistol that he calmed down. But there were sweeter moments too and, urged on by her mother, Ginger had succeeded in easing the performer away from some of his more self-destructive exploits with his rabble-rousing entourage.

Three months after their first meeting, Elvis popped the question. Sitting in a chair in his bathroom, he slumped to one knee and presented her with yet another fabulous ring, this one with a huge centre-cut diamond surrounded by six smaller stones.

'Ginger, I'm asking you. Will you marry me?' he said.

And so they set a date for the 'Wedding of the Century' for the following Christmas.

Always king of the big gestures, Elvis surprised his awe-struck daughter on Monday, 8 August 1977 by taking over the entire Libertyland amusement park in Memphis from the hour of 1.30am until 6am to throw a one-of-a-kind party. But this short-lived domestic contentment wasn't enough to rescue the star from the masochistic spiral that had left him a bloated caricature of the slim-line hunk of his youth. Knowing he had only a short break to recuperate before he had to go back on the road again, he did what he usually did when he felt pressurised and put upon—he downed more drugs and ate more food.

The night of 15 August was like many others at the time for Elvis. He came awake as the rest of the world was settling into bed. Ginger had gone with him to visit his dentist, Lester Hofman, at around 10.30pm, to have a filling checked.

After leaving the dentist, Elvis and Ginger scoured Memphis for a copy of *Star Wars* as a farewell gift for Lisa

Marie, who was due to leave Tennessee the following day to rejoin her mother back in Los Angeles. Just for once, Elvis didn't get what he wanted. He was told a private showing of the year's hottest movie was impossible. Instead, he bought Lisa Marie a miniature motorcar to drive around the grounds.

They didn't get back to Graceland until after 2am and Elvis lounged around, restless, before waking up his first cousin, Billy Smith, and his wife, Jo, for a 4am racquetball game. The match didn't last long, with Elvis barely moving and playfully trying to hit Smith with the ball.

As he often did before he retired upstairs, Elvis sat at the piano he had placed with a couple of chairs on the other side of the court's glass wall. It was just Elvis and his piano doing what he loved best. First, he crooned 'Blue Eyes Crying in the Rain' and then 'Unchained Melody'. They would be the last two songs he ever performed.

After going up to his room with Ginger, he talked about her wedding dress. 'I've thought about your gown,' said Elvis, according to Ginger in her autobiography. 'The dress should have a high collar and I would like it to have small rosebuds with gold threads through it. I'm gonna have someone work on it in Los Angeles.'

Still, Elvis was wide-awake and sat up in his huge mono-grammed bed, reading a book. Just as he needed drugs to go on stage, he also needed them to relax. At about 6.45am, he called downstairs on the intercom for his sleeping medica-tion, which was brought up by his stepbrother Rick Stanley, who was on duty that morning.

Around 8am, Ginger was woken by Elvis calling down for another dose of drugs. This time, Stanley brought up his stan-dard pack of sleeping medication—eight pills that included

Quaaludes, Seconal, Tuinal, Amytal, Valium and Demerol—
which Elvis usually took before retiring. Even that clearly
didn't work because a third envelope of pills was delivered
about thirty minutes later by Elvis's Aunt, Delta Mae.

Only hours earlier, recalled Ginger, they had talked about
getting married and having children together. Now Elvis was
still hyped up and, at about 9am, he gave up and told his
young lover, 'Precious, I'm going to the bathroom to read.'

Ginger turned over and dozed off, thinking little of it.
It was hardly unusual for Elvis to be padding around his
Memphis mansion in his day-for-night world.

By that time, he had downed all three packets of the
smorgasbord of drugs he used to coax himself to sleep. It
wasn't until just before 2pm on 16 August 1977 that Ginger woke and wondered why Elvis was still not in bed next
to her. Confused and still half-asleep, she went over and
pushed open the door to his bathroom.

There was a TV set, two phones and a 7ft-wide circular
shower in the bathroom and it was so large that there were
even a couple of comfy armchairs, where Elvis would sometimes hold court. It was his inner sanctum and no one ever
entered without knocking first but there was no answer and
so Ginger walked in to get the shock of her life.

The King was on the floor, his blue pyjama bottoms
round his ankles. He'd fallen lifeless from the black, cush-
ioned toilet seat and his famous features were crumpled into
the three-inches-deep red shag carpet.

Ginger later recalled in her 2014 book, *Elvis and Ginger*,

I stood there for a few seconds so stunned. I started to
shake all over uncontrollably. I knelt down beside him

and shook him. I said, 'Elvis!' and my voice was trembling. There was no response.

I turned his head and he breathed out just once. His eyes were closed but his face was a purplish colour and swollen-looking. His tongue was sticking out of his mouth and he'd bitten down on it. I raised one eyelid and the eyeball was blood red—no white at all—and just staring vacantly.

Elvis looked as if his entire body had completely frozen in a seating position while using the commode and then had fallen forward, in that fixed position, directly in front of it.

His book lay open on the floor, close to a pool of vomit. It would later be claimed that Elvis was reading the Bible or a book about the Shroud of Turin. In fact, it was titled *Sex and Psychic Energy*.

Ginger called for help and Elvis's father, Vernon, came running to try to revive his son. 'Elvis, speak to me. Oh God, he's gone!' he cried.

It wouldn't be long before the whole world would learn of Elvis's ignominious fate and go into an unprecedented wave of mourning.

But even as paramedics rushed to Graceland in a vain attempt to save Elvis, the star's coterie could do little to protect little Lisa Marie, then just nine years old, from the truth. She ran in after hearing all the commotion.

'I closed the bathroom door so she wouldn't see him,' said Ginger. 'She said, "What's wrong with my daddy?" and I said, "Nothing's wrong, Lisa." She ran around to the other bathroom door to try to get in. We had to lock it.'

After the ambulance came to take Elvis away, Vernon called Lisa Marie over and tearfully told her, 'He's gone . . . your daddy's dead.'

'She screamed and I reached for her, but she ran out of the room,' recalled Ginger. 'Later I saw her walking around, still crying.'

When paramedics Ulysses Jones and Charles Crosby arrived at 3764 Elvis Presley Blvd after receiving the 2.33pm emergency call, they found as many as a dozen people gathered around the stricken star's body. He was still wearing his yellow pyjama top.

'From his shoulders up, his skin was dark blue,' said Jones in a report by the *National Enquirer*. 'Around his neck, which seemed fat and bloated, was a very large gold medallion. His sideburns were grey.'

The mask of death had changed Elvis so much that the emergency crew didn't recognise him at first.

'I knelt down to the body, checked his pulse and shined a pin light into his eyes—to see if there was any reaction. There was nothing. No pulse, no flicker from the eyes. Elvis was cold, unusually cold,' Jones continued.

One man said Elvis had OD'd and then another corrected him, claiming the singer 'had swallowed something'.

Crosby said in the same interview that it 'took five of us to lift him onto a stretcher. He must have weighed 250 pounds. The pajama top was unbuttoned all the way down and I could see the great big rolls of fat on his belly. It looked like he'd been dead for at least an hour.'

Just as the ambulance was about to leave, Elvis's personal physician, Dr George Nichopoulos, arrived and jumped into the back with the body and Elvis's road manager, Joe Esposito.

The nearest hospital was the Methodist Hospital South but Elvis's doctor insisted they went seven miles further, to the Memphis Baptist Hospital. He had two reasons for this. First, Elvis had been a regular at the Baptist Hospital and the staff had always been very co-operative in keeping his health problems private. Second, the hospital had one of the best emergency teams in Tennessee, with a reputation for bringing impossible cases back from the dead.

'The doctor kept shouting, "Breathe[,] Elvis . . . come on, breathe for me,' recalled Jones. 'All the way to the hospital the doctor had this look of sheer disbelief that this could happen to Elvis.'

The ambulance arrived at Baptist Hospital at 2.55pm and ER doctors worked feverishly on the King for twenty minutes but all their efforts were in vain. Rigor mortis was already setting in—a rigidity of the muscles that doesn't usually start until four hours after a death.

At 3.40pm, it was over. The doctors called the time of death.

One young nurse asked why the doctors had spent so long working on what was so clearly a hopeless case.

'Because it's Elvis Presley,' she was told.

It was left to Dr Nichopoulos to drive back to Graceland and break the news to the family and close friends, who were still hoping for a miracle. Sitting in the drawing room waiting for him were a barefoot Lisa Marie, Ginger, Vernon and various members of the household staff.

Jones accompanied him and remembered the grim scene.

Dr Nichopoulos walked in without saying a word. When Vernon noticed the doctor was carrying Elvis's things in a bag, Vernon sank back into his chair and sobbed, 'Oh no, no, I know he's gone!' The doctor nodded and the room was filled with hysteria. People were running all over the place crying and screaming and moaning. Little Lisa was running all over the house and crying, 'My daddy is gone! I can't believe my daddy is gone!' She ran halfway up the stairs and back again, then into the kitchen and out again. Ginger was walking around in a daze.

Elvis was just forty-two years old.

His dream about his mother had turned out to be chillingly accurate. Gladys also died at the age of forty-two, on 14 August 1958—almost nineteen years to the day before her son passed away.

DR NICK

To a potential assassin, Elvis must have looked an easy target in his final days. Blinking in the spotlight on stage in Alexandria, Louisiana in early 1977, he was a grotesque caricature of his once sleek, vibrant self. The great Elvis Presley had turned into a fat, fumbling buffoon, addicted to a daily regimen of destructive drugs and gut-busting feasts of fast food.

And ever present in that last ten years of the King's life was his personal physician, George Nichopoulos, known to everyone as 'Dr Nick'. At Elvis's beck and call day and night, Dr Nick reputedly wrote 10,000 prescriptions for his client in his final 12 months. These included shots of amphetamines, barbiturates, narcotics, tranquilisers, sleeping pills, laxatives and hormones.

As the grieving world fought to get to grips with the tragedy in the wake of Elvis's death, it was Dr Nick more than anybody else who was landed with most of the blame as the 'Dr Feelgood' who could never say no to his famous patient.

After Elvis died, Dr Nick was indicted in 1980 on fourteen counts of over-supplying drugs to him and other patients, including rocker Jerry Lee Lewis. Although acquitted of the charges, he was later struck off the Tennessee medical register and was even shot in the chest in 1979 while watching a football game by someone he assumed must have been an angry Elvis fan. He wasn't seriously hurt and nobody was ever arrested for the attack but the incident showed just how high emotions were running in the years after Elvis's death.

In much the same way as Conrad Murray would later take the fall for Michael Jackson's chronic addiction to sleep drugs, Dr Nick could never shake off the label of being The Man Who Killed Elvis.

In his defence, he claimed, as would Murray, that he simply 'cared too much'.

The effect of over-prescribing by Dr Nick and a coterie of other tame doctors Elvis had cultivated was to make the singer immensely vulnerable. A hitman wouldn't need a gun or a knife—just the addition of the wrong drug (or drugs) into his daily chemical cocktail.

Elvis was hardly a well man by this point. According to Dr Nick, writing in his memoir, the star suffered arthritis, gout, a fatty liver, an enlarged heart, migraines, constipation and a colon swollen to twice its normal size.

The doctor had met Elvis one Sunday in 1967 when he was on call at the local Memphis medical centre and was sent out to see the red-faced singer at his ranch about ten miles out of town. To his embarrassment, Elvis admitted he was saddle sore from riding his horses. He wasted no time in telling Dr Nick the drugs he needed to ease the pain. It wasn't long before he was giving his pleading patient injections of the painkiller Dilaudid, said to be five times more powerful than heroin.

Elvis would never touch street drugs—they offended his conservative views on preserving law and order and he'd seen too many musicians succumb to them. But prescription medication was different: they couldn't be wrong if they came from a doctor.

Speaking to me shortly before his death on 24 February 2016, at the age of eighty eight, Dr Nick told me he was still haunted by the scene of his friend and patient lying unresponsive on a bathroom floor.

'I just can't get it out of my mind,' said the former physician, who still lived in Memphis. 'I miss Elvis and I think about him almost daily,' he said. Despite giving 1,000 prescriptions for over 10,000 doses of drugs including amphetamines, barbiturates, narcotics, tranquilisers, sleeping pills and laxatives in the months before Elvis's death, Dr Nick bristled at accusations that he hastened the star's end.

'It hurts me,' he said in a halting voice at the home he shared with Edna, his wife of sixty-four years. 'It's not fair. I was the person trying to keep Elvis alive.'

Over the years, he struggled with health problems and bankruptcy. At one point, he was forced to sell prized mementoes given to him by Elvis, including the unique 'Taking Care of Business' necklaces that were only lavished upon members of the Memphis Mafia. Although Nichopoulis released a book in 2010, *The King and Dr Nick*, it sold poorly and did little to help his financial problems.

Right to the end, Dr Nick adamantly defended his controversial treatment of Elvis.

'A lot of people have written things that aren't true,' he contended. 'It wasn't the number of prescription drugs he was taking. He died because of his bowel problem.'

The disgraced medic, whose Tennessee licence was lifted in 1995 for 'over-prescribing', said Elvis's colon was swollen to nearly twice the size of a healthy intestinal tract. 'He suffered from bad constipation and blockage of the bowel,' explained Dr Nick. 'Doctors didn't diagnose that.'

He said his patient suffered in silence, despite having diarrhoea accidents during concerts and suffering from constipation that contributed to his huge weight gain. But he claimed Presley was too embarrassed by the idea of having an operation to fix his chronic problem. 'He was very macho,' said Nichopoulis. 'He thought he could handle almost anything.'

Dr Nick tried to arrange colostomy surgery for Elvis at the University of Memphis in the mid-1970s but the singer's 'ego' got in the way. 'He would have lost part of his colon and may have ended up needing a colostomy bag,' the physician explained. 'He wouldn't do that. But if he'd agreed to the colostomy then, he may still be alive today.'

Dr Nick said his fondest memories were of travelling as a VIP member of the King's entourage. 'I think of the fun times we had together,' he remembered. 'I miss those days.'

SALVATION!

Performing at the Louisiana Hayride early on in his career after his first three big hits in the mid-1950s, Elvis was in the wings, waiting to go on stage. On before him was country star George Jones, who was going through a fallow period and hadn't penned a hit for a while. To Elvis's astonishment, Jones sang all three of the young singer's chart-toppers, one after the other.

Passing the shame-faced country legend as he took centre stage, Elvis fell back on the gospel music that had been part of the fabric of his life since his childhood in Tupelo, Mississippi. Instead of 'That's Alright', 'Heartbreak Hotel' and 'Blue Suede Shoes', he sang three of his favourite gospel songs—and brought the house down.

The episode taught him two important lessons: that he had broken into the big time and that he could always fall back on his faith in times of challenge. Time and again in his roller-coaster life, the King relied on his love of gospel—and his bedrock faith in God—to get him through the tough times.

'I am not the King. Jesus Christ is the King. I'm just an entertainer,' he would tell fans at one of his Vegas shows in the early 1970s. 'Since I was two years old, all I knew was gospel music. That music became such a part of my life it was as natural as dancing. A way to escape my problems and my way of release.'

The great, untold tragedy of Elvis's final days was his re-discovery of his deep religious faith just when those closest to him feared he was lost. Friends revealed that, just before his death, Elvis had finally resolved to fire his manipulative manager, Colonel Tom Parker, and devote the second chapter of his life to doing 'God's work' and making his daughter, Lisa Marie, proud of him.

Sick and tired of the party lifestyle that had consumed him for so long, Elvis turned his back on Las Vegas and, after years of threatening to axe Parker, he'd finally confronted him and told him he was going it alone. According to a Presley insider, Elvis had decided to turn his back on rock'n'roll, at least for a while, to become a gospel performer.

As a child, he attended the First Assembly of God Church in East Tupelo and would squirm from his mother's clutches to run up front and watch the choir close-up. 'Gospel music is the purest thing there is on this earth,' he would say later. The only Grammys Elvis won were for gospel songs and many fans remember him as much for 'How Great Thou Art' as they do for 'Jailhouse Rock'.

Although he said the Holy Bible was his favourite book, Elvis admitted he had gone off-track as a Christian during much of his adult life, never joining a church. He said he didn't drink because of his faith but showed few other outward signs of any religious devotion, despite believing he'd seen the face of God smiling down on him on a trip to the Arizona desert in 1965.

Elvis once told his friend, Pat Boone, 'I wish I could go to church like you.' After Boone told him he could, Elvis replied, 'No, they wouldn't leave me alone. I would distract the minister.'

His salvation came as he reached rock bottom in the weeks before he died.

Rick Stanley, Elvis's stepbrother, claimed that, the night before Elvis died, he prayed, 'Dear Lord, please show me a way. I'm tired and confused, and I need your help.' Stanley said the singer looked at him and said, 'Rick, we should all begin to live for Christ.'

Hours later, Elvis was found dead in his Graceland bathroom.

ELVIS'S DEATH—TIMELINE
16 AUGUST 1977

12.30am: Elvis and girlfriend Ginger Alden return to Graceland after 10.30pm dentist appointment.

2.15am: Elvis calls Dr Nick to request more painkillers, complaining about toothache. Elvis's stepbrother, Ricky Stanley, drives to the all-night pharmacy at Baptist Memorial Hospital and returns with six Dilaudid pills.

4am: Elvis wakes up first cousin Billy Smith and his wife, Jo, to play a game of racquetball.

4.30am: Elvis moves to a nearby piano and performs 'Unchained Melody' and 'Blue Eyes Crying In The Rain'.

6am: Elvis decides to go up to his bedroom with Ginger and takes his first packet of prescription pills designed to help him sleep.

6.45am: Elvis takes his first packet of sleeping medication.

8:00am: Still unable to sleep, Elvis asks for another packet of drugs.

8.30am: His Aunt Delta Mae brings up a third pack of pills.

9am: Elvis takes the book he's been reading—*Sex and Psychic Energy*—and goes into his bathroom. 'Don't fall asleep in there,' Ginger calls after him. His last words were, 'OK, I won't.'

2pm: Ginger wakes up and sees Elvis is still gone. After knocking in vain, she goes into the bathroom and finds his lifeless body on the floor in front of the toilet. She screams for help. First, Memphis Mafia employees Al Strada and Jo Esposito try to help revive Elvis and then his father, Vernon, arrives.

2.33pm: Emergency 911 call for help.

2.35pm: Lisa Marie comes in and yells, 'What's wrong with my daddy?'

2:55pm: Elvis arrives at the Baptist Medical Center in Memphis.

3:40pm: The star is pronounced dead.

4:00pm: The world learns that the King is dead.

7.00pm: Autopsy begins.

8.00pm: Dr Nick and Shelby County Medical Examiner Jerry Francisco read the results of the autopsy—even though it was still continuing. The cause was given as a Cardiac Arrhythmia due to an undetermined heartbeat. There was no mention of drugs (although toxicology tests would later reveal fourteen types of drug in Elvis's system, ten of them in significant quantity).

ELVIS DIDN'T NEED TO DIE

Elvis was secretly plotting to get back together with ex-wife Priscilla at the time of his death—and the King's closest friends believe to this day he wouldn't have died if his last wish had come true.

'I'm miserable. I want my family back,' he told Priscilla. 'I miss the family times we had. Lisa needs her mom and dad together.' Calling his ex-wife by his pet name for her, 'Satnin' (a slang word he used for her skin being soft as satin), the King admitted he hoped to woo her back, despite already being engaged to twenty-year-old Ginger Alden.

Shirley Dieu, who was a trusted member of the star's inner circle, revealed the meeting in her 2014 book, *Memphis Mafia Princess: Living in 'The Elvis World'*.

'I called Priscilla,' she later told me. 'She had told me about their last conversation but she didn't put it in her own book. When I called, she said she was happy for me to include it in mine. Enough time had passed. I am so privileged that she trusted me with this.'

Elvis's desperate plea wasn't the first time he'd tried to woo back the woman he'd first met while he was overseas in the US army. Priscilla was a fourteen-year-old living in Germany when she won his heart. He always regarded her as the great love of his life and was desperate to win her back. And it probably would've happened—if only he had survived.

'At that point, I think she was pretty ready for a relationship. Elvis was too. They were both kind of getting rid of other relationships,' says Shirley, who still wears the diamond-studded 'TLC' necklace given to her by the 'Jailhouse Rock' legend.

'I know that's what we all wanted. We all would have loved for the two of them to get together.'

As girlfriend of Elvis's road manager, Joe Esposito, Shirley toured with the singer for the last three years of his life. She saw first hand how loyal and generous Elvis was to his friends. She also witnessed his vulnerability with women and tried to wean him away from the prescription medications that ultimately claimed his life.

Breaking down in tears, Shirley said, 'Elvis was a wonderful person. It saddens me when I hear the terrible things people say about him. And Priscilla went through a lot and still does, even now.'

In her book, Shirley writes that Priscilla's last meeting with Elvis came when she visited Graceland with their daughter, Lisa Marie, in the summer of 1977. Priscilla took the trip because she was curious about Ginger, who was described as being a dead ringer for Elvis's ex-wife in her younger days. 'If you ever saw Elvis waiting for the arrival of Priscilla, you would know how he got when she was coming by, like a teenage boy waiting for his high school sweetheart. There was always anticipation as he tried eagerly to impress her somehow,' she writes.

Priscilla told Shirley how she went upstairs at Graceland to look for Elvis.

'When Elvis proceeded to the dressing area of his bathroom, Priscilla heard him calling her name. Priscilla told me that is when she knew he needed help,' Shirley explains.

> He was standing in front of the mirror and he kept saying, 'Can you hear that? Listen to that, 'Cilla, can you hear it?' He seemed to be delusional, she told me.
>
> Then he turned to Priscilla and abruptly said, 'I've never planned to marry Ginger, Satnin. I'm miserable. I want my family back.'

After talking for some time, Priscilla left Graceland to return to Los Angeles. It was the last time she saw Elvis alive. When she returned to Memphis for the funeral, Shirley was on the flight with her from LA.

Esposito, who was Elvis's right-hand man and confidante from their days together in the US army, confirmed Shirley's story. He remembers that, weeks before the King died, Priscilla and Lisa Marie were staying at the Howard Johnson hotel down the street in Memphis because she didn't want to intrude at Graceland. Elvis insisted she visit him at the house they'd once shared. 'They visited upstairs in Elvis's bedroom for over four hours, reminiscing about old times and talking about what she was doing, while Ginger waited in the kitchen,' he says.

Esposito recalls the couple having long 'middle-of-the-night phone talks. They even recaptured some of the close-ness they had shared.' And Presley had hoped that, one day, Priscilla would be back for good.

Like the rest of the 'Mafia', Esposito wasn't a fan of Ginger. After Elvis died, he worked as road manager for stars including Michael Jackson, The Carpenters, John Denver and The Bee Gees. But even living in retirement following the death of his wife, Martha, he remained in close touch with Priscilla and another of Elvis's former lovers, Ann-Margret.

Shirley says there were three women in Elvis's life that really cared about him—Linda Thompson, the long-time girl-friend he'd recently split from before turning to Ginger; his former co-star and lover, Ann-Margret; and Priscilla. 'Those three women would have been there for him no matter what. He knew they would be there for him and take care of him.'

MURDER, LIES & COVER-UPS

Millions of mourning Elvis fans around the world breathed a sigh of relief when Memphis Medical Examiner Dr Jerry

T. Francisco announced, on 21 October 1977, that the beloved King of Rock'n'Roll had died from 'hypertensive heart disease'. It meant they could dismiss all the lurid tales of their hero's excesses—for women, drugs and fatty food—that had sullied his reputation in the days following the tragedy.

A heart attack was, after all, the kind of calamity that could kill the cleanest living of superstars. And Elvis's devoted admirers would much rather remember the fresh-faced, polite young stud in 'Blue Suede Shoes' than the shambling, fat junkie who had long been a disappointment to more 'Suspicious Minds'.

But no one really believed that was the full story—it wasn't even close.

Elvis's manager, Colonel Tom Parker, his wife, Priscilla, and the Memphis Mafia closed ranks to preserve the King's image—conspired in an elaborate cover-up to hide the real reasons behind the King's death. It was a manoeuvre that was perhaps only possible in the Deep South, which always re-garded Elvis as a prodigal son. To throw people off the track, the star's body was even listed at the morgue as 'Ethel Moore'.

Incredibly, the code of silence remains just as strong to this day, as the full autopsy results for Elvis's death have only ever been shown to his closest family and advisors. Had it not been Elvis Presley, the body would have been taken directly to Shelby County Morgue after being 'found dead' at the scene and an official post-mortem would have been carried out and the results made public. By taking him to the Elvis-friendly Baptist Hospital, his personal physi-cian, Dr George Nichopoulos, and the family could better control what information was released to the media.

As a result, for more than three decades of speculation has run rife over the icon's true cause of death.

The most widely held belief is that he collapsed after suffering a killer medical 'perfect storm' brought on by his drug dependency, his obesity and a weak heart. But some of the wilder theories include suicide as a result of a cancer diagnosis or his despondency over his fading career, that he was felled by a fatal karate chop to the windpipe, backed up by chronic constipation, and even that he faked his own death.

What is certain is that there was a concerted effort to prevent the authorities—and ultimately, the public—from learning the truth about Elvis's drug addiction. It also seems likely that he could have been saved had Ginger Alden, his fiancée who was sleeping in the bedroom, heard his fall from the toilet. Medical experts agreed that Elvis would probably not have died immediately.

Quizzed about the possibility that drugs were involved in the death, Dr Francisco, while acknowledging they had been in Elvis's system, added, 'Had these drugs not been there, he would still have died.'

The controversy raged on for thirteen years before Dr Eric Muirhead—a pathologist who helped carry out the autopsy on Elvis's body—came forward to insist that, while the singing legend did have an enlarged heart and some coronary artery disease, the real cause of death was a deadly cocktail of drugs. He revealed the autopsy found a total of fourteen different types of drug in Elvis's body, including ten times the normal dosage of codeine and toxic levels of Quaaludes. The sensational claims caused a storm, with Dr

Francisco being accused of whitewashing his findings to preserve Elvis's good-guy image.

In a bid to quell the critics once and for all, the State of Tennessee called in Dr Joseph Davis, then the Chief Medical Examiner for Dade County, Florida, to make the definitive examination as an independent pathologist.

Dr Davis was given access to all of Elvis's medical records, as well as the original autopsy results and another one carried out exclusively for the Presley family. He wrote his report in 1994, seventeen years after the showman's death, but to this day, it remains locked in a Tennessee vault, shrouded in secrecy because of the state's privacy laws concerning death records. His only public statement essentially cleared Dr Francisco by saying he didn't intentionally conceal any of the facts when he claimed Elvis had died from natural causes.

'There is nothing in any of the data which supports a death from drugs. In fact, everything points to a sudden, violent heart attack. He was grossly obese, which put an enormous strain on the heart,' Dr Davis insisted.

The scene itself tells you what happened. The position of Presley's body told me that he was about to sit down on the toilet when the seizure occurred. He pitched forward onto the carpet and was dead by the time he hit the floor. It takes hours to die from drugs. The only way drugs could have killed Elvis Presley that fast was if he were shooting up a lethal dose of heroin.

To be fair to Dr Francisco, his investigation was hampered from the start.

The contents of Elvis's stomach and throat had been flushed away by mistake in the ER at Baptist Memorial Hospital. The bathroom where the King took his last breath had also been cleaned up.

Someone had systematically scrubbed the bathroom and adjacent sitting room of all pills, bottles and papers. Even Elvis's vomit, which could have revealed a lot to investigators, was washed out of the carpet.

Paramedic Ulysses Jones went back to Graceland a few hours after rushing Elvis to hospital because he'd forgotten an item of equipment. 'I'd left a piece of medical equipment upstairs in the bathroom and I went to get it,' he recalled. 'Remembering the mess I had found the bedroom and the bathroom in, I was really surprised to find everything neat and tidy and not a thing out of place.'

Medical Examiner's office investigator Dan Warlick was horrified to find the scene was cleaned up before he arrived. After examining dozens of bathrooms in the course of his work, he wryly commented that it was the first he'd ever seen when there were absolutely no drugs, even if it was just cough drops or aspirin.

All that was left to show Elvis had died in the bathroom was a vomit stain on the carpet about nine feet from the toilet. Warlick found several guns—part of Elvis's extensive collection—in the bedroom, as well as a couple of empty syringes, but even the bed had been made.

The results of toxicology tests, which reveal the drugs in the body, were not even back when Dr Francisco reached his verdict. He signed the death certificate citing hypertensive heart disease with narrowing of the arteries as a contributing factor. However, Dr Muirhead claimed that, apart from codeine and Quaaludes, other drugs found in Elvis's system included amitriptyline, nortriptyline, morphine, diazepam, diazepam metabolite, ethinamate, ethchlorvynol, amobarbital, phenobarbital, pentobarbital, meperidine and phenyltoloxamine.

The day before Elvis died, Dr Nichopoulos wrote him a staggering eight different prescriptions for around six hundred pills, many of them narcotics and controlled substances. They were said to include 100 Percodans, 20cc of liquid Dilaudid and 50 Dilaudid tablets (extremely strong painkillers sometimes given to late-stage cancer patients), 112 Amytal sleeping pills, 150 Quaalude tranquilisers, 178 Dexedrines and 100 Biphetamine tablets.

On the same day—15 August 1977—Elvis was given a bottle of codeine tablets by his dentist, Lester Hofman, in case he suffered any pain resulting from a filling.

Elvis was allergic to codeine; his personal nurse, Marion Cocke, and ex-lover, Linda Thompson, both later told investigators that he reacted to the drug by breaking out in a rash and became short of breath and panicky. One theory is that he may have mistaken codeine for the Dilaudid tablets he took to try to get to sleep on the day of his death.

Or were the similar-looking off-white pills switched on purpose by a mystery assassin?

DEATH-SCENE CLEAN-UP—THE TRUTH AT LAST

Members of the Memphis Mafia cleared a box full of Elvis's medications out of the King's Graceland bathroom as part of a clean-up in the hours after his death. That's the shocking secret bared by the star's closest friend and road manager, Joe Esposito, who admitted he removed the drugs in an attempt to preserve Elvis's image.

Speaking from his home in Las Vegas, the best man at Presley's wedding to Priscilla says he deliberately lied about where he found the dying music legend. After the tragedy, Esposito, now in his seventies, told the world's press that Elvis's body was on a bed and not in the bathroom where the singer had fallen after collapsing on the toilet. He didn't want Presley's millions of devoted fans conjuring up the image of their hero dying in this way.

'I stated "bedroom" instead of "bathroom" because I was simply trying to protect Elvis' privacy,' explained Esposito. 'It was always our job to protect Elvis, regardless of the circumstances.'

Esposito revealed his shock as he tried in vain to revive his friend after finding him lying face down on the carpet with his pyjamas around his ankles. One of the first on the scene, he helped medics carry the 260-pound star to an ambulance and sat with him on the way to the hospital.

After doctors were unable to save Elvis, Esposito hurried back to Graceland. He hoped to prevent the King's reputation from being tarnished by the humiliating manner of his death—and the drugs that surrounded him.

'I went up there and got them all [the medication bottles] out of the bathroom and put them in a box and put them away someplace. I had to get them out of there,' he explained to me. 'The thing about it was that he took a lot of different medicines. He really did. So he took more than he should be taking. That's what happened. It was a very sad day.'

Esposito, who still proudly wears the 'TCB' (Taking Care of Business) necklace given to him by Elvis, says the star died from a fatal reaction to the drug cocktail he took daily to help him sleep.

Shirley Dieu, Esposito's girlfriend at the time, was in LA when the superstar passed away. She didn't see the death scene but believes Elvis may have died from an allergic reaction to codeine. Shirley insists the Memphis Mafia only wanted the best for their friend, saying, 'Whether we did it right or we did it wrong, we still tried with all of our hearts to save him. We failed.'

WHAT REALLY HAPPENED?

The Gambino crime family murdered Elvis to prevent him from spilling the secrets of the Mob's most lucrative ever multi-billion-dollar scam.

It may seem a far-fetched scenario, particularly all these years after Elvis died, but examination of the FBI records and inside information about the probe into one of the world's biggest ever white-collar scams makes it a chilling possibility that the King was 'whacked' by organised-crime bosses desperate to prevent their lucrative fraud schemes from being busted.

So many aspects of Elvis's death still don't add up and so much confusion still surrounds the cause. A Mafia hit would explain why the singer took a drug—codeine—that he knew he was allergic to. It would also provide a strong sense of redemption for his family, friends and the millions of fans who believed in him and felt strongly that he deserved better than an ignominious end on the toilet in his Graceland home.

Here is how I believe the Mob literally got away with murder on 16 August 1977 by successfully covering up the assassination of the world's most famous and best-loved entertainer. According to an organised-crime source, the killer received a king's ransom for his murder mission, possibly totalling more than $1 million. Sneaking into the music legend's innermost sanctum, the shadowy assassin only needed to be armed with the knowledge of a medical Achilles' heel that would prove fatal for Elvis. Although the singer was battling an addiction to a bathroom-cabinet's worth of prescription meds—a habit he had sworn to conquer in his final days—he had a serious allergy to codeine painkillers.

By switching Elvis's Dilaudid pills—tablets closely resembling codeine and part of the nightly cocktail of drugs the singer took to help combat his rampant insomnia—the killer could achieve something that would be impossible with a bullet or a knife: a bloodless murder with no telltale clues.

Although $1 million for the 'hit' was a lot of money, particularly back in 1977, it was small change compared to the estimated $2.5 billion the gangsters risked losing if Elvis testified in public about the heroic efforts he made to help the FBI probe codenamed 'Operation Fountain Pen' that uncovered a chain of mammoth frauds around the world.

The star-turned-crime-buster was due to give evidence to a Grand Jury in the case on the day he died, focusing worldwide attention on the white-collar scams the Mafia had gone to enormous lengths to keep out of the public eye. By silencing Elvis, the godfathers who masterminded the elaborate frauds hoped to keep the criminal conspiracies out of a spotlight that would have brought the full force of the law crashing down on them.

As it turned out, Elvis's death dominated the news for months, overshadowing details of the FBI operation. While small-time crooks further down the chain were arrested and charged—including scam artists who tried to steal Elvis's aircraft—none of the Mafia bosses who pulled the strings in 'The Fraternity' ended up facing the music.

Not one but three Mob families are thought to have been tied into the hitman plot.

The boss suspected of ordering the 'hit' was Paul Castellano, the heavyweight head of the Gambino family, who would himself be infamously whacked at Manhattan's Sparks Steak House in 1985 by 'Teflon Don' John Gotti. Castellano was married to boss Carlo Gambino's sister and, when Gambino died in 1976, he ruled that his brother-in-law should take over the reins of the most powerful of New York's five crime families. Facing fierce opposition from inside his own wise-guys operation, Castellano took control of all white-collar crimes, including stock embezzlement and other big money rackets, leaving the more traditional Cosa Nostra activities to long-time underboss Aniello Dellacroce.

When Castellano learned Elvis had been helping the FBI in Operation Fountain Pen, he would have worried that the money-spinning frauds that he was overseeing—and which were his power base in the family—would be in ruins if the involvement of a celebrity of Elvis's stature was revealed, claimed a Mafia source. Castellano was regarded as more of a businessman than a crime boss and he needed to make a big move to stamp his authority on his rebellious subordinates, who had backed Dellacroce for the leadership.

'By whacking Elvis he could save his criminal operations and send a message that he meant business at the same time,' speculated the insider. His enforcers, say Mob historians, were a crew run by Roy DeMeo and Anthony 'Nino' Gaggi, who were allegedly responsible for between seventy four and two hundred murders during the late 1970s and early 1980s. Another killer for the Gambinos was Sammy 'The Bull' Gravano, who admitted to nineteen murders when he turned government witness and helped jail thirty six of his former Mafia associates, including Gotti, who took over from Castellano as head of the family.

Even now, Omerta—the Sicilian Mafia's traditional law of silence—has ensured the identity of Elvis's assassin remains a closely guarded secret. But experts say that, to get permission to target Elvis in Memphis, Castellano would have needed the blessing of Carlos 'The Little Man' Marcello, the New Orleans-based godfather who kept an iron grip over Mafia operations in the south.

There is no way something like this could happen without Marcello knowing about it,' said another authority on the Mob's murderous past. 'Marcello wasn't as high profile as the New York godfathers but he was just as powerful, if not more so. If one of the most likely conspiracy theories surrounding JFK's death is to be believed, it was Marcello who ordered the President's death in Dallas in 1963. He hated the Kennedys for deporting him from the US and for trying to crack down on his criminal activities.

If Castellano went to him saying Elvis had to be killed because billions of dollars in crooked revenue was at risk[,] then he would almost certainly have asked for a fee in return for permission to move on his turf. He could even have provided one of his own people.

One problem would have been Vincent 'The Chin' Gigante, head of the Genovese family in New York, who was a huge Elvis fan.

'I loved the times when we put on Elvis,' says his youngest daughter, Rita, whose dad earned his 'Oddfather' sobriquet by feigning mental illness in a bid to escape the clutches of the law. 'I didn't care if he was in his bathrobe and his slippers and whatever—he'd get up and start dancing to Elvis. He couldn't sing a word—forget it. But he'd try,' she said in a 2012 interview with the *New York Daily News*.

Unlike Marcello, however, Gigante wouldn't have had the power alone to outvote Castellano and prevent a hit on his hero. Piecing together clues from various sources, including court papers, the official autopsy and informed sources—much of it ignored or misread in the tumultuous aftermath of the death—it seems certain the killer would have been armed with deadly inside information about Elvis's pill regime to help pull off the 'perfect crime'.

Investigators say it's impossible to know after all these years whether the assassin broke into Graceland or got inside help. What is clear is that Elvis swallowed a huge dose of codeine—a drug he knew full well would kill him.

No one in the King's entourage believed for one moment that he would take his own life. Indeed, Elvis was more determined than ever to be a good dad to Lisa Marie and kick the drugs that had turned him into a shambling hulk of his former magnetic self.

More than anything, said his old friends, Elvis's epiphany in risking his life for his country by working with the FBI to hunt down the bad guys had renewed his zest for living. It was simply against everything he believed in—particularly his strong religious beliefs—to commit suicide, they insisted.

But it wouldn't be difficult for the killer to know Elvis's mind was often scrambled as he struggled through countless nights to get some sleep, especially if he or any of the wise guys had a contact on the inside of their target's famously large entourage. And it certainly wouldn't be hard for a light-fingered intruder to switch the bottle of Dilaudid Elvis was given by his prescription-drug supplier, Dr Nick, with codeine, which can be lethal if taken in large enough quantities.

The singer took Dilaudid religiously as part of his 'sleep cocktail'—and yet the pills were found untouched in his bathroom after he died. Question marks have also been raised over the activities of Elvis's personal dentist, Lester Hoffman, in the icon's final hours.

Hoffman—who boasted of being gifted a Cadillac Seville by his famous patient—told in later interviews how he once performed a root canal on Elvis without anaesthetic, saying the singer meditated to control the pain. Elvis had a 10.30pm appointment with Dr Hoffman on 15 April 1977, to get his teeth cleaned and a couple of cavities filled. The picture of the King leaving the dentist's office was the last snapped of him alive.

Although Hoffman denied prescribing any anaesthetic, he fell under suspicion for possibly providing Elvis with codeine-based painkillers in case he suffered any pain following the routine procedures. If that was, indeed, the case, was it an innocent mistake? Or did the late dentist play some role in the death plot, perhaps unwittingly providing the drugs that were switched by the killer to cause the superstar's demise?

'It wouldn't have been difficult for the killer to have slipped out again in the chaos after Elvis's body was discovered. It was mayhem,' said a source.

It would have been even easier if he had some inside help. It's not the type of crime the Mob was ever going to talk about because Elvis was so hugely popular and it would turn the public against them in just the way they feared would happen if he was allowed to give his Grand Jury testimony.

But there are a lot of people who were very close to Elvis who have been convinced for years that he was murdered. It is the only explanation that makes sense. Elvis had been taking prescription meds for so long he was like a seasoned chemist—he knew exactly what he was putting into his body. He would never knowingly have taken codeine so there is only one realistic conclusion—he was murdered.

Sources say Elvis's independent autopsy report—sealed by the family until 2027—will prove that the King was, indeed, tricked into swallowing a massive overdose of codeine.

Although he died before he was able to give evidence to put the scammers away, Elvis's behind-the-scenes co-operation with Operation Fountain Pen wasn't in vain. The probe helped the FBI open leads in seventeen different offices and crack fifty cases across the globe, according to the agency's website.

Suzanna Leigh—the 1960s starlet who appeared with Elvis in the 1966 movie *Paradise, Hawaiian Style* and later worked as a VIP tour guide at Graceland—became convinced the King was murdered by the Mob after launching her own investigation.

'I soon learned Elvis had in fact been part of one of the largest FBI investigations of the Seventies, codenamed Fountain Pen,' she wrote in her 2011 book, *The Flip Side of Paradise*.

'Scores of federal agents worldwide had investigated it, and Elvis was due to give evidence. The FBI was meant to be protecting Elvis when he died.'

She insisted that Vernon Presley, who died in 1979, was always convinced his son was murdered and says she was told by Elvis's former security chief, Dick Grob, that a codeine overdose caused the death.

'It doesn't matter what other things they say he died of—that is what he really died of,' Grob told her, adding that, on the night of the death,

> there was pandemonium in the streets, with distraught fans and journalists arriving from all over the world. There were about 200,000 people outside the gate. If the police had said they suspected Elvis had been murdered, there would have been a lynching. The police tried to get a handle on things, but so much stuff was walking out the door. A lot of things disappeared that night and were sold later. Someone even washed the carpet where Elvis had fallen. Imagine that—cleaning up before the police arrived? It could only have been someone really close to Elvis that could have ordered that.

Suzanna adds in her book that she was forced to leave Memphis after surviving two murder attempts: one when someone opened fire above her head and another when her car was sabotaged. Her home was also broken into and a dog was stabbed in what she believed was a warning for her to stop making inquiries.

'In Dick Grob's opinion, it was organized by the Mob,' she said. 'He told me they did not want Elvis or his father to appear in court because of all the media interest it would create, so they must have got someone inside the house. That's what Vernon believed all along, said Dick.'

THE MAFIA PLOT TO STEAL ELVIS'S PRIVATE JET

Elvis took his December 1970 appointment by Richard Nixon as a special roving federal agent very seriously. He was willing, he wrote in a letter asking for the White House meeting, to do whatever was necessary to serve his country, although he did want a small something in return. 'I can and will do more good if I were made a Federal Agent at Large and I will help out by doing it my way through my communications with people of all ages. First and foremost, I am an entertainer, but all I need is the Federal credentials.'

In the December 1970 letter, Elvis insisted he had the necessary qualifications: 'I have done an in-depth study of drug abuse and Communist brainwashing techniques and I am right in the middle of the whole thing, where I can and will do the most good.'

Perhaps it wasn't all good. British writer John Parker speculates that the singer's envy of The Beatles—and his belief that they, along with the likes of Jane Fonda and the Smothers Brothers, were corrupting America's youth—prompted

Nixon's subsequent persecution of John Lennon, in which he tried to get the British music icon deported in the mid-1970s.

Nevertheless, with his credentials in hand, Elvis ordered his entourage to investigate hoodlums and Mafia gangsters in Las Vegas—further provoking the wrath of the wise guys who wanted him gone. But it was the saga of Elvis's airplane—one of three he owned—that earned him the gratitude of the Feds . . . and may have ultimately signed his death warrant.

Hard as it is to believe after all the millions he earned throughout his career, Elvis was faced with the prospect of going broke in the summer of 1976, when his father, Vernon, who watched over the King's financial affairs, suggested selling off one of the private planes that he never used.

Always a big spender, Elvis had gone crazy giving cars and other gifts to hangers-on to mask his unhappiness with the way his life was heading. After Vernon started looking into what to do with the Lockheed JetStar, he became suspicious about the kind of people who were interested and confided in his son about his concerns.

It was the perfect opportunity for Elvis to make good on his pledge to the President to help uphold the law. He went to the Feds as an informant and agreed to advertise the plane for sale as bait to tempt out the crooks.

Elvis can't have known, when he first made contact with the FBI, that the scam artists seeking to con him out of his plane were among the biggest fraudsters in the world and part of a Mob-connected gang calling themselves The Fraternity that the Feds already had their eye on.

In the FBI file on the case, The Fraternity is described as 'a loosely knit group comprised of approximately 30 to 40 of the world's top con-men'. Although Vernon was the one who made contact with the fraudsters, insiders said Elvis made sure he was closely involved and informed of every development. Risking his own life, he gave the go-ahead for two FBI agents to go undercover as part of Operation Fountain Pen and meet up with the gangsters. He also signed over the plane to the men—knowing they were all about to be arrested by the FBI almost as soon as the deal was done.

At the Feds' request, Elvis and Vernon—who was his son's financial advisor—agreed to keep the Lockheed JetStar up for sale in the Miami newspapers as bait to try to catch Fraternity fraudsters, who they knew targeted super-rich movie stars, bankers and entertainers as the perfect fall guys for their crooked white-collar schemes. The crooks believed celebrities had more cash than common sense and shied away from embarrassing publicity once they discovered they'd been conned.

Ringleader Fred Pro took the bait and came up with an elaborate plot to buy the plane, refurbish it and lease it back to the Presleys and then lease it out again to confound the taxman and make Elvis a $1,000-a-month profit.

The file reveals that Pro's co-conspirator, Phil Kitzer, met with two undercover FBI agents as a part of the sting operation. The three men flew on the same National Airlines flight from Miami to New York on 5 May 1977 and didn't acknowledge one another until they had all booked into Manhattan's Mayflower Hotel, where Kitzer took the undercover agents to meet Pro in another room.

Kitzer said the two undercover agents were 'good guys to know' and would help smooth over any potential problems with the 'outfit'—meaning the Mob families in New York and New Jersey.

According to the FBI file, Kitzer told Pro that he thought stealing Elvis's aircraft was a 'mission impossible'. But after flying off with the plane, Pro called Kitzer from the air to boast that he'd pulled it off, unaware that the whole scam was being tracked by the FBI.

After grey-haired, bespectacled Pro took out a $1 million mortgage on the plane, he 'indicated he skated with the proceeds and left the bank holding the aircraft,' said the file. It was then that the Feds pounced, arresting Pro, Kitzer and their associates, said to have ties to Sam 'The Plumber' DeCavalcante, the reputed head of a New Jersey Mob family as well as a senior gangster in the Columbo Mob.

At about the same time, said the Presley insiders, Elvis became paranoid about his safety, wearing bulletproof vests and carrying around a gun at all times—even inside Graceland.

It's not as though his fears were ungrounded. Seven years earlier—in March 1970—the FBI investigated a kidnap-and-murder threat made against the King in Las Vegas by a caller who said a hitman had a gun with a silencer and was seeking revenge because the star had 'done him wrong'. Nothing ever came of the threat but it underlined just how vulnerable Elvis was, despite his army of ever-present bodyguards.

Following Elvis's death, the fraudsters were accused of racketeering and wire fraud and dealt with quietly after they agreed to plea agreements in return for lighter sentences. If avoiding publicity was the Mafia's motive in killing Elvis, they certainly succeeded.

By keeping the full details of the King's contribution to the battle against organised crime under wraps, the authorities have done Elvis a disservice. Now, all these years later, this sacrifice might finally explain why his life was so tragically cut short. If that was, indeed, the case, he at least died as a result of his brave decision to take on the bad guys and not, as has been reported for so long, as a hopeless drug-addicted shell of a man with no concern for anything or anyone other than himself.

PRINCESS DIANA

It is very easy to believe that Princess Diana was killed in August 1997 in a tragically unfortunate road accident caused by an irresponsible drunken chauffeur and a rabid pack of paparazzi hounding their most lucrative prey into an early grave. After all, inquests and investigations in London and Paris assured us that any suspicion of foul play was groundless. The people in power, the police chiefs, the judges, the politicians . . . they were adamant no stone had been left unturned. Life could be incredibly cruel but the Royal Family was moving on and so, too, should we.

This is what the British establishment would have us believe and, with all the cynicism and multi-culturalism of modern-day Britain, it is a nation that still wants desperately to trust in a system that has been forever run not by elected representatives but by the byzantine manoeuvring of what Diana herself liked to call the 'men in grey suits'.

These aristocratic power brokers, their roots dating way before the House of Windsor or, indeed, the House of Tudor, act with impunity. The allegiance is not to any God or populace; it is entirely to the state—and woe betide anyone seen as a threat. They pull their strings behind the scenes, just as they always have.

There is a reason the Queen surpassed Victoria to become the United Kingdom's longest-serving monarch—an astonishing feat considering her reign bridged the most transformative period in the nation's long and storied history. We look fondly on Her Majesty as a benign and dutiful but largely powerless figurehead.

Again, this is what we are supposed to believe.

Paul Burrell reportedly claimed that the Queen said to him there were 'dark forces at work' in Britain that he couldn't begin to understand. It is clear to me that there really are dark forces and that they are bound to protect the Royal Family against any threat, real or imagined, to its continuity. And have no doubt about this: Princess Diana was a threat to the Queen and the future of the monarchy; certainly the greatest threat in modern times.

You only have to take a cursory glance beyond what we have been spoon-fed about Diana's death by the authorities and the media to understand this was no ordinary car accident.

In fact, I am absolutely convinced it wasn't an accident at all.

As a very well informed friend asked of me when he learned I was taking a closer looks at the events on and around 31 August 1997, 'Ask yourself who benefited from Diana's death?'

Who, indeed?

Well, Prince Charles was able to marry his mistress, the patient and enduring Camilla Parker Bowles, and rehabilitate their image as a couple to the extent that she could be admired, if not loved, as his consort, should he become King. It is hard to imagine that would have been possible had Diana lived as an ever-present reminder of her ex-husband's cold indifference.

Similarly, the Queen survived her *annus horribilis* of 1992—in which Andrew Morton's tell-all book, *Diana: Her True Story*, was published; Prince Andrew separated from Sarah, Duchess of York; Princess Anne was divorced from Captain Mark Phillips; and Windsor Castle caught fire—and her emotional missteps in the aftermath of Diana's death five years later, to rebuild a stronger-than-ever foundation for her family, with Prince William and his popular wife, Kate, as its face for the future.

With Diana as a rival in the affections of the British public, it would have been a very different story. If she was, indeed, planning to marry Dodi Fayed—and I'm told she was—there was the very real spectre of an alternative monarchy uniting cultures and religions—Christian and Muslim—much more reflective of contemporary Britain. A stronger, more confident Diana could have pushed the Windsors, wittingly or otherwise, to the brink of irrelevance.

Even those convinced of royal culpability in Diana's fate refuse to believe the Queen, Prince Charles or Prince Philip would have signed her death warrant. That's simply not how things are done in the UK.

But while the Queen is the head of the Royal Family, Philip has always been the head of the family and it would have been eminently clear to the 'men in grey suits' and their henchmen in MI5, the domestic intelligence agency, and MI6, responsible for spy work abroad, that the 'Diana problem' was becoming untenable.

Of course, Prince Philip would never have suggested she should be done away with but that doesn't mean Diana wasn't murdered. And it doesn't mean that her tragic absence hasn't been a boon to the one-time House of Saxe-Coburg and Gotha (George V changed the name of his branch of the family to Windsor due to anti-German sentiment in 1917).

By the time she reached Paris on that fateful weekend, it was no longer a secret that the Princess was dating Dodi. The relationship may have been all of eleven weeks old but Diana appeared to be happy and Dodi told friends he had found the woman he wanted to be with for the rest of his life.

They were returning to London on the Monday with the intention of announcing their engagement. At least that was the plan. Diana was excited at the prospect of starting a new life with Dodi, with homes in Malibu, California and in Paris. Was the decision hastened because of an unplanned pregnancy? In her more reflective moods, Diana confessed she longed for a baby girl.

I don't know the answer to that (perhaps the only people who did know were Diana and Dodi themselves)—any evidence that may have confirmed a pregnancy was destroyed in the immediate aftermath of her death. But to those who dismiss the suggestion and claim Dodi was just a passing whim, I'd remind them she gave her lover her 'most prized possession'—a pair of her late father's cufflinks—one of the few belongings of his that she was bequeathed.

Maybe they would have delayed the marriage announcement. After all, the princes, William and Harry, had to be told and life as a royal divorcee was rarely uncomplicated, especially where it concerned matters of the heart. There is a possibility Diana would have second thoughts. She could have given back the £11,600 engagement ring Dodi chose for her with such care from Repossi jeweller's shop, across the square from the Ritz hotel in Paris, the afternoon before the crash.

But the shady defenders of the state—the protectors of the royal status quo—would be very aware of the risks. Once the proposal was made public, it would be out of the bag and there would be no stuffing it back. The 'oily bed-hopper', as Philip allegedly referred to Dodi, could have one day been stepfather to the King and that simply couldn't be allowed to happen.

The only way to guarantee that was to ensure Diana never returned to London.

THE LEGEND

The sound of laughter rang out across the stone terrace of the grand stately home that had been in Diana's family since the sixteenth century.

The annual Althorp pheasant hunt in the Northamptonshire countryside was over for the day and a sixteen-year-old Diana, all giggly and slightly overawed to be on her own with Prince Charles, was teaching the playboy heir to the throne how to tap dance.

To him, it was an amusing diversion and little more, although he was sufficiently entranced by the fresh-faced teen to ask her to show him around the Spencers' gallery of Old Masters. To Diana, it was the beginning of the fairytale.

Charles had always known Diana as one of the flock of children who played with his younger brothers, Andrew and Edward, when they spent the holidays as neighbours in Sandringham, the Royals' summer getaway in Norfolk, about three hours from London.

The impromptu tap lesson on the terrace of November 1977 was, perhaps, the first time he'd thought of Diana as anything other than a wearisome child. Aged thirty and indisputably the biggest bachelor catch on the planet, he was romancing princesses, heiresses and society beauties, not schoolgirl virgins.

But friends said Diana had loved Charles since she was a young girl. While others worshipped actors and soccer stars, she already had her knight in shining armour, even when he didn't notice her at all.

Even if Charles did feel some small spark for Diana back then, it would have been further complicated by the fact that he was dating her older sister, Sarah, whom he'd met several months earlier at the Royal Ascot House Party.

That relationship ground to a halt after Charles accused Sarah of blabbing to the media. Meanwhile, Diana moved into a London flat—60 Coleherne Court in the Royal Borough of Kensington and Chelsea—with a group of friends and started work as an assistant at an upmarket nursery school (she left school without any academic qualifications).

While settling comfortably into the trendy 'Sloane Ranger' set of young London socialites, Diana, perhaps with one eye still on her elusive prince, was determined to keep her chastity intact. That would certainly come into play later as she began to emerge as a very real contender for the role of future Queen.

Diana's next meeting with Charles at the English country estate of Commander Robert de Pass, a friend of Prince Philip, in the summer of 1980 appeared to be a matter of blind chance. But it was anything but. The commander's son, Philip, had invited Diana thinking she would be a 'young blood' to amuse Charles, the guest of honour.

According to biographer Andrew Morton, Diana touched a deeper chord with Charles, perhaps for the first time, when they sat chatting after he played a polo match. Recalling Earl Mountbatten, who was killed in an IRA bombing the previous year, she told Charles, 'You looked so sad when you walked up the aisle at Lord Mountbatten's funeral. My heart bled for you when I watched. I thought, "It's wrong. You're lonely. You should be with somebody to look after you."'

In all of Charles's previous romantic relationships, the weight of his duty as future King overshadowed thoughts of his own happiness. He told one former girlfriend, Laura Jo Watkins, the American daughter of a US rear admiral, that they could never stay together because the Queen would not approve.

For his family, at least, love wasn't a necessary factor. It was all about suitability and duty, particularly since the abdication of the last Prince of Wales, King Edward VIII— Elizabeth's uncle—to marry the American socialite Wallis Simpson was still relatively recent history.

But the incurably romantic Diana believed wholeheartedly in love, so much so that she ignored the warning signs that, even at that early stage, might have warned her to tread more carefully when her prince came wooing. If Charles had any doubts that he could have anything in common with this largely uneducated and, to his mind, superficial 'filly', Diana didn't share those reservations and ardently encouraged his hesitant advances. More to the point, his grandmother, his parents and their coterie of advisers liked the idea of Diana. They liked her lineage, her family, her lack of any real sexual past and, consequently, any skeletons in her closet.

Diana may have wondered why Charles's 'friend', the very married Camilla Parker Bowles, was always with them on 'dates' but it clearly didn't concern her that much and, anyway, things were moving so fast she barely had time to ponder this. By September of 1980 the press had got wind of the budding romance and her life would never again truly be her own.

Despite his reputation at that time for being something of a rake, albeit a gentlemanly one, Charles didn't try to bed Diana before their marriage.

Charles invited Diana on a sailing weekend on board the Royal Yacht *Britannia*, moored in Cowes on the Isle of Wight, in the summer of 1980 and, soon afterwards, she was on her way to Balmoral, the family's Scottish residence, to meet the parents.

Royal biographer Ingrid Seward said that, although Charles made the odd 'clumsy pass', the new couple spent most of their time with his older friends. 'There were no candlelit dinners, no lavish gifts and certainly no intimacy,' she added.

The inevitable proposal, when it came on 6 February 1981, was similarly unromantic. Diana was invited to drive herself to Windsor Castle, where Charles asked to meet her in the sparsely furnished nursery dining room. 'There were no candles on the white tablecloths, and the food was cold poached salmon and salad and fresh fruit. There wasn't even any champagne,' wrote Seward in *Diana* (1998). 'When he asked her, Diana burst out laughing, thinking he was joking, but she quickly agreed, saying, "I love you so much, I love you so much." Typically of Charles, he immediately ran upstairs to ring his mother.'

Later that night, Diana drove herself back to her London flat to break the news to her friends, whose joyous screams and whoops were in stark contrast to Charles's somewhat dour acknowledgement of her acceptance, dutifully reporting her reply to the Queen.

The announcement was made three weeks later, on 24 February 1981, with a photo call on the lawn of Buckingham Palace for Diana to show off her exquisite eighteen-carat sapphire-and-diamond engagement ring. But while the public around the world celebrated the news, behind closed doors clues that life as a royal bride wouldn't be quite so rosy were gradually dawning on Diana.

Speaking to the press, Diana said that she was very much in love with Charles, only for him to add, 'Whatever love means.'

As time would tell, it clearly meant two very different things to both of them but, again, Diana paid the remark little heed at the time. She was too busy trying to handle the onslaught of interest in her every movement and, for a young woman already struggling with a fragile self-esteem, the pressure was taking its toll. Her self-worth wasn't helped when Charles, his hand around her waist, suddenly pulled it free, exclaiming his bride-to-be had become rather 'chubby'. Later, Diana saw pictures of herself in the media and believed she looked fat.

The eating disorders that would plague her for the rest of her life began in earnest as she began secretly purging her food. Between the first fitting with designers David and Elizabeth Emanuel for the wedding dress and her last, Diana's waist shrank from 29 inches to 23½. The bulimia left her wasting away but, bizarrely, no one appeared to notice. Everyone was too caught up in the fairytale to want to hear the increasingly ugly truth, it seemed.

Soon afterwards, Diana found a bracelet in an aide's office that Charles had bought for Camilla, engraved with the initials 'GF' for the nicknames they had for each other, Gladys and Fred. Camilla's presence loomed ever larger in the shadows. Still, according to Seward, Diana summoned up enough excitement to ride a bicycle around the Palace grounds on the eve of her wedding, shouting, 'I'm marrying the Prince of Wales in the morning!'

Diana herself remembered the lead-up to the big day rather differently. She told biographer Andrew Morton that she didn't think she was happy.

We got married on Wednesday and on the Monday we had gone to St Paul's for our last rehearsal and that's when the camera lights were on full and a sense of what the day was going to be. And I sobbed my eyes out. Absolutely collapsed and it was collapsing because of all sorts of things . . . The Camilla thing rearing its head the whole

way through our engagement and I was desperately trying to be mature about the situation but I didn't have the
foundation to do it and I couldn't talk to anyone about it.
I had a very bad fit of bulimia the night before . . . I was
sick as a parrot that night. It was such an indication of
what was going on.

By the time Diana spoke to Morton, the Royal marriage had
fallen apart, so it was hardly surprising she was so jaundiced
that she struggled to remember any good coming out of it.

But the fairytale was still alive on the morning of 29 July
1981 as hundreds of thousands of people crowded into the
heart of London to celebrate the 'Wedding of the Century'.

'I was very, very calm, deathly calm,' Diana told Morton.
She'd spent the previous night at Clarence House, the Queen
Mother's official London residence. 'I felt I was a lamb to
the slaughter. I knew it and I couldn't do anything about
it,' she added. 'It was all so grown up. Here was Diana, a
kindergarten teacher, getting married. It was so ridiculous. I
had to see the funny side, otherwise I would have burst into
tears.'

Traditionally, Royal nuptials had been held at Westminster
Abbey but the venue was switched to St Paul's to fit the
2,700 VIP guests. Diana unveiled her elaborate ivory silk
taffeta and antique lace gown, with a 25-ft (7.62 m) train
(which was so long her courtiers had trouble squashing
it into the glass coach she rode in to the ceremony). The
couple had been dating for less than a year, yet their marriage was being heralded as a magical diversion from the
troubles of the world and everyone was caught up in it—
even Diana. During her vows, Diana got Charles's names

mixed up, calling him Philip Charles Arthur George instead of Charles Philip Arthur George. In turn, Charles fluffed his lines, saying, '. . .with all thy goods I share with thee,' instead of, '. . .all my worldly goods I share with thee.'

On the balcony of Buckingham Palace later, the crowd was roaring for a kiss from the newly-weds. 'They want us to kiss,' Diana told Charles, who seemed at first unwilling to give in to his subjects' request. Then, his usual reserve softened by the huge wave of public adoration, Charles demurred. 'Why ever not?' he said, pulling his new wife towards him for the most iconic kiss ever.

So Diana had her Prince Charming and, despite her misgivings, she still had reason to hope that her dream of a long and happy marriage would become reality. Within months of the wedding, she would provide Charles with his first son, William, the heir he wanted above all else, followed by a second son, Harry, in September 1984.

Just before the wedding, the Queen gave Diana an emerald necklace and a diamond-and-pearl tiara that had once belonged to Queen Mary—a sure sign that she was entrusting the future of the monarchy to the young bride. But the storm clouds that were held at bay by the pomp and glory and circumstance of the Royal wedding were about to break. And Diana's short-lived optimism wouldn't last beyond her honeymoon.

PRINCESS DIANA FACT FILE

1. Diana failed her O-levels twice and didn't have any academic qualifications.
2. Her father, Earl Spencer, won custody of Diana and her three siblings following his 1969 divorce from his wife,

Frances.

3. Diana's £28,000 engagement ring—fourteen magnificent solitaire diamonds surrounding a twelve-carat oval blue Ceylon sapphire set in eighteen-carat white gold—was passed on to her son William's future wife, Kate Middleton, in October 2010. It's now estimated to be worth in excess of £300,000.

4. Diana's stepmother, Raine, Countess Spencer, was the daughter of the bestselling romance novelist Barbara Cartland.

5. She once invited supermodel Cindy Crawford over for tea because Prince William had a crush on her.

6. Diana supported over one hundred charities, including Centrepoint, National AIDS Trust and Children with Leukaemia.

7. On 29 July 1981 750 million people in 64 countries watched Diana's wedding to Charles on television.

8. Her funeral 16 years later had 2.5 billion TV viewers.

9. Diana was buried in a long black dress and holding rosary beads given to her by Mother Teresa.

10. Thirty-six oak trees symbolising each year of her life lead to her final resting place on an island in an ornamental lake in Althorp Park. Four black swans 'guard' the grave.

THE END OF THE FAIRYTALE

For any woman, it would be the ultimate betrayal. Standing in a pale grey dress with a veiled pillbox hat, the mistress stood to one side of the aisle, right in the sightline of the bride in white.

This was Diana's 'vivid' memory of the final moments before she exchanged vows with a waiting Prince Charles in front of the Archbishop of Canterbury at St Paul's Cathedral on the biggest day of her life.

She remembered looking up to see Camilla Parker Bowles, with her son, Tom, standing on a chair. By this time, she already recognised that Camilla—whom she would come to nickname 'The Rottweiler'—was a threat to her happiness. What she could not know then was just how little Charles really loved her and how much he resented being pushed into marriage with a woman he felt he had almost nothing in common with.

'I was furious,' Diana would say later of her emotions, after learning too late that Camilla was on the wedding guest list. 'I wanted to turn and run. If I'd had the courage[,] I would have hitched up my dress and bolted out of the church.' Much later, she would famously say, in a BBC *Panorama* interview with Martin Bashir, 'There were three of us in this marriage, so it was a bit crowded.'

Within days of beginning her honeymoon, the Princess was facing the harsh reality of her predicament as the bride of convenience to a man who expected her to stay silent as he carried on with his life exactly as he wanted, with his much older mistress most definitely in tow.

Departing a London still bathed in post-wedding fever, the newly-weds went by train to Broadlands, the Hampshire estate where the Queen and Prince Philip spent time as a young couple. Once there, Charles immediately unpacked seven novels by his favourite author, South African philosopher Laurens van der Post, and settled down to start reading them. 'I thought, you know, it was just grim,' Diana told biographer and confidant Andrew Morton. 'I just had tremendous hope in me, which was slashed by day two.'

'It was like an icy wave biting her in the face,' wrote Tina Brown in *The Diana Chronicles* (2007). 'The oldness, the coldness, the deadness of royal life, its muffled misogyny, its whispering silence, its stifling social round confronting sycophantic strangers, this is how it would be until she died. Nothing else can explain the violence of her panic.'

The next stage of the honeymoon on board the Royal Yacht *Britannia* was, if anything, even worse. Her bulimia attacks became 'absolutely appalling', with Diana purging up to four times a day. Then, to cap it all, she was taken up to Balmoral, the Scottish estate where the Royals traditionally retire for the summer, where she continued her honeymoon in the company of the Queen, Prince Philip, the Queen Mother, Charles's three siblings, Anne, Andrew and Edward, and other members of the family. It was nothing like the romantic escape Diana had dreamed of her whole life and, when she begged Charles to return to London, he quickly shot her down. After all their efforts to bring Diana into the royal fold, the family, too, was beginning to suspect a rocky road ahead. 'Look at her sitting at that table glowering at us!' the Queen reputedly told a dinner guest one night, according to Tim Clayton and Phil Craig, authors of *Diana: Story of a Princess* (2001).

In her biography, Tina Brown quotes a former member of Charles's staff as saying, 'When I think of the young, beautiful, newly-married Princess of Wales at this time, I see her sitting up abruptly in the middle of the night in the Spartan spaciousness of her bedroom at Balmoral and uttering a long, bloodcurdling scream.'

Diana saw her pregnancy as a way out of the lonely path stretching out in front of her and threw herself enthusiastically into motherhood. She gave birth to William on 21 June 1982 and Harry was born two years later, on 15 September 1984. The royalists were happy—Diana had done her job, providing 'an heir and a spare'. According to Ingrid Seward, those early years leading up to Harry's birth were 'the happiest in their whole relationship'. But Charles quickly tired of the domesticity and refused to break things off with Camilla. He and Diana spent more and more time apart and the strain began to tell in public.

What Charles and the Royals had not reckoned for, however, was just how popular the 'People's Princess' had become. The Prince struggled to win over the public, his stilted, awkward persona making him appear out of touch and elitist. By contrast, Diana's warmth and compassion won her the nickname 'Queen of Hearts' and so passionate was public support that her popularity was rivalling that of the Queen.

With Charles refusing to give up Camilla, Diana eventually started looking for love outside her marriage, beginning with an affair with her riding instructor, army officer James Hewitt, and leading to a succession of other lovers. Long before it became public knowledge, I was sent by the *Daily Mail* to interview a former military groom who had worked with Hewitt and wanted to sell lurid details of the illicit affair. At that time, the Royal Family's tenuous relationship with the media was still hanging by a thread and the decision was made not to publish, to spare Diana's blushes and maintain a respectful relationship with the Palace. That, too, was about to change.

All the time, Charles and Diana kept an outward charade of a contented marriage—an arrangement Charles would have been happy to continue for the sake of appearances. But Diana was losing patience with her cold, unfeeling husband. 'When Charles tried to kiss her at a polo match, she deliberately moved her head away as she knew the gesture was a sham and that he was just playing to the cameras,' wrote Seward. A series of photographs documented the deterioration of the relationship over the years, each one showing the couple looking increasingly unhappy and further apart.

In late 1991 Diana found love letters from Camilla that proved her worst fears. According to Andrew Morton, one read, 'My heart and body both ache for you'. Another excoriated Diana and urged Charles to rise above the attacks from 'the onslaughts of that ridiculous creature'. Morton's book, written with Diana's discreet co-operation, was published in June 1992. It caused an immediate sensation by claiming that Diana had attempted to commit suicide five times in despair over her marriage.

Buckingham Palace went into spin overdrive to try to limit the damage by decrying the claims, only for it to be established that Diana was the source for the stories. She was said to have thrown herself down the stairs, cut her wrists with a razor, cut her chest and thighs with a knife, thrown herself at a glass cabinet and cut herself with a lemon slicer in tormented cries for help.

The publication in Britain of a transcript of an intimate conversation between Diana and her lover James Gilbey—called 'Squidgeygate' because of Gilbey's affectionate name for Diana—heaped more embarrassment on all concerned. It was swiftly followed by the leaked 'Camillagate' tapes, which included humiliating details of Charles's exchanges with Camilla, including one likening himself to a tampon.

Any sense of propriety the media had for the Royals was gone. It was open season.

Later that year, on the couple's final joint trip to India, Diana was deliberately photographed alone outside the Taj Mahal, as a symbol of her independence from Charles.

In December 1992 Prime Minister John Major formally announced the separation in Parliament. The couple remained married as they struggled to find a way out of the crisis without causing irreparable harm to the monarchy but, after Diana went on TV in 1995 to admit her affair with Hewitt and question Charles's ability to be King, the Queen had seen enough and urged the pair to divorce.

The divorce was finalised on 28 August 1996.

The fairytale was over.

THE MURDER

Diana never stood a chance.

From the moment she arrived in Paris on Saturday, 30 August 1997 on board a private jet with lover Dodi Fayed, there was no way the beloved Princess was going to be allowed to leave the City of Lights alive.

The royal rebel knew her life was in peril and took every precaution possible to combat an assassination attempt. But she was battling an unseen enemy and, if she was somewhat paranoid in her final months, she had every right to be. She wasn't some naïve outsider jumping at shadows—she was trapped inside an establishment she not only distrusted but also feared.

There is very real evidence, suppressed by the authorities

and the mainstream media, that the British intelligence and elite military—the SAS—were involved in a plot to murder Diana. It's inconclusive but certainly enough to build a persuasive case.

The establishment would dismiss such claims as nonsense, although Diana herself certainly believed there were those who were capable of putting her in jeopardy.

I can say that a thorough examination of the facts reveals that the events of that night point to a much more sinister alternative to the highly questionable finding that the crash was a simple accident, a chance of fate, or a case of the Princess being at the centre of a perfectly deadly storm.

All these years after the tragic death of a princess, an alliance of conspirators continues to maintain its code of silence. But here, for the first time, is a detailed account of the events of 30 August 1997, compiled with the help of sources and friends of Diana who believe this—and not the official timeline—tells the real story of how the Princess's killers got away with murder.

DIANA'S DEATH—TIMELINE

3.20pm: Diana, thirty-six, and Dodi, forty-two, are met by Henri Paul, deputy head of security for the Ritz Hotel, on their arrival from Sardinia at Le Bourget Airport. The paparazzi have been tipped off and are waiting.

4.35pm: The couple arrive at the Ritz with the photographers in hot pursuit.

6.00pm: Dodi goes to pick up an engagement ring—adorned with the words 'Tell Me Yes'—he had ordered for Diana from exclusive Parisian jeweller Repossi. According to Dodi's father, former Harrods boss Mohamed Fayed, Diana had accepted his son's marriage proposal and was pregnant with his baby.

7.00pm: Diana and Dodi sneak out the back door of the hotel to go to his apartment off the Champs-Elysées.

7.05pm: Paul leaves the Ritz. Suspected of being a paid informant for the French Direction de la Surveillance du Territoire—or DST intelligence agency—and for Britain's MI6, he is thought to have checked in with his spymasters to report on Diana's location and the couple's plans for the night.

9.30pm: Diana and Dodi return to the Ritz after their attempt to enjoy a quiet romantic dinner is wrecked by photographers. Thirty lensmen follow them back to the hotel.

10pm: Diana—looking upset at the media attention—and Dodi leave the hotel restaurant after ten minutes and dine in the Imperial Suite. They decide to return to his apartment.

10–11pm: Paul downs two strong Ricards—an aniseed-flavoured pastis—while chatting with Diana's bodyguards, Kez Wingfield and Trevor Rees-Jones, at the Bar Vendome at the Ritz while they wait for Dodi and Di to reappear. Ritz CCTV will later show that Paul did not appear in the least intoxicated.

11pm: Paul is spotted chatting with the paparazzi outside the Ritz.

11.37pm: Paul tells the two bodyguards that he has devised a decoy plan, sending the two cars the couple had been using all day—a Mercedes and a Range Rover—out the front with the bodyguards while the hotel security boss drives the couple out the back in an unmarked car. The guards complain that the plan would leave Diana without any protection and they insist on one of them—Rees-Jones—going in the car with Diana and Dodi.

11.45pm: With the decoy plan agreed, a three-man team of military mercenaries is suspected of sabotaging the brakes and steering on the second Mercedes, which Paul will drive out from the back of the hotel.

31 AUGUST 1997

00.20am: The sabotaged Mercedes is brought around to the back of the Ritz and Paul gets in the driver seat, with Rees-Jones next to him. Diana and Dodi get in the back. In a startling omission from the usual practice, there is no back-up car following in case of emergency.

00.21am: Paparazzi tipped off by Paul photograph the Mercedes and set off after it through the streets of Paris.

00.25am: One of the mercenaries shines a blinding light in Paul's eyes, causing him to lose control of the Mercedes, according to the murder theory. Eyewitness François Levistre later tells *The Times* that, moments before the crash, he saw a 'flash of light'. At the same time, the two other killers—one in a white Fiat and the other on a motorcycle—try to crowd Paul off the road, one of them swiping the Mercedes. Neither vehicle was ever traced, even though white scratches were found on the side of Diana and Dodi's car and French police confirmed it was manufactured between 1983 and 1987.

00.25am: The Mercedes smashes into the thirteenth pillar of the Pont de l'Alma underpass. Paul and Dodi are beyond help. Diana and her bodyguard are critically injured but still alive.

00.26am: First on the scene is photographer Romuald Rat. He took Diana's pulse and told her help was on its way.

00.27am: ER doctor Frederic Mailliez is driving by when he sees the carnage and rushes to help.

00.32am: Ambulance and fire service arrive. Eight

photographers at the scene are arrested.

01.25am: The ambulance containing Diana finally leaves for the hospital—after nearly *one hour*! Her heart has stopped.

01.30am: Dodi is pronounced dead.

01.55am: Ambulance stops for medics to inject adrenalin into Diana's body in a bid to keep her alive. Unidentified men are seen entering the vehicle.

02.06am: Ambulance arrives at Pitié-Salpêtrière hospital, where doctors carry out open-heart massage for nearly two hours, trying, unsuccessfully, to heal a tear in the Princess's pulmonary vein.

04.00am: Diana is pronounced dead.

Writer and investigator John Morgan claims a clandestine committee of top Royals was behind the murder plot. Other sources suggest the Queen was kept in the dark to protect her.

Morgan—author of *How They Murdered Diana: The Shocking Truth* (2014)—insists the secret services assassinated Diana with official approval. Diana was a 'loose cannon', he writes. And she had to go.

'Princess Diana cannot rest in peace whilst her killers walk free and the people who ordered this assassination and the ensuing massive cover-up live in peace—and are not brought to account,' he says in conclusion.

LIES & COVER-UPS

A sinister conspiracy to cover up the truth about Diana's death still holds strong today, despite two showcase inquests in the United Kingdom and the biggest ever police investigation in French history.

According to a source with close links to the international intelligence services, Diana's enemies didn't stop at murdering the Princess—they also ordered the killings of her assassins to ensure they took the secret to their graves.

Diana was alive when paramedics reached her in the tunnel. Whether or not you believe sinister forces were at play, it is very reasonable to conclude that, had the Princess been rushed to hospital without delay, she may well be alive today.

French police officer Sébastien Dorzee arrived at the scene with a colleague around 12.30am. 'Blood was coming out of her mouth and nose,' he said.

> You could see a deep wound to her forehead. At the same time she was rubbing her stomach. She must have been in pain. She turned her head towards the front of the car and saw the driver. She became agitated. Then she put her head down again and closed her eyes. Minutes later, she asked Dorzee's fellow medic, Xavier Gourmelon, 'My God, what's happened?'

Police and independent investigators have been stymied at every turn by a wall of silence over crucial questions that remain unanswered nearly two decades after the car crash that stunned the world.

One possible key to solving the murder mystery once and for all: hundreds of documents from an internal CIA and FBI probe into the death have been sealed for reasons of national security and locked away at the US National

Archives centre in College Park, Maryland, and an official report filed by British Embassy staff in France in the aftermath of the 1997 tragedy has been heavily censored to hide names and important information that could support the homicide allegations.

Investigative sources claim witnesses have been bribed and threatened to keep quiet about what they know. French officials, medical staffers and people linked to a band of elite mercenaries are all receiving hush money to muddy the waters, say the insiders.

'At least a dozen people in France and Britain have received big money to stop them from telling the world what they know about Diana's death,' claimed one informed source. 'Each one knows a piece of the puzzle which, when put together, proves the Princess's murder was covered up and made to look like a terrible car accident.'

Russian author Gennady Sokolov claims three senior officers from the British spy agency MI6 arrived in Paris shortly before Diana died. In his book, *The Kremlin v The Windsors–Palace Spies of the Secret War* (2013), he claims the 'hit' was subcontracted out by British spooks to a band of paid assassins.

'It was clear for me that the fatal crash was NOT just an accident,' he said. 'The executioners all must have been liquidated. Some of the witnesses disappeared in the strangest manner.' He said to blame driver Henri Paul for the death was 'total nonsense'.

Sokolov claimed the killers used 'the Boston Brakes' method to sabotage Dodi and Diana's Mercedes. He explained that the killers planted 'a tiny electronic system with a transceiver' that 'disabled the steering wheel and brakes' via a radio signal. The investigative writer suspects an agent masquerading as a paparazzo on a motorbike triggered the signal. Sokolov added that thorough testing after the crash was prevented by powerful insiders—just as evidence from the car was destroyed in a mysterious fire and key laptops from the probe were lost.

The cover-up conspiracy helped pervert the course of justice so completely that an initial French investigation and a Metropolitan Police inquest ruled the crash an accident and a 2007 British Coroner's inquest found it was an 'unlawful killing' but blamed driver Henri Paul and the paparazzi. The inquiries—costing the British taxpayer over £60 million—dismissed and overlooked evidence pointing to a more sinister reason for the tragedy.

Former MI6 agent Richard Tomlinson told the second inquest into the death that he was aware of a colleague's proposal to kill Serbian leader Slobodan Milošević by using a strobe light in a tunnel to distract his driver, causing a crash. 'It was what we called "knock-them-off tactics",' he explained. 'The driver was blinded by a laser flash gun in a tunnel, where high speed ensured a crash.'

But Tomlinson's claims were dismissed by senior intelligence chiefs who sought to malign the former spy's reputation.

Dodi's father, Mohamed Fayed, charged that the inquest proceedings in London were biased to prevent the truth about the conspiracy from coming out.

'This is not an accident. It is a plot, an assassination,' he insisted.

For years, the authorities refused to release the official file detailing the events leading up to the royal beauty's tragic passing. When it was finally made public in 2014, the document was heavily censored, with any clues to the truth wiped from the record. 'If ever there was a blatant attempt to hide the truth about Diana's death, this is it,' says a source that befriended Diana in the course of her doomed marriage. 'Censoring this dossier proves the British and French governments engineered a massive cover-up that continues to this day.'

DIANA PREDICTED HER OWN MURDER— AND NAMED PRINCE CHARLES

'This particular phase in my life is the most dangerous. My husband is planning "an accident" in my car, brake failure and serious head injury in order to make the path clear for Charles to marry.'

Written with chilling foresight just ten months before her untimely death, Diana put her fears that she was the target of a sinister death plot down on paper as 'insurance' for the future.

Frightened and lonely, she knew the letter would never be taken seriously while she was alive but, filled with foreboding, she was determined to fight back against the Buckingham Palace machine that had been trying to break her ever since her highly publicised split from Charles.

'I am sitting here at my desk today in October, longing for someone to hug me and encourage me to keep strong and hold my head high,' she wrote. 'I have been battered, bruised and abused, mentally by a system for 15 years now, but I feel no resentment. I carry no hatred. I am weary of the battles, but I will never surrender. I am strong inside and maybe that [is] a problem for my enemies,' she continued.

The handwritten letter—the most compelling docu-ment suggesting the Princess's death was no accident—was handed to her trusted butler, Paul Burrell, for safekeeping.

'I'm going to date this, and I want you to keep it,' she wrote to Burrell. 'Just in case.'

Burrell claimed that, at the time Diana penned the letter in October 1996—two months after her divorce from Charles was finalised—she was wracked with anxiety and believed someone had bugged her apartment in Kensington Palace. She feared the royal hierarchy believed that, as long as she was on the scene, Charles could never properly move on.

Diana was enjoying huge public support but Burrell said she had an 'overpowering feeling that she was in the way'. It was as if the stronger she became, the more she was regarded as a modernising nuisance. 'I have become strong and they don't like it when I am able to do good and stand on my own two feet without them,' she added in the letter.

Indeed, Diana became so paranoid about her safety—cor-rectly, as it turned out—that she persuaded Burrell to help her pull up the floorboards at her home so they could search for hidden spy bugs. She also fired her police detail because she didn't trust them.

Tragically, the Princess's cry for help was never read during her lifetime. On 31 August 1997 her worst fears came true in the nightmare car crash that stunned the world.

Diana's prophetic words wouldn't be revealed for another seven years, when Burrell belatedly divulged the contents of the letter in his book, *A Royal Duty*.

Diana was so afraid she'd fall victim to a plot to tamper with her car that she told her lawyers about her fears.

The Princess insisted the conspirators intended to 'get rid of her' or leave her 'unbalanced' and were also targeting her love rival, Camilla Parker Bowles.

A note of the meeting was handed over to Scotland Yard less than three weeks after the Paris car crash—but Paul Condon, then Metropolitan Police Commissioner, and David Veness, who was in charge of the Royalty and Diplomatic Protection Group, kept it secret for six years. They didn't hand the note over to French investigators probing the 'accident' and only revealed its existence after Diana's handwritten letter predicting her own death was published as part of the serialisation of a book by her former butler, Paul Burrell.

The Princess described her concerns in a meeting with the late Lord Mishcon, head of the London law firm Mishcon de Reya, and two of his senior partners, Sandra Davis and Maggie Rae, in October 1995.

In an outburst that took the solicitors by complete surprise, Diana said she believed the Queen was about to abdicate in favour of Charles and claimed the Prince's true love wasn't Camilla but former royal nanny Tiggy Legge-Bourke, who, she claimed, had had an abortion.

So perturbed was Mishcon that he made a full note of the conversation. He wrote,

Her Royal Highness said that she had been informed by reliable sources, whom she did not want to reveal, as they would very quickly dry up if she did, that: A: The Queen would be abdicating in April and the Prince of Wales would then be assuming the throne, and B: Efforts would then be made, if not to get rid of her, be it by some

accident in her car, such as prepared brake failure or whatever, between now and then, at least to see that she was
so injured or damaged as to be declared 'unbalanced'. She
was convinced that there was a conspiracy and that she
and Camilla Parker Bowles were to be put aside. She had
also been told that Miss Legge-Bourke had been operated
on for an abortion and that she, HRH, would soon be in
receipt of 'a certificate'.

I told HRH that if she really believed her life was being
threatened, security measures, including those on her car,
must be increased.

Miss Rae later told the London inquest into the death, 'It
was very clear in my own mind that she thought she was
going to be killed.'

At that same inquest, Michael Mansfield QC, representing Mohamed Fayed, claimed police deliberately held
on to the 'Mishcon note' to cover up the involvement of
the British authorities in the death. He addressed Veness
with,

It didn't need Sherlock Holmes, you don't need to be
experienced in the job, that once Lord Mishcon walks
through the door on 18 September, you knew that this
was relevant, didn't you? Were you just sitting on this
note because you knew full well that the security services
or agents of the British state, maverick or otherwise, had
been involved and you didn't want this investigated?

The former police chief said he 'rejected' the allegation
'completely'.

THE AUTOPSY

If Diana was, indeed, pregnant at the time of her death, all trace of the foetus was destroyed by not one but two embalmings carried out within hours of her death.

The French authorities claimed the first—illegal—embalming was hurried through because the Princess's body was deteriorating in the summer heat and officials wanted her to look 'presentable' to Prince Charles and Diana's sister, Lady Sarah McCorquodale, who were flying to Paris to take her back to Britain.

But the effect of the embalming—which began at 2pm on 31 August 1997, ten hours after Diana was officially declared dead, and lasted two hours—was to totally obliterate any evidence of a pregnancy.

Jean Monceau, who did the controversial embalming in France, admitted at the London inquest in 2007 that the procedure was illegal. The reason the body wasn't taken to a refrigerated mortuary was because there was insufficient security.

According to Monceau, British Consul General Keith Moss gave the go-ahead but Moss would later say that he didn't realise the French meant to embalm the Princess.

However, a radiologist at the Paris hospital allegedly saw a six to ten-week-old foetus in the Princess's womb. A nurse was also said to have seen the embryonic child. Needless to say, neither was called to give evidence at either inquest.

The claim that Diana was pregnant would seem to tally with photographs of her in a leopard-print swimsuit, holidaying in the South of France fourteen days before the crash that show an unmistakable bump around her abdomen.

Sources also tell me that the Princess had visited a leading London hospital in the strictest secrecy for a pregnancy scan just before that photo was snapped.

Friends of the Princess have strenuously refuted the claim—also made by Dodi's father—that Diana was carrying a child at the time of her death. Sir John Burton CBE, former coroner to the Royal Household, who carried out the British autopsy, also claimed there was no evidence of a pregnancy.

EMBASSY TOP-SECRET DOCUMENTS

A heavily redacted British Embassy log from the night Diana died reveals how long it took for Prince Charles to respond after learning his former wife had perished in the Paris car crash.

Despite the heavy censorship of the documents, the timeline shows that the Prince of Wales was alerted to the tragedy at 1am—three hours before the death was officially pronounced. But Charles didn't turn up at the Paris hospital until 5pm—sixteen hours later—even though it was just a one-hour flight away.

Private investigators discovered that the blacked-out names on the log applied to Charles and Diana's sisters, Sarah and Jane:

17.00: CENSORED arrives at the hospital with CENSORED and are given a guard of honour on the steps . . . were introduced to hospital staff. They made a point of talking to the junior staff—nurses, admin, assistants, etc.—and circulated among them for more than 40 minutes.

17.40: CENSORED spent a few private minutes with the Princess.

The log—only released following years of legal campaigning—describes how the news was 'immediately relayed' to various officials, including the Queen, who was at the time at Balmoral Castle in Scotland with Diana's sons, William, then fifteen, and Harry, twelve. It gives no details about who gave the order to give up trying to keep the battling Princess alive. The report says only, '03.45: Diana's life support machine is switched off.'

COVERING THE TRACKS

Celebrity photographer James Andanson, who followed Diana's every move in the week before her death, was thought to have committed suicide when his burned corpse was discovered in the wreckage of a car in the French countryside. But the search for answers in the Princess's death-crash mystery took another suspicious turn when it was revealed that the paparazzi millionaire had, in fact, been murdered.

'I saw him at close range and I'm absolutely convinced that he had been shot in the head, twice,' declared Christophe Pelat, the fireman who discovered the body.

Andanson, who had boasted of working for the French and British secret services, had been in Sardinia during the last week of August 1997 as Diana and Dodi idled in the Mediterranean, and then returned to France on 30 August. But he was nowhere to be seen in the aftermath of the 'accident' and later claimed he wasn't anywhere near the scene of the tragedy. Less than six hours after the fatal crash in Paris, and for reasons that have never been revealed, Andanson boarded a flight at Paris's Orly International Airport, bound for Corsica.

He came under suspicion after numerous witnesses said they saw a white Fiat Uno speed into the tunnel and bump Diana's Mercedes from behind, causing the crash. Paint and plastic from the Uno was later found in the wreckage and the car was traced to Andanson.

He denied any involvement and kept a low profile until his death three years later in thick woodland, near Montpelier in the South of France. There were reports that the fifty-four-year-old's head had been detached from his body and that he had a hole in his temple.

A month later, laptops and cameras were stolen by armed men from the Sipa photo agency representing him. Some sources believe that Andanson was killed to prevent him talking about his role in the conspiracy, or perhaps that he snapped a photo proving the wreck was no accident. Yet still the authorities stuck to their story that Diana had been the victim of fate and not murder.

THE SMOKING GUN

Afraid for her life and unable to trust even those closest to her, Princess Diana left a secret smoking-gun video, pointing the finger of suspicion from beyond the grave at the plotters whom she believed wanted her dead.

In the final months of her life, she was convinced that high-profile establishment figures were conspiring to have her murdered.

According to a close friend of the Princess, a sympathetic British spy tipped her off that she was in danger and warned that a rogue team of agents from MI6—the UK's equivalent of the CIA—could strike at any time.

She allegedly put the tape in a 'safe' place so that her sons William and Harry could learn the truth if she was silenced. Diana had made no secret of the fact that she feared the establishment plotters would go to any lengths to end what many of them believed was the threat she represented to the future of the monarchy.

What she hadn't guessed was that she had also made some very dangerous foes through her charity work helping some of the world's most tragic victims of war.

Not only was Diana's growing popularity threatening the age-old traditions of the Crown but her high-profile campaign to ban landmines following a headline-making trip to Angola early in 1997 was costing a cadre of Middle Eastern arms dealers a small fortune in lost sales. The British security services had the connections for a 'Black Op' targeting the Princess and the arms dealers had both the motive and the funds to make it possible.

Ex-Harrods owner Mohamed Fayed, Dodi's father, has long been convinced that Diana and his son were murdered by British security services at the behest of establishment forces.

In an emotional appearance at the inquest into the deaths, Fayed said Diana had 'suffered for twenty years from this Dracula family'. He claimed he was 'sure' Charles knew what was going to happen.

According to the Egyptian tycoon, this was 'because he

would like to get on and marry his Camilla and that is what happened. They cleared the decks. They finished her. They murdered her. He married his crocodile wife and he is happy with that.

'It was slaughter, not murder,' he told the court, adding that 'French intelligence helped the British intelligence to execute their murder.'

It has never been made public whether or not Diana's sons ever got the opportunity to see their mother's bombshell recording—or, indeed, if it has ever been recovered.

One informed source said a police raid on Paul Burrell's home, ostensibly to recover property belonging to Diana, was, in fact, contrived to seek out the secret tapes, supposedly also including potentially damning material concerning Charles's personal life, stored in 'a mahogany wooden box'.

'The box was recovered and the contents, including the tapes, were never heard from again,' said the insider. 'Although other of Diana's belongings were seized, the raid was all about the mahogany box.'

A friend of Diana's claimed, 'She was genuinely in fear of her life. She told me the spy who tipped her off named names—senior intelligence officials known to Buckingham Palace.'

Diana received the same warning from a former bodyguard who worked for the elite police Royal Protection Squad. He even called her while she was on the Fayed yacht with Dodi, just days before she died, and confirmed she was under surveillance by the CIA, as well as MI6—'Di wanted to talk about the conspiracy on video in case something happened to her. She told me she put the video somewhere safe.'

THE FALL GUY

The hotel security chief blamed for causing Diana's death was secretly drugged at the Ritz bar as part of a plan to make him the fall guy.

Investigators believe a cocktail of drugs designed to cause an instant high and impair vision and physical reaction was slipped into Henri Paul's drink as he sat waiting to drive Diana and Dodi back to Dodi's apartment.

Paul knocked back two shots of pastis, a strong anise-flavoured French aperitif, while sitting at the bar with Diana's bodyguards Trevor Rees-Jones and Kieran Wingfield. Friends said that wasn't an unusual tipple for Paul—and certainly not enough to make him drunk. Yet when he went outside to chat to photographers and tip them off about the Princess's travel plans, his behaviour was described as bizarre and 'euphoric'.

After the tunnel tragedy, Paul was found to be three times over the French DUI limit. Discovered in his bloodstream, according to a Paris prosecutor's report, was a mix of the anti-depressant Prozac and Tiapride, a prescription medicine for recovering alcoholics.

Experts say the combination of the drugs and alcohol would have left Paul with the feeling that he was 'invulnerable' while, at the same time, his reflexes and reaction time would be markedly slowed and his vision would be impaired, particularly at night and while driving at high speeds.

Some sources have also claimed that Paul's blood samples were tampered with and perhaps even came from a different body.

CAMILLA'S FINAL INSULT

Consumed with grief after hearing that Princess Diana had been fatally injured in Paris, there was only one person Prince Charles could call on for comfort as the enormity of the tragedy became clear.

The first message alerting Charles to Diana's accident came through to Balmoral, the Royals' Scottish getaway, at 1am on Sunday, 31 August 1997.

According to biographer Penny Junor, the Queen urged her son not to wake William and Harry after their mother's death was confirmed. So the Prince turned to the woman he'd relied on for much of his adult life when things went wrong or he needed advice.

He called Camilla.

As ever, her words were 'a great comfort' to Charles as the world woke to the news of the death of the Princess. Any semblance of a friendship between the two women in Charles's life had long been destroyed by Diana's understandable resentment and anger over his refusal to give up his long-time love.

But Camilla understood as well as anyone else the devastating effect Diana's death would have on her sons and on the way Charles would be perceived, at least in the immediate future. Privately, she must also have understood that the outpouring of grief over the popular princess would jeopardise her immediate hopes of enjoying a public life with Charles after years of skulking in the shadows. But both would have known that, if they bided their time—and Camilla was nothing if not patient and faithful—their dream of marriage could finally be realised.

Just the previous month, on 18 July, Charles had taken the huge step of organising a fiftieth birthday party for Camilla at his Highgrove home in Gloucestershire. Through his friends, he'd even tipped off photographers to record her arrival—and her departure the following morning. The newspapers in Britain, which, in the past, had routinely favoured Diana and reviled her rival, had begun to warm to the idea of Charles and Camilla, even if few doubted they would ever be allowed to marry.

Now the couple would have to rethink their strategy. If the previously untouchable Queen could draw the wrath of her people by her refusal to break with tradition and fly the flags at half-mast at Buckingham Palace after Diana's death (because no flag was normally flown when the monarch was not in residence), what chance did Camilla stand?

The resurrection of every last detail of Diana's doomed marriage sent Camilla back underground and, for a while at least, it seemed that Charles was faced with the not unfamiliar choice of either giving her up or relinquishing his claim to the throne.

But, as we have already seen, their relationship is nothing if not resilient. Camilla wasn't seen publicly for eight months and, even then, it was only to attend the May 1998 wedding of her godson, Henry Dent-Brocklehurst. The breakthrough came with the help—of all people—of Prince William. He had never met Camilla, for obvious reasons, and his mother had made him very aware of her scorn for 'the other woman'.

But William must have been also aware that, as far as his father was concerned, Camilla was 'non-negotiable'. Her children, Tom and Laura, were already fast friends of the boys, and Penny Junor explains in her book, *Prince William: Born to be a King* (2012), that the first meeting happened on 13 June with an introduction by Charles at St James's Palace. William had already lost his mother—who can forget the lonely figure the then-fifteen-year-old Prince painted walking mournfully with his brother behind Diana's funeral cortege to Westminster Abbey—and wouldn't want to risk losing his father as well.

The Prince of Wales told Camilla: '"He's here: let's just get on with it,"' wrote Junor.

> So he took her up to William's flat, introduced them and left them alone to talk for about half an hour. At the end of the encounter, Camilla came out saying: 'I need a drink.' She said the young Prince decided to break the ice because he and Harry were planning a surprise fiftieth birthday party for their father for the night of 31 July.
>
> The Prince was moved to tears by his children's thoughtfulness, but what touched him most was their seating plan: they'd placed Camilla next to him. To be fair to Camilla, she never tried to be Mummy but she was the 'other woman' and she was there and taking Daddy's time. It wasn't all happy families for quite a long time, but William was happy to see his father happy.

But there were still many in the Palace—and the country—who were not so forgiving and Camilla was later excluded from Charles's official fiftieth birthday celebrations.

Slowly and not so steadily, Camilla's reintroduction continued, helmed by the Prince's deputy private secretary/spin doctor Mark Bolland. It was a long, painstaking business. In January 1999 Charles and Camilla made their first appearance together since Diana's death when they attended a party at The Ritz in London for Camilla's sister, Annabel. Later in July, she was at her first royal engage-ment as Charles's guest at a Buckingham Palace dinner for American contributors to his foundation. It was another two years before the Queen finally gave her blessing by meeting Camilla at a party Charles threw for the former King Constantine of Greece at Highgrove.

By all accounts, it was a brief and formal audience but the ice had been broken.

Camilla was back in the fold.

A BRITISH SNIPER'S CONFESSION

A former sniper in Britain's elite SAS military unit finally unlocked the Diana murder mystery when he revealed that Special Forces soldiers killed the Princess.

'Soldier N' confided to his wife that an SAS squad flashed a blinding light at Diana's driver, Henri Paul, to cause the Paris-tunnel crash—a technique used to tackle terrorists.

The claims were investigated by Scotland Yard after the man—who has not been named for security reasons—and fellow SAS sniper Danny Nightingale were court-martialled after being arrested for hiding illegal guns and ammunition in the house they shared in Hereford, where the crack regiment is based.

The sniper's wife later backed the claim, revealing she was offered £500 in hush money. But even this wasn't enough to force a new probe—the British authorities ruled there was insufficient 'credible evidence' that the SAS was involved in the deaths.

As the saying goes, they would say that, wouldn't they?

This wasn't some random squaddie seeking attention. Soldier N was a member of one of the most respected and deadly military units in the world and had been expected to kill for his country with impunity. The authorities tried to dismiss him as a 'loose cannon' and yet the military was happy to use him as a prosecution witness in the case against his former friend, Danny Nightingale.

Nightingale, who was not covered by the identification ban, saw service in Northern Ireland, Bosnia, Lebanon, Turkey, Syria, Libya, Afghanistan and Iraq. The cagier Soldier N would say only at trial that he had fired 'many pistols' and been on more tours than he could remember. This was not a man prone to bragging.

The SAS murder revelation was included in a seven-page letter written by Soldier N's mother-in-law in September 2011 and sent to military bosses because she was concerned for her daughter's safety.

The sniper's wife was interviewed by Detective Chief Inspector Philip Easton and she was said to have given 'a compelling account' of what her husband told her on several separate occasions.

Before their marriage collapsed, the soldier also told his wife about the existence of a shadowy unit within the SAS, known as 'The Increment', which comprises troops from the SAS and SBS for the purposes of carrying out lethal operations on behalf of MI6. There was a form that could be filled out and left with cash in a 'box' for specific details for covert operations for anyone interested in doing 'private jobs'.

'They put in the box the name, address and details of what they want done and then one of them who wants to earn extra money takes the details out of the box and does that job,' explained the wife.

She later claimed that she was given a brown envelope stashed with notes by an SAS officer, who told her to 'keep quiet about Diana.'

'The threatening and sinister way that the SAS dealt with me made what my husband had said about the regiment's role in Diana's death all the more believable,' she added.

I had never been handed £500 before and told to keep quiet about the payment and what it was for. They wanted me to keep quiet about Diana and SAS operations but I couldn't stay silent about something so serious. The payment was deeply suspicious and made me very uncomfortable. The fact that they stayed silent about Diana compounded my belief that my ex-husband had told me the truth in 2008 when he talked about an SAS soldier directing a beam of light into the eyes of Princess Diana's chauffeur as their Mercedes entered the Pont d'Alma road tunnel. My husband had added that[,] after the SAS had caused the car to crash, a soldier had run back to the wreckage and looked inside to see how badly Princess Diana was hurt. Apparently[,] he then gave a signal to a colleague that their mission had been successful. So now I'm convinced that this operation is the SAS's big secret.

The two snipers were charged over illegally stashing away guns at their home that they had taken as trophies on missions abroad.

Soldier N admitted the offences and was sentenced to two years at the Military Corrective Training Centre in Colchester, Essex. He was also discharged from the army.

If the murder claims were so off the mark, one would expect that Soldier N's SAS brothers would have disowned him. In fact, quite the opposite occurred. Despite his former wife's claims, he refused to discuss the Diana case and served out his time. On his release, the decorated Special Forces veteran was welcomed into the SAS Association—the exclusive club for former members of the elite unit—with open arms.

WHAT REALLY HAPPENED—AND WHY?

Diana was murdered. There's little doubt in my mind that a highly trained team of professional assassins was ordered to ensure the Princess didn't make it through the night.

Whether you choose to believe that her car's brakes were compromised, a bright light was shone in Henri Paul's eyes or another vehicle intentionally drove the speeding Mercedes into the tunnel pillar, it is scandalous that it took so long to get Diana to hospital.

Then again, the stakes were incredibly high and some sources suggest that two mystery medics were recruited as 'insurance' by British secret-intelligence service MI6.

'Diana survived the crash and was murdered in the ambulance,' claims John Morgan, author of *How They Murdered Princess Diana: The Shocking Truth* (2014).

He said ER staff tried their best to save Diana—but she didn't get to La Pitié-Salpêtrière hospital until *one hour and forty one minutes* after the collision. By then, doctors had no chance of saving the dying Princess because the killer medics and the other plotters 'had already sealed their fate'.

'One of MI6's key strategies was to delay treatment,' added Morgan, who said the medics exaggerated the Princess's low blood pressure diagnosis 'as a pretext to start pumping catecholamines into Diana's system.' The effect was to boost her blood pressure, which, in Diana's case, increased the pressure on the internal injuries that killed her.

Morgan also claimed that the ambulance stopped en route to the ER and a witness saw the vehicle 'rocking' after one of the medics got out of the front passenger seat and climbed in the back beside the stricken Diana.

When John Hinckley shot Ronald Reagan in 1981, the US President suffered a similar wound—a pulmonary vein tear—and survived. There's no valid reason to think Diana couldn't have been saved.

Accepting the crash wasn't an accident, the obvious question is: who would go to such extraordinary lengths to silence her?

According to some extremely well informed sources, including one of Britain's top trial lawyers, her brave stand against the deadly landmine menace could have effectively signed her death warrant.

Michael Mansfield QC, who represented Mohamed Fayed in the inquest into the death of his son Dodi, said Diana claimed she had an 'exposure diary' in which she was going to unmask the people most closely involved with the British manufacturing of landmines.

'I think everyone remembers she raised the profile of the landmines,' Mansfield told an audience at the Hay Festival in Wales in 2010.

Everybody is aware that the British involvement in the arms trade, particularly landmines, is and was a huge vested interest. It seems to me she had planned various visits. She had already been to Angola [and] she was going to Cambodia later in the year. She was going to set up an institute for the victims of the landmines that had been exploded. A large number of landmines had been manufactured by the British and a witness who knew her well claimed that she had an exposure diary in which she was going to expose the people most closely involved in the British arms trade. It seems to me that is not unrelated [to her death].

In an apparent reference to the mahogany box that sources say went missing from Paul Burrell's home following a police raid, Mr Mansfield said there was a missing box of papers that could contain key information relevant to the investigation.

'Nobody really knows what was in it,' he said. 'The box exists but when it was opened there was nothing in it and everybody has forgotten what was in it. I don't know what was in it. It is said there were papers in there, it may have been the diary or notebook she was keeping in relation to the arms trade or it may be other correspondence between the royal family and herself.'

Landmines are hidden explosive devices that are buried in the ground and designed to be detonated when a person steps on or near them, causing indiscriminate death and horrific injuries. They can lie dormant for decades, long after a conflict has ended. In the sixty countries where landmines remain, an estimated four thousand people a year are killed or wounded. Many of the victims are children.

Although her royal duties were stripped from her following the divorce from Prince Charles in 1996—she also agreed to relinquish the title of 'Her Royal Highness' and any future claims to the British throne—and Diana had cut down on her charity work, she remained committed to ridding the world of the landmine menace and was prepared to take great risks to draw attention to the dangers they represented, despite being called a 'loose cannon' and ill-informed on the subject by senior British lawmakers.

Seven months before she died, Diana brought worldwide attention to the landmines crisis by visiting Angola, which was still littered with the explosives as a legacy of the country's decade-long civil war. Wearing protective clothing, she watched workers clear mines around Kuito, believed to be the most heavily mined city in the world.

Diana followed up her journey to Angola with a later visit to war-torn Bosnia, championing the anti-mine cause until her untimely death. The landmines arms merchants, with their own reason for wanting the campaigning Princess out of the way, would be the perfect choice to distance the plotters from the murder. With the weapons dealers paying the assassins, there wouldn't be a discernable link to any establishment figures.

Further muddying the waters, the 'merchants of death' were understood to have close ties to the Kremlin. According to intelligence sources, Russian agents may have even played a part in the conspiracy and offered a safe harbour for the killers until the worldwide shock and outrage over the tragedy subsided.

Speaking in 2010, Mr Mansfield insisted, 'I felt very strongly there was more to this case than a mere accident.'

He said the inquest result also left question marks over the cause of the death, stating,

> The verdict of the jury was not accidental death. The jury had that option and chose not to take it. They came back to unlawful killing contributed to by the paparazzi and following vehicles. The interesting thing is most immediate vehicles were driven not by paparazzi but people they have never managed to trace.

'The idea of murdering someone to protect your business interests is unthinkable to most people,' said a source. 'But arms dealers are peddling weapons of death and destruction every day. Diana may have been a princess with admirers around the world, but to these people she was merely a pawn in a very dangerous game of chess and they wanted her out of the way.'

All of which brings me back to the question I was asked at the outset of my investigations into Diana's death. Who benefited from the demise of a woman who was loved and treasured by so many?

The answer to this question, I believe, will lead to the truth.

MICHAEL JACKSON

'They're going to kill me, they're going to kill me.'
The wailing came from the second floor of the $100,000-a-month (£75,000) rented home in the upscale Los Angeles neighbourhood of Holmby Hills, where Michael Jackson tried to hide away from a prying world.

Jackson was convinced his life was in danger and his son, Prince, heard him cry out in panic more than once. For all his fame and all his millions and in spite of the three young children he adored, the King of Pop was falling apart. The weaker he became physically, the greater his paranoia.

If he was eaten up by guilt over his inappropriate behaviour towards the little boys left in his care in his Neverland years, he never let on. But he would collapse in tears after calls with his business partners or the hangers-on who leeched the life out of him in his later years. He worried that everyone was after his money. In his mind, at least, danger lurked around every corner.

No one—not even his conspiracy theorist sister, LaToya—would seriously suggest Jackson was being literal. There was no shadowy assassin waiting to knock off the fifty-year-old Peter Pan.

But there are still people to blame.

There are the doctors who enabled his deadly addiction to prescription drugs. Conrad Murray was a disgrace to medicine and the one who carried the can with his four-year involuntary manslaughter sentence for killing Jackson but he was just the tip of the iceberg. There was a whole cabal of star-struck doctors all too ready to feed Jackson with whatever drugs he wanted. Anyone who heard the singer's drug-addled voice played on a tape during Murray's 2011 trial was all too aware of the damage done.

Dermatologist Arnold Klein, Jackson's 'friend' for more than thirty years, perhaps did more than any other physician to enable the star's crippling prescription-drug addiction—certainly more than Murray, who was a relative newcomer to Jackson's inner circle.

In the three months before the star's death, he was injected with the painkiller Demerol an astounding fifty one times by Klein, visiting the doctor's clinic almost daily with no legitimate medical reason other than to get his fix. Eyewitnesses said he would often be so out of it when he left Klein's offices that he could hardly talk or walk.

Larger-than-life Klein—who died in October 2015—was certainly no shrinking violet and played up his relationship with Jackson to the full. Yet he was never charged in connection with the singer's ultimately deadly addiction.

I'm told Jackson 'died' at least three times in the eighteen months before his death on 25 June 2009. Each time, frantic staff brought him back to life. On one occasion, his body-guards did CPR; on another, doctors pumped his stomach.

He ingested an astounding 10,000 pills in his final 6 months, revealed the same source. It's not like the singer was blind to the dangers—he kept an oxygen tank by his bed in case he stopped breathing.

In his final days, says his long-time make-up artist, Karen Faye, Jackson was so thin and frail his beating heart could be seen through his skin.

Forget *Soul Train* (on which The Jackson 5 performed 'I Want You Back' under a giant 'Jermaine' banner), Michael was the *gravy* train for his brothers and his father. Many years later, he would recall how his father, Joseph, would beat him.

Three weeks before Michael died, his father reportedly turned up at the house wanting his superstar son to sign an agreement for a pay-per-view television show for the *Return Of The Jackson 5*.

Michael allegedly told a friend, 'I'm not in The Jackson 5—that's a thing of the past.'

The demons summoned by Jackson's desperate—even perverse—determination never to grow up were the root causes leading to the lifestyle that ultimately killed him. His health deteriorated so badly at the end that he couldn't perform some of his trademark dance moves. He couldn't sleep—he could barely function at all. This was no big secret.

Michael Jackson should be alive today. He should have been saved from himself in the weeks, months and years before his death and he undoubtedly should have been saved the night he died.

The fact he wasn't is the biggest scandal of all.

THE LEGEND

There was a reason Michael Jackson looked so joyful when he was on stage with his brothers as a boy—if he performed well, it would please his disciplinarian father.

It didn't take long for steel worker Joseph Jackson to work out he had a potential goldmine in Michael, the seventh of nine children living in a three-bedroom house in blue-collar Gary, Indiana, a tough industrial city near Chicago.

Right from the age of one, when he would dance around in his nappy with a baby bottle in one hand to the thumping rhythm of the family's washing machine, it was clear Michael had a musical gift.

And Joe Jackson was determined to maximise it.

His brothers were already singing together in 1963 when their mother, Katherine, noticed Michael's strong, clear voice and told her husband, 'I think we have another lead singer.' The next year, he amazed parents and staff at his elementary school with his performance of 'Climb Every Mountain'. Michael may have only been five years old but Joe made him lead singer, replacing his elder brother, Jermaine.

That certainly didn't mean he got any preferential treatment. If anything, his father was even harder on him.

Indeed, Joe was so focused on making his sons stars that he wouldn't let them play sports, date, or even hang out with their friends.

A mischievous, fun-loving child, Michael once threw a shoe at his father after a spanking, earning himself an even harder beating.

There was no time for play; it was all work. When Michael was six, the brothers won a big talent contest, with Michael kicking off his shoes in the middle of the song 'Barefootin'', delighting the crowd. More talent contests and paying gigs followed, with Joe eventually changing the group's name from The Ripples and Waves Plus Michael to The Jackson 5.

The family group delighted fans around the world after signing on with Motown Records in 1969 and made history the following year as the first act to reach Number One in the Billboard chart with their first four singles—'I Want You Back', 'ABC', 'The Love You Save' and 'I'll Be There'. Before Michael left the group for good in 1984, the group had seventeen Top 40 singles but he had already been flexing his muscles as a solo artist and would achieve even greater success on his own.

His 1982 album, *Thriller*, is the bestselling album of all time and *Off The Wall* (1979), *Bad* (1987), *Dangerous* (1991) and *HIStory* (1995) are all right up there in the world's sales charts. But Jackson's influence extended way beyond the estimated 400 million records he sold in his lifetime. His distinctive musical and dance styles made him an enduring cultural touchstone. Songs like 'Billie Jean', 'Thriller' and 'Beat It' provided a backdrop to a generation.

The hard work had paid off—but at what cost?

It would be years before Michael would find the courage to go public with the experiences of his childhood. By then, the damage had been done. 'I began to be so scared of that man,' writes Taraborrelli in *Michael Jackson: The Magic, The Madness, The Whole Story, 1958-2009* (2010), describing Michael's recollections of his father. 'In fact, I guess it's safe to say I hated him.'

'It was that hate that was instrumental in perhaps the weirdest aspect of the singer's life—the constant transformation of his appearance, turning a cute and bubbly Afro-American boy into an image-obsessed, eccentric pop star,' wrote Taraborrelli. In other words, Michael did everything possible to distance himself from his father—to the extent of changing his face and skin colour so he didn't look anything like him.

The singer first spoke openly about the beatings at the hands of his father in a 1993 interview with Oprah Winfrey. He admitted that he had often cried from loneliness and he would vomit on the sight of his father. He said Joe also verbally abused him, making jibes about his fat nose—a key factor in his subsequent plastic surgery. Ten years later, Michael told British journalist Martin Bashir that his father would sit in a chair holding a belt, watching the brothers rehearse. 'If you didn't do it the right way, he would tear you up, really get you,' he added.

Michael would spend most of his adult life trying to recapture that lost youth but it was always a losing battle. His father had stolen it from him and there was no going back.

THE FBI FILES

The 333-page file on the King of Pop was opened after the FBI was asked to provide back-up in the police probe into his alleged molestation of kids. The documents include new information about Jackson's creepy behaviour around young boys, including an account by a Canadian couple travelling on the same train as the star and a twelve or thirteen-year-old on 7 March 1992.

'Jackson was very possessive of the boy at night,' said the woman, according to one file. She added that she and her husband grew even more suspicious of the singer's behaviour when they 'heard questionable noises through the wall'.

'She was concerned enough to notify the conductor of her suspicions,' it adds.

The FBI was asked to analyse a homemade VHS tape titled, *Michael Jackson's Neverland Favorites: An All-Boy Anthology.*

The file also includes threatening notes in 1992 from a deeply disturbed fan named Frank Paul Jones, who said he was willing 'to commit mass murder at a Michael Jackson concert if necessary in an attempt to kill Michael.'

FALL FROM GRACE

Even for Michael Jackson it was bizarre behaviour.

With the spectre of a future behind bars lifted, the King of Pop leaped on top of a car outside a California courtroom and danced to celebrate his acquittal on child-molestation charges.

In the joy of the moment, perhaps he thought his troubles were over. But it was a hollow victory. A jury might have cleared him of child-abuse charges but the court of public opinion was not convinced. And it wasn't just his tainted reputation that took a heavy hit. The stressful five-month trial had taken an enormous toll on Jackson's already fragile health, and the cost of mounting the defence and maintaining his ridiculously lavish lifestyle had sent him deep into debt.

In truth, that ill-advised celebratory car-roof jig probably marked the beginning of the end for the star. He would never again approach the heights of his legendary career and the deterioration of both his mental and physical state accelerated from that point on.

Still, Michael's relief that sunny day on 13 June 2005 was understandable. For the second time in ten years, he had overcome charges that he had abused young boys left in his care.

The first time around, he'd managed to bury the scandal under the whopping $22 million (£13 million) he paid to Jordan Chandler in return for his silence after the thirteen-year-old's family sued him in 1993. After claiming Michael fondled the boy during sleepovers at the star's Neverland ranch, the Chandlers took the money and allowed the matter to drop.

But no amount of money could cover up the scandal after a 2003 British documentary, *Living With Michael Jackson*, showed Michael holding hands and discussing sleeping arrangements with thirteen-year-old cancer patient Gavin Arvizo. The boy's parents had gone to the authorities—and this time, there would be no out-of-court settlement.

Michael's own words to Martin Bashir in the documentary were bizarre and hurt him badly: 'The most loving thing to do is to share your bed with someone you know,' he told Bashir. 'When I see children, I see the face of God. That's why I love them so much,' he told US interviewer Ed Bradley in another interview.

He was charged with seven counts of child sexual abuse and providing alcohol to the boy in 2003 but was adamant he'd been framed. 'Before I would hurt a child I would slit my wrists,' he said.

After the trial, Michael walked away a free man, only for his health, his finances and his career to collapse. Already he was battling the skin disease vitiligo and lupus, an incurable connective-tissue condition. Both took a greater hold and a report said he had emphysema, gastrointestinal bleeding and needed a lung transplant. Sometimes he was so exhausted and frail he used a wheelchair.

To combat the fatigue and frustration, he upped his doses of painkiller medication. Compounding his health slide, the huge fortune he'd amassed over his long career had all but disappeared, leaving him a reported $400 million (£300 million) in the red.

Thriller may have been the bestselling album of all time and, in a shrewd business move, Michael outbid Sir Paul McCartney in 1985 for the rights to many of The Beatles' songs—an asset worth an estimated $1 billion—but legal fees, lawsuits and obsessive overspending meant he had to face the possibility in 2007 of putting his precious Neverland ranch up for sale.

His dancing days were effectively over; it was downhill from there.

MICHAEL JACKSON FACT FILE

1 Michael Jackson admitted to Oprah Winfrey to having two nose jobs.
2. He had booked a meeting in one of the Twin Towers on the morning of 9/11 but overslept and missed it, according to brother Jermaine.
3. His album, *Thriller*, sold 50 million copies worldwide—more than any other album in history. Seven of the nine tracks were Top 10 singles in the US. In all, Jackson has sold more than 300 million records.
4. On flights, he would ask for wine to be served in Diet

Coke cans so kids wouldn't know he drank alcohol.

5. *Home Alone* star Macaulay Culkin is godfather to two of Jackson's children. Former *Oliver Twist* child star Mark Lester claims to be godfather to all three children.

6. Michael's famous lean in the dance for 'Smooth Criminal' was made possible through a special patented anti-gravity illusion shoe.

7. Jackson paid $47 million for the publishing rights to The Beatles back catalogue in 1985 and sold a share of the rights to Sony in 1995 for $95 million.

8. He was an honorary director of Exeter City Football Club.

9. Twitter, Wikipedia, and AOL IM all crashed at 3.15pm on the day Michael Jackson died.

10. At least a dozen devastated fans committed suicide after learning of Jackson's death.

LONDON CALLING

Michael Jackson wept as he told how he wanted to make a triumphant record-breaking comeback in England so that he and his children could 'stop living like vagabonds'.

A financial firm that owned the 'note' on Neverland ranch touted the original idea of a monster engagement at London's O2 Arena. Put simply, they wanted their money and, while Jackson had the propensity to spend wildly while offstage, he was still able to pull in millions by going back to what he did best—performing.

The O2 worked on several levels: it was one of the world's biggest showcase venues, large enough to house such an event, and a good fit for promoters AEG Live. Jackson also agreed to it because Prince had performed twenty one sell-out dates there and he was determined to one-up his old rival.

But the real reason was because he was tired of moving around in the aftermath of his child-abuse acquittal and wanted to settle down in one place in the English countryside.

The singer would only agree to the extra concerts if he could live in a country estate with more than sixteen acres, a running stream and horses. 'He didn't want to be trapped in a hotel suite, no matter how beautiful. He wanted to give the children a pastoral, country-living vibe,' said AEG Live president Randy Phillips.

Jackson shook hands on the deal on Halloween 2008, arriving at the meeting with his three children, Prince, Paris and Blanket, all wearing dress-up costumes.

Initially, he agreed to thirty one concerts—ten more than Prince—and, when the first ten nights went on sale to test the water, they all sold out instantly. The triumph went right to Jackson's head and he decided to eviscerate Prince's marathon residence by playing a fifty-date run in London, insisting the Guinness World Records should have a representative there on the final night to record an event 'that will never happen again'.

Every night sold out in a matter of minutes. 'More than 250,000 people were still in the queue after the 50 shows sold out. That would have been enough to sell out another 50 shows,' noted Paul Gongaware, then joint-CEO of AEG Live.

However, rather than becoming energised and invigorated by the immense challenge of the 'This Is It' comeback concerts, Jackson quickly became paralysed with fear at the prospect of failure. He was terrified the concert promoters were going to 'pull the plug' on the tour, according to his friend and producer Kenny Ortega. Giving evidence in the case against Murray, Ortega told how he became increasingly worried about Jackson's health in the days before his death.

Ortega was working with the star to put together the spectacular shows but Jackson wasn't showing for rehearsals and turned up 'completely incoherent' on 19 June 2009.

The experienced producer, who had worked with Jackson on his 'Dangerous' and 'HIStory' tours, said he gave him food, put a blanket around him, massaged his feet and put a heater in his room. 'He appeared lost. I did feel that he was not well at all,' he said.

Jackson was like 'a lost boy', he wrote in an email to AEG. 'He's terribly frightened it is all going to go away. It would shatter him if we pulled the plug. I believe that there was a meeting to say that[,] if Michael didn't attend rehearsals, we would not be able to open in London,' he added.

The singer appeared to improve after another crisis meeting and was back on form for rehearsals on 24 June, the night before his death. He was telling friends how he hoped that, after the London dates, he would be able to bring 'This Is It' out into the world and possibly back to the United States. He also wanted to develop feature films based on his hits 'Thriller' and 'Smooth Criminal'. All he had to do was hold his nerve until he was back on stage for the first time in a decade in front of the people he loved and who loved him—his fans. If he could just get to that point, he truly believed everything would work out.

This was going to be his absolution. He needed to feel the love after all the pain of the past few years.

The O2 rollercoaster ride was still on track . . . but not for much longer.

EMAILS THAT REVEAL
THE TRUTH ABOUT THE KING OF POP

A cache of 250 confidential emails reveal Michael Jackson's inner turmoil as his dream of a big comeback turned into a nightmare. The messages—key evidence in the failed wrongful-death lawsuit brought by Jackson's mother, Katherine, and his children against concert promoters AEG—detail the star's devastating deterioration as he raced against time to be ready for the planned London concerts.

They underline the concern top AEG executives had about Jackson's increasingly fragile health and his ability to fulfil his lucrative concert contract.

Even before the deal was struck, AEG Live executive Paul Gongaware warned, in a September 2008 email before a scheduled meet with Jackson in Las Vegas, for his colleagues to wear casual clothes, 'as MJ is distrustful of people in suits', and expect to talk 'fluff' with 'Mikey'.

Asked whether Jackson could deliver, AEG Live boss Randy Phillips wrote, 'He has to or financial disaster awaits.'

In mid-June, a month before the shows, the singer was missing rehearsals, slow picking up dance routines and would have to lip-sync some of his biggest hits, the execs complained in messages.

'There are strong signs of paranoia, anxiety and obsessive-like behavior. I think the very best thing we can do is get a top Psychiatrist in to evaluate him ASAP,' wrote the show's director, Kenny Ortega, who had known Jackson for twenty years. 'It is like there are two people there. One (deep inside) trying to hold on to what he was and still can be and not wanting us to quit him, the other in this weakened and troubled state. I believe we need professional guidance in this matter,' he added.

But Phillips dismissed the request, putting his trust in Jackson's personal doctor, Conrad Murray, 'who I am gaining immense respect for as I get to deal with him more. This doctor is extremely successful (we check everyone out) and does not need this gig so he [is] totally unbiased and ethical.'

THE 911 TAPE

The emergency call from 100 North Carolwood Drive in Los Angeles was little different from the millions received by the rescue services each day. Although it was the first clue to the world that Michael Jackson had taken his last breath, his name isn't mentioned once, perhaps because of concern that news of the tragedy would leak out.

After his own efforts to save the star failed, Conrad Murray finally told bodyguard Alberto Alvarez to call an ambulance at 12.20pm on 25 June. Here is a transcript of that conversation:

Operator: Paramedic 33, what is the address of your emergency?
Caller: I need an ambulance as soon as possible, sir.
Okay, sir, what's your address?

Los Angeles[,] California, 90077.

Carolwood?

Carolwood Drive, yes.

Okay, sir, what's the phone number you are calling from?

Sir, we have a gentleman here that needs help. He's stopped breathing, he's not breathing and we are trying to pump him, but he's not, he's not. . .

Okay, okay, how old is he?

He's 50 years old, sir.

Okay. He's not conscious, he's not breathing?

Yes, he's not breathing, sir.

And he's not conscious either?

No, he's not conscious, sir.

Okay (pause). Alright, is he on the floor, where's he at right now?

He's on the bed, sir, he's on the bed.

Okay, let's get him on the floor.

Okay.

Okay, let's get him down to the floor. I'm gonna help you with CPR right now, okay.

We need him . . . we need a. . .

Yes, we're already on our way there. We're on our way. I'm gonna do as far as I can to help you over the phone. We're already on our way. Did anybody see him?

Yes, we have a personal doctor here with him, sir.

Oh, you have a doctor there?

Yes. But he's not responding to anything to no . . . no . . . he's not responding to the CPR or anything.

Oh, okay. Well, we're on our way there. If your guy is doing CPR and you're instructed by a doctor[,] he has a higher authority than me. And he's there on the scene.

Okay.

Did anybody witness what happened?

No, just the doctor, sir. The doctor's been the only one here.

Okay, so did the doctor see what happened?

Doctor, did you see what happened, sir? (inaudible voice) Sir, just, if you can please. . .

We are on our way. We are on our way. I'm just passing these questions on to my paramedics, who are on their way there, sir.

Thank you, sir. He's pumping, he's pumping his chest but he's not responding to anything, sir. Please.

Okay, okay, we are on our way. We are less than a mile away and we will be there shortly.

Thank you, sir, thank you.

Okay, sir. Call us back if you need any help. Thank you.

MICHAEL DIDN'T HAVE TO DIE

Michael Jackson didn't have to die.

Emotionally exhausted, weighing just 136 pounds and only able to sleep with a cocktail of powerful knockout drugs, in his final weeks, the King of Pop was a tragic shadow of his former self. But the doomed superstar would still be alive today if it wasn't for the lies, the greed and the indifference to his failing physical state by those surrounding him.

The master showman—so drained he could barely sing and dance at the same time. No one—certainly not his personal physician, Conrad Murray—stepped in to catch the falling star when he needed it most.

Katherine, the singer's ageing mother and the one relative he still looked up to, believed the promoters behind his thwarted comeback should shoulder the blame, launching a doomed multi-billion-dollar bid for damages against entertainment giant AEG for 'putting its desire for massive profits from the Tour over the health and safety of Michael Jackson.'

Hundreds of millions of pounds were, indeed, at stake when AEG Live lined up Jackson for a hugely anticipated comeback tour that was to start in London in the autumn of 2009. A huge publicity machine cranked into gear to tell the world that, after all the sensational headlines, the humiliating child-molestation trial and the wacky stories about his private life, Jackson was ready to return to the stage— the one place the magic always happened. The big problem was that one very important person wasn't so convinced he could pull it off—Jackson himself.

His health had been declared 'excellent' in January 2009, soon after he signed up for the tour, although, when asked in a medical questionnaire whether he had 'ever been treated for or had any indication of excessive use of alcohol or drugs', Michael circled 'no'—a blatant lie, since the singer had, in the past, dropped out of at least one tour for prescription-drug treatment.

And a series of confidential emails sent between the bigwigs at AEG—the firm promoting the planned concerts at London's O2 Arena—revealed the legendary star was reduced to a 'basket case' as he rehearsed for the shows.

In March 2009, just days before the tour was announced, promoter Randy Phillips, the head of AEG Live, found

Jackson so sloshed on booze in his London hotel room that he had to dress him.

'MJ is locked in his room, drunk and despondent,' Phillips wrote to AEG president Tim Leiweke, who was in the US. 'I [am] trying to sober him up. I screamed at him so loud the walls are shaking. He is an emotionally para-lysed mess riddled with self-loathing and doubt now that it is show time.'

If his friends and family knew how badly the star was spiralling in the ensuing months, they didn't appear to do anything to persuade him to cancel the tour and take a break to seek treatment and spend more time with his children. In the run up to the opening concert, the promoters expanded the number of shows from 10 to 50.

Just five days before Jackson died, the director of the ill-fated 'This Is It' shows was sounding the alarm even louder than before. In the early hours of 20 June 2009 Kenny Ortega sent a panicked email to Randy Phillips saying the star appeared too 'weak and fatigued' to rehearse and was 'trembling, rambling and obsessing'. But AEG wasn't about to throw in the towel.

'You cannot imagine the harm and ramifications of stop-ping the show now,' Phillips wrote later. 'It would far out-weigh "calling this game in the 7th inning."'

AEG co-CEO Paul Gongaware wrote to Phillips saying, 'We cannot be forced into stopping this, which MJ will try to do because he is lazy and constantly changes his mind to fit his immediate wants. He is locked. He has no choice . . . he signed a contract.'

The company would later claim successfully in court, through their lawyers, that the singer was quite capable of taking responsibility for his own affairs. But Jackson's close friends said he was already putting massive pressure on himself and was a performance perfectionist, refusing to accept second best. His chronic insomnia meant he lay awake for hours, exacerbating his insecurities with a relentless tiredness he couldn't shake off.

Jackson insisted that AEG hire Dr Murray as his personal physician for the London shows, at roughly $150,000 a month. The cardiologist was deep in debt and in danger of having his home repossessed.

He began giving Jackson nightly doses of propofol—a powerful surgical anaesthetic meant only for use in a hospital—to help him sleep. The doctor's dangerous drug regimen, together with AEG's determination to keep the O2 concerts on track and Jackson's rapidly deteriorating condition, created a perfect storm of chaotic circumstances that threw the star's life into a tailspin.

Jackson spent the last night of his life doing what he had always done: performing. He ran through a full slate of songs at the Staples Center in Los Angeles as the rehearsals began to come together. But he was such a bag of nerves when he returned to his Holmby Hills mansion that he couldn't sleep.

Murray tried giving his patient a 10-mg tablet of Valium, then 2 mg of sleep-inducing lorazepam, followed by another 2 mg of midazolam, another sleep aid. He bumped up the dosage of lorazepam and midazolam but all to no avail.

At one point, Jackson stood and urinated into a jug and then lay down and tried again to sleep.

At 10.40am on the morning of 25 June 2009, the singer was still awake. Murray went to his fall-back drug and administered propofol. Jackson was finally able to close his eyes and go to sleep. He would never awaken.

MICHAEL'S FINAL HOURS
25 JUNE 2009

12.30am: Jackson's black Escalade pulls into the driveway of his Holmby Hills home after rehearsals for his 'This Is It' tour wrap up at the Staples Center in downtown Los Angeles. Despite the warmth of a June evening in southern California, the star is shivering with the cold. The heating in his second-floor bedroom is cranked up high and a fire burns in the fireplace.

1am: Jackson tells Dr Conrad Murray that he's tired and feels fatigued, adding, 'I'm treated like I'm a machine. Let me just have a quick shower and change and I'll come back to you.'

1.30am: Jackson is given one 10-mg Valium tablet. Murray rubs Jackson's body with cream to treat the singer's vitiligo—a condition that discolours the skin. He takes doses of two sedatives: lorazepam and midazolam. It doesn't help him get to sleep.

2am: Murray injects his patient with 2 mg of the sedative Ativan, using an IV drip.

3am: Jackson dozes off for between ten to fifteen minutes after Murray persuades him to try meditation. 'Let's change the lighting of the room, let's lower the music . . . let me rub your feet and try to relax,' Murray tells his sleepless patient before injecting him with 2 mg of another sedative, Versed.

3.15am: Jackson is wide-awake again.

10am: Increasingly frustrated at his inability to sleep, Jackson begs Murray to give him some 'milk'—his pet name for the white-coloured hospital knockout drug propofol. 'He was hysterical,' said Murray. 'He was begging me, "Please, Dr Conrad, I need some milk so I can sleep." This went on for hours.' Murray initially says no.

10.40am: The singer is finally asleep but only after Murray is persuaded to give him 25 mg of propofol, using his IV, together with the local anaesthetic lidocaine.

10.50am: Murray leaves the room to go to the bathroom, later claiming that all of Jackson's vital signs were good.

10.52am: Murray returns to find Jackson has stopped breathing and unsuccessfully attempts CPR while his patient lies lifeless on the bed.

11.18am: According to police, Murray makes the first of three phone calls spanning forty seven minutes.

12.12pm: Murray calls Jackson's personal assistant, Michael Amir Williams, and leaves a message telling him to 'get here right away.'

12.22pm: 911 call made.

12.26pm: Paramedics arrive at the house.

1.08pm: Paramedics give up attempts at CPR at the scene after forty two minutes.

1.13pm: Ambulance arrives at Ronald Reagan UCLA Medical Center with Jackson still in full cardiac arrest.

2.26pm: Michael Jackson is pronounced dead at the age of fifty.

LIES & COVER-UPS

It was every child's worst nightmare.

Prince Michael and Paris ran into Michael Jackson's bedroom after hearing there was an urgent problem with their dad.

Seeing her father unconscious on the bed, his mouth open and his eyes staring blankly back at her, Paris, then just eleven years of age, screamed out, 'Daddy!'

Prince Michael, who was twelve at the time, stared in disbelief, his whole world falling apart around him.

Jackson's shocked bodyguard, Alberto Alvarez, hurriedly shepherded the children out into the adjoining foyer, telling them that everything was going to be all right.

But he couldn't have been more wrong.

The star's personal physician, Conrad Murray, was at his stricken patient's side, giving him CPR with one hand—a fundamental mistake, say experts, who insist two hands are necessary to jumpstart a stalled heart back to life. Despite his doctor's flailing efforts, Jackson was dead—and the cover-up was already underway.

When he discovered Jackson had stopped breathing before noon on 25 June 2009, Murray quickly realised he was in deep trouble. It didn't help his case that he was on the phone at the time. While Jackson was taking his last breath in his bedroom, Murray was outside in the hallway, chatting on the phone with cocktail waitress Sade Anding.

Anding, who first met Murray at a Houston, Texas, restaurant, was talking about her day with the doctor when she realised he was no longer listening. 'I heard mumbling sounds and coughing and voices. I kept saying, hello, hello, are you there? But I didn't get any reply,' she recalled.

Earlier that morning, Murray had left a message on the phone of Michelle Bella, an exotic dancer he met in Las Vegas the previous year. He'd also been called by another ex-girlfriend, Bridget Morgan, but didn't pick up. In all, he was on the phone for forty six minutes of the hour before Jackson died.

And it didn't end there. Murray was also on the phone to his then-girlfriend, Nicole Alvarez, at 1.08pm, when he was travelling in the ambulance with Jackson to the hospital, still pushing paramedics to try to revive the lifeless singer.

'I remember him telling me that he was on the way to the hospital with Mr Jackson and for me not to be alarmed. He didn't want me to be worried because he knew I would hear through the news and I would be upset,' Nicole said later. Murray went on to call his girlfriend four more times through the afternoon.

As he attempted in vain to wake the patient he'd tried so hard to put to sleep, Murray knew that chatting on the phone to his girlfriends was the least of his worries if Jackson died. He had to hide the drugs.

At his 2011 manslaughter trial, the Los Angeles jury heard that the frantic doctor stopped in the middle of attempting to revive the star to order Alberto Alvarez to hide bottles of drugs. Among the items he tried to hide was an IV bag containing what appeared to be propofol, the anaesthetic that was ultimately discovered to have killed Jackson. 'I was standing at the foot of the bed and he reached over and grabbed a handful of vials. He said, "Here, put these in a bag,"' said the bodyguard.

He claimed Murray, who was kneeling on the floor next to Jackson's body, picked up the vials from a wooden nightstand. 'I got a bag and opened it and he placed the vials in the bag. He proceeded to instruct me to place that bag in a brown grocery-type bag. He then pointed to the IV stand

and said for me to grab one of the bags on the IV stand and put it in a blue bag.'

By then, Paris was in the next room, curled up in a ball and sobbing. Prince Michael stood next to her, hoping against hope that his father would wake him from the terrible nightmare.

It was not to be.

THE LONG GOODNIGHT

Paramedics took just five minutes to rush to Michael Jackson's gated mansion after receiving the 911 call. But when they arrived, they discovered the star was already dead—and probably hadn't been breathing for at least twenty minutes.

Paramedics Richard Senneff and Martin Blount said they found Jackson lifeless and Dr Conrad Murray evasive about what had happened to his patient. Murray insisted Jackson wasn't taking any medication. When pressed, he said he gave the star lorazepam to help him sleep. 'It didn't add up,' said Senneff. The paramedic recalled that Jackson's pupils were dilated, his skin was cold and his eyes were dry.

He said the fifty-year-old entertainer looked like 'a hospice patient'.

However, Senneff added that Murray insisted Jackson had only just lost consciousness and had no medical problems other than dehydration. The paramedic was instantly suspicious.

He had a doctor in the house and an IV hooked up. It didn't seem normal. I asked him how long since it happened and he said, 'It just happened right when I called you.' That meant to me that we had a really good chance of saving the patient. It meant we had a good chance of restarting the heart.

The team of paramedics carried out two-handed CPR, ventilated Jackson with a machine to push air into his lungs and hooked him up to a heart monitor. They also gave him three rounds of drugs to try to jumpstart his heart.

But nothing they did had any effect.

A second paramedic, Martin Blount, testified at Murray's criminal trial that he found it strange when the physician insisted his famous patient wasn't on medication, especially since he saw a hypodermic needle and three bottles of lidocaine in the bedroom.

Blount said Murray put the bottles in a bag before they left for the hospital.

'Did you ever see those bottles again?' a prosecutor asked.

'No, sir,' he replied.

Senneff said there was no change in Jackson's condition in the entire time—forty five minutes—he was attempting to save him, from arriving at the star's house to getting him to the hospital's emergency ward. Emergency doctors at the University of California Los Angeles Hospital tried everything they could think of to save the stricken singer, even though they knew they would need a miracle.

They still carried on trying for one hour and thirteen minutes to bring him back to life after he'd already been diagnosed as being clinically dead. Hospital staff tried CPR, pumping oxygen into his lungs, and used three different heart-starting drugs, but all to no avail.

'Mr Jackson died long before he became a patient,' said casualty doctor Richelle Cooper. In all the time she was trying to revive Jackson, Dr Cooper said she never detected a pulse.

Murray made no mention to the paramedics or to the hospital doctors trying to save Jackson's life about the propofol he'd administered to the star to combat his chronic insomnia just hours before his dramatic collapse.

Coroner's investigator, Dr Elissa Fleak, later revealed that she discovered bottles of propofol hidden away in bags she found in a cupboard in the star's bedroom. She also found an empty vial of the drug on the floor by the bed and an array of different sedatives and prescription painkillers in medicine bottles.

Hampered by the delay in calling for help, the doctor's ineptitude and his cover-up to hide his alarming treatment, the paramedics and ER doctors never really stood a chance of saving the star.

DR DEATH

To many of his devoted patients, Conrad Murray was a caring doctor who would offer treatment for free to the poor. But his secret double life as a deadbeat dad and a compulsive womaniser led him to take a lucrative job as Michael Jackson's personal drug doctor.

Desperate for cash to pay his mounting debts, Murray took the post helping Jackson beat his raging insomnia—which effectively meant injecting Jackson with nightly doses of the knockout sleep drug that ultimately killed the world's biggest star.

Murray's million-dollar Las Vegas mansion was about to be repossessed after he fell roughly $100,000 (£60,000) behind with the mortgage in 2009 when Jackson asked him to travel to London with him as his full-time physician, official documents reveal. His two medical practices in Nevada and Texas faced over half a million dollars in court judgements and he was late paying a $50,000 personal loan and thousands of dollars in child support. The Grenada-born doctor's spiralling debts were the reason Murray demanded around $4 million from Jackson when he was first offered the job, said friends. He later settled for just over $100,000 a month.

Murray has fathered at least seven children with six women, most of them out of wedlock. According to court records, he has also been sued for various claims, including breach of contract and unpaid child support. While still living with his doctor wife, Blanche, and their two children in Las Vegas, he was also paying the $1500-a-month rent on a flat in Santa Monica, California for his actress lover, Nicole Alvarez.

Murray met Alvarez when she was working as an exotic dancer at the Crazy Horse Too club in Las Vegas. He had moved to Sin City after an affair with a married nurse, Nenita Malibiran, who worked with him at the same San Diego hospital and who conceived a child by him.

Murray was born on 19 February 1953 to a poor single mother and was raised by his grandparents on a farm in Grenada, moving to Trinidad when he was seven. When he arrived in the US, he went to university and medical school in Houston and Nashville, before working as a cardiologist in San Diego.

He married his first wife, Zufan Tesfai, in 1984 and got divorced four years later after having a child with mistress Patricia Mitchell, who accused him of a 'fraudulent breach of trust'.

In 1994 he had another brush with the law when he was arrested for domestic violence against Janice Adams, who also had two daughters with him, while he was a cardiologist working at the University of Arizona in Tucson.

He met his current wife, Blanche, while both were attending the same medical school.

On the morning of Jackson's death, Murray was on the phone to Sade Anding, a cocktail waitress he met in Houston, and two stripper ex-girlfriends—Michelle Bella, from Spearmint Rhino Gentlemen's Club, and Bridgette Morgan, from Cheetah's—testified in court that they got calls from the doctor while he was supposed to be caring for the star.

Murray's current mistress, Nicole Alvarez, started dating the doctor after giving him a private lap dance in her strip club's VIP lounge.

Sade Anding, who was talking to Murray when he discovered Jackson had stopped breathing, also said that, the first time she met the doctor, he gave her a $90 tip for a $9 drink. 'He told me he was very successful. He said the song "I'm Coming Up" is the theme of his life—that he came up from nothing to where he was now. But he said nothing about a girlfriend and all these children,' she said.

He later gave her a cash gift of $300 and a cheque for $400 on nights out together. 'Looking back, I think he was hoping I'd join him on the bed but I said I had to go,' she added.

Another Vegas model, Maggie Goldstein, claimed Murray flew her on an all-expenses paid trip to the Caribbean. 'I was one of ten models and promotions girls hired by Conrad Murray to fly to a Trinidad and Tobago resort in 2005 to publicise a new energy drink, Pit Bull, that Murray was producing with a partner,' she recalled.

'Conrad had a ball. He was up into the early hours, drinking, having fun and posing bare-chested with the girls. He brought along a girlfriend, Bridget, a black singer from Los Angeles. I was shocked to later find out he was married,' she added.

Released from prison in 2013 after serving half of his four-year sentence for killing Jackson, Murray maintained he was not responsible for the star's death.

The 6-ft 5-in tall physician was found guilty of involuntary manslaughter and stripped of his medical licence but he insisted, in a 2013 interview with the *Daily Mail*, that he had such a strong relationship with Jackson that the wounded singer allowed him to hold his penis every night because he was incontinent and had to be fitted with a catheter. 'I tried to protect him but I was brought down with him,' he claimed.

Murray claimed he was successfully weaning Jackson off the hospital drug propofol when tragedy struck.

He told me there were doctors in Germany that gave it to him. I didn't agree with this at all, but Michael wasn't the kind of man you can say no to. He would always find a way.

So I acquired propofol and gave it to him over a two-and-a-half month period as I weaned him off it, which I finally achieved three days before he died. He begged me for the drug because he wanted to sleep, because then he didn't have to think. He was in crisis at the end of his life, filled with panic and misery. I would sit with him when he was on a propofol drip. It's a very fast-acting drug that disappears from the body quickly. Fifteen minutes after the drug is administered, it's gone. I gave him very light, light sedation.

'I did not kill Michael Jackson,' he claimed. 'He was a drug addict—Michael Jackson killed Michael Jackson.'

MICHAEL'S PRIVATE PAIN

Drugged and despondent, Michael Jackson's distinctive high-pitched voice is almost unrecognisable as he slurs into a tape recorder. But the message is clear enough: how this fifty-year-old man-boy felt the pain of abandoned children because he never had a childhood himself.

In an eerie recording from beyond the grave, the King of Pop tells how important it was to him that his planned comeback concerts at London's O2 Arena were a triumph.

'Elvis didn't do it. Beatles didn't do it. We have to be phenomenal. When people leave the show, when people leave my show, I want them to say, "I've never seen nothing like this in my life,"' he declared.

He wanted his fans to hail him as 'the greatest entertainer in the world'.

Conrad Murray made the recording on his iPhone using an iTalk application while the star was under the influence of propofol.

'My performances will be up there helping my children. I love them. I love them because I didn't have a childhood. I had no childhood. I feel their pain, I feel their hurt. I can deal with it,' Jackson says in a slow, faltering tone. 'Heal the

World', 'We Are the World', 'Will You Be There', 'The Lost Children' . . . these are the songs I have written because I hurt, you know, I hurt,' he adds.

The singer tells how he planned to take the millions he would make with his 'This Is It' tour to build the 'biggest children's hospital in the world', with a games room and a movie theatre. 'Children are depressed in those hospitals because there is no game room, no movie theatre. They're sick because they're depressed. Their mind is depressing them. I care about them, them angels. God wants me to do it. I'm going to do it, Conrad,' he adds.

'Don't have enough hope, no more hope. That's the real generation that's going to save our planet, starting with, we'll talk about it—United States, Europe, Prague.

My babies, they walk around with no mother. They drop them off, they leave—a psychological degradation of that. They reach out to me—please take me with you. I want to do it for them. That will be remembered more than my performances. My performances will be up there helping my children and always be my dream.'

Asked by Murray if he is OK, Jackson says, 'I am asleep.'

The recording was made on 10 May 2009, just six weeks before Jackson's death.

THE AUTOPSY

The only spotlight on Michael Jackson's final appearance on earth was the harsh glare in the Los Angeles Medical

Examiner's office. Taken just before the autopsy on the day he died, a photograph showed a very different picture to the public face the star had put on at rehearsals less than twenty four hours earlier at the Staples Center.

Lying on a white shroud, his neck, arms and ankles covered in thirteen puncture marks, there was a red bruise in the middle of his chest where doctors had tried in vain to restart his breathing. A bandage covered his nose and his stick-thin 5-ft 9-in, 136-pounds frame was naked.

'He was healthier than the average person of his age,' Los Angeles Deputy Medical Examiner Dr Christopher Rogers said later, adding that there was no sign of any fat or cholesterol on the walls of Jackson's heart. He ruled the cause of death was homicide as a result of acute propofol intoxication.

The fifty-one-page autopsy report did not dwell on Jackson's penchant for plastic surgery but it confirmed that the fifty-year-old pop icon went to great lengths to maintain his youthful image. 'The decedent's head hair is sparse and connected to a wig,' the report stated. Jackson also had tattooed-on black eyeliner and pink lips.

The report concluded that the star was weakened from a number of different illnesses when he died, including 'chronic lung inflammation, respiratory bronchiolitis, diffuse congestion and patchy hemorrhage of right and left lungs'.

In addition to propofol, the autopsy revealed that Jackson had a virtual pharmacy flowing in his veins, with traces of lidocaine, diazepam, nordiazepam, lorazepam, midazolam and ephedrine in his blood.

The report also reveals how, on 5 August 2009, six weeks after Jackson's death, coroner's officials travelled to Forest

Lawn Memorial Park to take hair samples from Jackson's head 'for potential toxicology testing'.

In the presence of Jackson's sister, LaToya, 'samples were collected by plucking with gloved hands'. Jackson, who was viewed in a 'secured lobby', was 'supine in a yellow casket with blue lining. The majority of the decedent was covered with multiple white towels/sheets leaving only the hands and top of the head exposed'.

Cardiologist Dr Alon Steinberg, who carried out an expert inquiry into Jackson's death for the California Medical Board, claimed the star would be alive today had Murray not been 'grossly negligent' in providing the basic standards of care.

'All these extreme deviations, giving propofol in the wrong setting without proper equipment or personnel, not making proper preparations, not calling 911 in a timely manner, not keeping records, all directly impacted on Mr Jackson's life,' he told the jury at Murray's criminal trial.

When you monitor a patient[,] you never leave their side, especially after giving them propofol. It's like leaving a baby that's sleeping on your kitchen counter top. You would never do it because there is a chance the baby could wake up and fall off or grab a knife or something. You just don't do it.

BACK AT NUMBER ONE

Michael Jackson was virtually broke when he died, telling friends that even his biggest asset, the lucrative Beatles' catalogue, was 'mortgaged up to the hilt'. But the moment he died, the money started rolling in and it hasn't really stopped.

Five years after his death, he was listed by *Forbes Magazine* as the top earning dead celebrity of 2014, having raked in more than $140 million. He earned more than twice as much as Elvis Presley, who died in 1977 and came in second with $55 million, and three times more than cartoonist and *Peanuts* comic-strip creator Charles Schulz, who took third place with $40 million.

And according to *Forbes*, 'Few celebrities prove the point that there is [financial] life after death better than Michael Jackson.'

It was Jackson's second straight year atop the list. He regained the title in 2013, a year after being pushed into second place by his close friend in life, actress Elizabeth Taylor.

Two Cirque du Soleil shows, 'Immortal' and 'One', account for much of Jackson's earnings, along with his music catalogue and publishing empire. Taylor, who died in 2011, came in at number four with $25 million, while reggae singer Bob Marley completed the top five, with $20 million in earnings in the year to October 2014. Marley died of cancer at the age of thirty-six in 1981.

TOHME OR NOT TOHME

In the year before Jackson's death, little happened around the beleaguered star without the knowledge and acquiescence of a mysterious advisor called Dr Tohme Tohme.

Tohme was Michael's gatekeeper and he carefully controlled who got to see his first and only celebrity client. For managing Jackson's affairs, according to court papers, he was paid $35,000 a month (£26,000) plus 15 per cent of 'all gross compensation received by [Jackson] for his services within the entertainment industry, including live performances, merchandising, electronic arts, recorded and live telecasts, motion pictures, and animation projects'.

For a superstar with the earning power of Michael Jackson, that's some deal. But before the money could roll in, the singer had to start singing again. Paranoid and vulnerable and unable to shake off the taint of suspicion pervading the child-abuse claims, he was hardly in the mood to get back on stage.

According to his sister, LaToya, Jackson was seriously afraid that he would be assassinated if he ever performed live again. But Tohme had other ideas.

Jackson was introduced to Tohme by his brother, Jermaine, in the spring of 2008 after defaulting on a loan for his Neverland ranch property in central California. He was in danger of losing not only his home but also his ownership stake in The Beatles music catalogue and his memorabilia.

Tohme found an investor to bail Jackson out and, as a result, the repossession was allayed and he was asked to become the star's manager.

'From the outset of Tohme's involvement, it was evident that, due to a variety of pre-existing personal problems, Jackson's professional career was in the throes of a potentially destructive downward spiral,' say court papers filed as part of a court battle Tohme fought with the Jackson Estate over commissions he claims he was owed.

'Tohme immediately set out to reverse that spiral and build Jackson's career. Tohme convinced Jackson that he should leave the negative environment of Las Vegas, where he and his family were living, and move to the healthier and more hospitable environment of Los Angeles.'

The papers say Tohme persuaded the star he needed to go back to work to 'earn the money required to clear away the cobwebs of the financial bind he was in'.

It was Tohme who co-ordinated Jackson's move back to LA, handled all the bills and hired and fired his famous client's staff. He axed all of Jackson's existing security staff and brought in an entirely new crew. He dealt with the media and any problems the family encountered. He made himself indispensable.

When the idea of concerts at London's O2 Arena had first been proposed in 2007, Jackson dismissed it because he didn't want to go on tour. But the child-molestation charges he faced would play a part in his eventual decision to agree to the London dates two years later. Sheikh Abdullah of Bahrain had covered a 'substantial portion' of Jackson's defence costs and, after the acquittal, the singer and his family moved to the oil-rich Middle Eastern country, where they lived at the Sheikh's expense.

While living in Bahrain, Jackson signed a deal with the Sheikh giving him 'the exclusive right throughout the world to any and all of Jackson's new creative undertakings'. This contract, says the court file, 'operated to preclude Jackson from recording, performing, or otherwise pursuing any sort of artistic activity without first obtaining the consent of the Sheikh'.

When Jackson left Bahrain in 2006, the Sheikh sued his old houseguest in London, demanding $7 million (£5.2 million) in damages and insisting the star should not be allowed to perform without his permission, as per the contract. Even if he wanted to make a grand comeback, the star's hands were tied.

Having been instated as Jackson's business guru, Tohme made it his mission to free his client from the constraints of the contract and he is clearly a man used to getting his way. 'Tohme succeeded in orchestrating a settlement agreement that resolved the London lawsuit,' said the court file, adding that, as long as Jackson paid 'the agreed upon settlement amount', he would be allowed to perform again.

The catch was, of course, that, to pay the Sheikh the $3 million required to make the contract go away, Jackson would have to perform—something he hadn't wanted to do in 2007. But, of course, there was money to be made for everybody, including Dr Tohme. Colony Capital, the investment company he'd brought in to pay the promissory note on Neverland ranch, also had to be paid.

The die was cast; whether he really wanted to or not—or, indeed, if he was capable—Jackson was offered the O2 dates again and this time he really couldn't say no.

Tohme—described as a 'hard negotiator'—and Colony Capital representatives met with tour promoters AEG Live and, after a series of meetings, a deal was struck that was lucrative for everyone . . . including Jackson.

Tohme is still claiming he is owed his 15 per cent management fee for the work he did for Jackson from mid-2008 onwards—a cut of the star's posthumous revenue that runs into hundreds of millions of pounds. The estate's lawyers see it very differently. They have argued that the singer had signed agreements that gave Tohme 'unfair financial compensation' and say Jackson fired him in March 2009. The long-running litigation has yet to be resolved.

Described alternately as a Lebanese financier and 'ambassador at large' for the country of Senegal, Tohme undeniably got Jackson out of some sticky spots and laid the groundwork to make the 'This Is It' concerts possible for his weary client.

But was Jackson emotionally or physically capable of going through with the tour he'd turned down just two years earlier?

SLEEPLESS

Michael Jackson went without sleep for an eye-popping sixty days—possibly the only human ever to stay awake that long.

Testifying at Jackson's wrongful-death trial in Los Angeles, Charles Czeisler, a Harvard Medical School sleep expert, said the King of Pop was knocked out night after night on the hospital anaesthetic proposal but that he never actually snoozed off.

Although a patient on propofol comes around refreshed, they haven't actually been to sleep!

Dr Czeisler told jurors he has never heard of any person who has gone sixty days without Rapid Eye Movement (REM) sleep, which is vital to keep the brain and body alive. 'The symptoms that Mr Jackson was exhibiting were consistent with what someone might expect to see of someone suffering from total sleep deprivation over a chronic period,' he explained.

The expert said he'd never heard of a patient being given sixty consecutive nights of propofol infusions but added that laboratory rats died after five weeks of getting no REM sleep. He estimated Jackson would have died before his eightieth night of being injected with the drug, which is only normally administered in a hospital setting.

Dr Czeisler, a sleep consultant to NASA and the CIA—and who has also worked with The Rolling Stones—told the court that the drug does not offer REM sleep and disrupts the normal sleep cycle. 'It would be like eating some sort of cellulose pellets instead of dinner,' he explained. 'Your stomach would be full, and you would not be hungry, but it would be zero calories and not fulfil any of your nutrition needs.'

He claimed the star's lack of REM sleep could, eventually, have taken his life within days had he not collapsed on 25 June 2009. 'Depriving someone of REM sleep for a long period of time makes them paranoid, anxiety-filled, depressed, unable to learn, distracted and sloppy,' Czeisler testified. 'They lose their balance and appetite, while their physical reflexes become ten times slower and their emotional responses ten times stronger,' he added, according to CNN.

Those symptoms are strikingly similar to descriptions of Jackson in his last weeks, as described in emails from show producers and testimony by witnesses in the trial. Show staff reported that he became thinner, paranoid and forgetful, and was heard talking to himself. The brain needs seven to eight hours of sleep every night to repair and maintain neurons. Learning and memory also happen when you are asleep, Czeisler said. Without it, the sufferer completes tasks less successfully.

The sleep expert explained the human brain needs seven to eight hours of sleep to repair and maintain neurons every night. 'Like a computer, the brain has to go offline to maintain cells that we keep for life, since we don't make more,' he explained. 'Sleep is the repair and maintenance of the brain cells.'

THE FATHER OF BOTOX

Michael Jackson first met dermatologist Arnold Klein in 1983, at a time when he was arguably at the height of his powers, soon after the release of *Thriller*.

The Beverly Hills physician, nicknamed 'The Father of Botox', had also carved out a hugely lucrative niche for himself in Hollywood and worked with scores of celebrities, including Elizabeth Taylor, Dolly Parton, Goldie Hawn, Dustin Hoffman, Sharon Stone and Cher.

The two men considered themselves friends and Klein would join Jackson and his family on almost every holiday.

Their first meeting came just months before the singer required major facial work when his hair caught on fire while he was filming a Pepsi commercial. 'I spent the night at the hospital, in his room, just telling him what it is like to be burned, because I was badly burned as a two-and-a-half-year-old kid. That's how we really bonded,' Klein told *Vanity Fair* in a 2012 interview. He also claimed credit for diagnosing Jackson with lupus and vitiligo, a disease that causes the loss of colour in the skin.

Perhaps in those early days, Klein was a great help to the star, who suffered great pain as a result of the burning incident. But Jackson's problem with pain medication began right there—and their thirty-plus years of friendship marked his serious decline in health from the vibrant, exuberant, ground-breaking performer of his early years as a solo artist in the early 1980s to the drug-addled skin-and-bones shell of his final years.

Many of the hangers-on and the doctors harnessed to fill his prescription needs came and went during this slow but insidious fall from greatness but Klein was a constant. He shared in his friend's good times and stood loyally by him in the bad . . . and all the time, he fed him the drugs that Jackson was soon unable to do without.

Consequently, Jackson couldn't do without Klein.

Klein, who liked to style himself as 'the world's greatest dermatologist', gave the singer regular treatments with wrinkle-filler drugs like Botox and Restylane. But while Jackson's vanity may have been piqued by these treatments, the real reason for his daily visits to Klein's offices was for his injections of Demerol pain medication.

In one 3-day period in 2009, from 21–23 April, Jackson—using the alias Omar Arnold—was treated with 775 mg of the drug. Klein also treated his client to reduce 'excessive perspiration' by injecting Botox into his groin and armpits, again accompanied by the requisite painkiller jabs.

The last visit was just three days before Jackson died.

According to addiction expert Dr Robert Waldman, insomnia is a 'very common complaint' in patients withdrawing from drugs like Demerol. Dr Waldman, who works with addicts in Los Angeles and testified as an expert witness during the 2011 Conrad Murray trial, said withdrawals from Demerol also caused sweating, an increased heart rate, bone and muscle pain, chills, nausea, anxiety and severe restlessness—all symptoms Jackson complained of in his final days and weeks.

Klein insisted Demerol was never the problem, blaming propofol as the Doomsday addiction. The dermatologist claims he knew of a number of doctors who fed Jackson's 'milk' habit. What he didn't say was that he himself numbered among them.

Testifying in 2013 at the wrongful-death suit brought by Jackson's mother and children against AEG Live, Debbie Rowe, the singer's one-time dermatological nurse and mother of two of his children, said Klein and Jackson's other doctors competed to see who could give him the most powerful pain meds. 'Michael had a very low pain tolerance, and his fear of pain was incredible, and I think the doctors took advantage of him that way,' she testified.

'These idiots were going back and forth the whole time not caring about him,' she added.

Rowe was concerned that Jackson was not getting better. 'Klein was not doing what was best for Michael,' she said. 'The only physician who ever cared for Michael was Allan Metzger.' (Metzger was Jackson's internist, who was treating the star for lupus.)

On the witness stand, Rowe claimed both Klein and another Jackson doctor administered propofol to the singer. Klein also gave the anaesthetic to five or six other patients, she said.

Klein conceded he gave Jackson Demerol, a narcotic painkiller, but he insisted, in an interview with ABC News in America, that other people were to blame for giving him propofol. 'People have drugs of choice, sir,' he said. 'His choice was propofol. Unfortunately, when you're at that level of wealth, doctors will do anything for you. So I'm just telling you that this has been a long problem.'

In interviews, he portrayed himself as the good guy, much in the same way as Conrad Murray. They were the ones trying to get Michael back on track, just as long as he kept paying them and they kept providing him with the drugs he wanted.

Klein recalled one occasion when he chartered a plane to Las Vegas when he heard the singer was being administered the knockout drug at a hotel and threw out the doctor concerned. Another time in Hawaii, Klein said he and a nurse slept on the floor of Jackson's room to prevent him getting propofol from a plastic surgeon.

Speaking to Headline News Network in the US, the dermatologist also said he once 'saved' Jackson in New York after a doctor combined propofol and another drug, which made the star 'go running down the street'.

It hardly matters here but Klein, ever the self-promoter, strongly hinted after Jackson's death that he was the biological father of both Prince and Paris, the singer's eldest children. He went so far as to post strikingly similar photos of Prince and himself as a teenager on Facebook, with the caption, 'Hmmmm'.

As more details emerged of his drug pandering to Jackson, Klein's rich and famous clients deserted him and he was forced to declare bankruptcy. The celebrity culture that he had preyed on recognised his role in Jackson's demise, even if the authorities were willing to overlook it.

Klein, who died from natural causes in Palm Springs, California in October 2015 at the age of seventy, was never called to account officially for the way he abused his position as a doctor and his Hippocratic Oath not to harm by helping to turn the most celebrated entertainer in the world into a helpless drug addict.

WHAT REALLY HAPPENED?

The assumption in the aftermath of Jackson's death was that Dr Conrad Murray was the only doctor to have injected the singer with propofol and that, given the caveat that he was acquiescing to the wishes of his demanding patient, he was largely to blame when it all went wrong.

But the truth is that he was secretly being administered with the hospital-grade amnesic drug—nicknamed the 'milk of amnesia'—for at least twelve years before it killed him. This wasn't some new experiment in combating insomnia he'd drafted in Murray to oversee; Jackson was extremely well acquainted with the drug—and with its dangers.

I'm told two German anaesthesiologists were brought in by Jackson's tour team to inject him with propofol in a Munich hotel in July 1997. In between concerts, he hadn't been able to sleep and was desperate for some help after the sedatives he normally used didn't have any effect.

After eight hours of propofol-infused sleep, he was hooked and had a second treatment following his second Munich show. From then on, whenever he couldn't sleep, he cried out for his 'milk'. If the doctor *du jour* wouldn't provide him with it, he'd find one who would.

Back in 1998 Dr Christine Quinn was summoned to a Beverly Hills hotel by Jackson, who asked her to get him some propofol, saying the best sleep he'd ever experienced was while under the drug. She refused, telling him, 'The sleep you get with anaesthesia is not real sleep; not restful sleep.'

As we have already seen, Arnold Klein was alleged in court to have given Jackson propofol.

Two months before he died, the star was warned that he might not wake up if he took propofol but he brushed aside the concerns, saying, 'I'll be OK. I'll be safe as long as I have someone to monitor me with the equipment while I sleep.'

Nurse practitioner Cherilyn Lee said she rejected Jackson's pleas for her to give him the powerful anaesthetic at a meeting at his house in April 2009. Then, just four days before the singer's death, Lee got a call from Jackson's bodyguard, Fareem Muhammad, who told her his boss wanted to see her.

'One half of him was hot and the other half was cold. I told him they should take Michael straight to hospital,' she said, remembering that 'shivering and trembling' were among propofol's side effects. 'Another of the symptoms I discovered was memory loss. I knew I was working with a great entertainer. But he said, "I would never forget my lines."'

Jackson had first asked if she could get him Diprivan—the commercial name for propofol—telling her he'd first experienced its effects during an operation in hospital. 'Based on his experience in surgery, he said, "I know it will knock me out,"' she said.

She didn't know anything about the drug at first but, after consulting with a doctor, she warned Jackson it was too dangerous to use at home. 'It was not for use in a home setting and it was not a sleep aid,' she said during the Conrad Murray trial. 'I told Michael, "No one who cares about you or has your best interests at heart is going to give you this. What if you don't wake up?"'

But that wasn't going to stop him. Jackson was a doctor shopper hooked on prescription drugs and used as many as nineteen aliases. These included the names of his personal chef and assistant, author Jack London and 1930s exotic dancer Josephine Baker.

Like many largely law-abiding citizens, he would never consider taking street drugs such as cocaine, heroin or even marijuana. But painkillers were prescribed by doctors—how could that be wrong?

Despite a two-year investigation into Jackson's death and an independent probe into the prescription-medication abuse revealed in the Jackson case, Conrad Murray was the only doctor ever charged in relation to the star's passing.

Other doctors were suspected of having provided the singer with propofol. One of them—thought to be Arnold Klein—was quizzed by federal agents but never prosecuted. No evidence was found against anyone other than Conrad Murray.

From Elvis to Jackson, celebrities have fallen foul of prescription-medicine bandits in the medical profession. The assumption is that many, many more members of the public suffer similar fates that we just never hear about.

Michael Jackson was killed by his abuse of prescription drugs and every single doctor who illegally prescribed him medicine he didn't need should have been in the dock alongside Conrad Murray to pay the price for what they did. Only by sending that kind of message do we stand any chance of ridding ourselves of the greedy parasites who profit from the misery they cause to the patients they are sworn to protect.

Jackson wasn't alone in his addiction. The White House said in 2015 that 120 Americans a day die from drug overdoses, most of them involving legal prescription drugs—that's more than the number of people killed each day in car crashes in the United States.

This was an opportunity not only to bring all culprits behind Jackson's death to justice but also to put doctors around the world on notice that overprescribing potentially deadly painkiller and anxiety medication will not be tolerated and carries a heavy penalty if uncovered.

The possibility that something positive could have come from Jackson's death was squandered. Doctors who share the blame for his spiral into addiction escaped justice.

We were left with a wonderful catalogue of songs and generations of memories from a performer who gave so much joy to so many. The great scandal is that he was allowed to self-destruct by the very people who should have saved him from himself.

CONCLUSION

So much has been written about these five iconic deaths that it has become virtually impossible to see the wood for the trees. It is for this very reason that I have deliberately cut through the dense foliage to put forward my case for what really happened in each of these shocking incidents.

Hindsight is a wonderful thing and the public are not the only ones to jump to conclusions in the aftermath of a celebrity's death; investigators often fall into the same trap and dig holes that they can't—or won't—climb out of.

Sometimes a cover-up can be as simple as the authorities wanting to sweep the whole affair under the carpet and move on—a possible explanation for the official lone-wolf assassin theory in the aftermath of the JFK shooting.

But often, suspicions persist.

In the case of these five legendary figures, we've become so immune to all the conspiracy theories and tell-all memoirs that we've lost sight of the facts. For some very powerful people, that is exactly what they intended.

The police, the media and the establishment collude to protect their own vested interests in so much of what goes on beneath the radar in what many naïvely believe to be a free and open society.

Secrets are allowed to lay fallow for years but they never go away. They are fed by lies. And it can be the very people who keep them secret who decide when they should be exposed.

To get to the truth about matters of consequence in Britain and the United States, you must first get past the guardians of the 'Establishment'—one old, the other comparatively new but both fiercely protective of the status quo.

Both Marilyn Monroe and Diana were iconic figures, adored by their public, and both had the potential to rock the establishment. They had no intention of slipping off quietly into the sunset.

Do I personally think JFK and his brother Robert were involved in Marilyn's death? No, I believe that, despite the shenanigans, in their private lives they were fundamentally decent men. Nor do I believe that the Royals were in any way connected to Diana's death.

This doesn't mean, however, that the shadowy 'men in grey suits'—as Diana referred to the 'Establishment' enforcers behind the scenes in the UK—and their counterparts in the United States were not capable of acting independently.

Desperate men can do some desperate things when everything they hold dear is threatened and, make no mistake, Diana and Marilyn both had the popularity to affect public opinion.

The idea that the Mafia could have been involved in three of these deaths may surprise some readers but they may be unaware just how deeply organised crime is ingrained into America's culture.

If the 'dark forces' in Britain are bound to protect power, the Mob is all about greed.

In their various ways, Elvis, Marilyn and JFK all jeopardised the lucrative niche the Mafia bosses had carved out for themselves. As you will have read, my evidence—both documentary and from interviews—linking them to all three deaths is hard to ignore.

Having read about the attempt to steal Elvis's plane and the fact that he died just as he was about to give evidence against the Mafia, you may still prefer to blame his demise on the self-destructive urges that propelled him to obesity and drug abuse. For someone with such experience of prescription meds to overdose on a painkiller he knew full well he was allergic to was either accidental or something far more sinister.

Like I say, I'm not trying to convince you; I'm just laying out the facts as they fell without any agenda.

Michael Jackson's death is a simpler one but with a message that is still being ignored, with tragic consequences.

Prince's death seven years later, in April 2016, also seems to have been the result of irresponsible pill-popping, just like that of his one-time rival and Elvis before them.

And yet still it goes on. Conrad Murray and the late Dr Nick were the scapegoats but who else was to blame?

We grew up with these legends; they live on in our memories through photos, film and TV footage that enable us to celebrate their achievements, even as we mourn their loss.

We can still see Marilyn's shimmering glamour and Diana's supermodel shyness, President Kennedy's shining self-belief and the snake-hipped mastery of the King and his thrilling, princely pop heir.

It shouldn't have ended this way; they all had so much still to give.

The real tragedy is that, in each of the five cases, we shall probably never know with absolute certainty what really happened.

David Gardner is a former *Daily Mail* Foreign Correspondent and author of *The Last of the Hitlers*, an account of his investigation to track down the last living direct descendants of Adolf Hitler in the United States. He also wrote a biography of the actor Tom Hanks and ran international news agencies in New York and Los Angeles. He was the first British print journalist into Baghdad during the first Gulf War of 1990–1, and has covered four presidential elections during his twenty years in America. He now lives in Laguna Beach, California, with his wife, Michelle, and their three children.